Understanding
the Enneagram

REVISED EDITION

BOOKS BY DON RICHARD RISO
AND RUSS HUDSON

Enneagram Transformations: Releases and Affirmations for Healing Your Personality Type (1993)

Discovering Your Personality Type: The Enneagram Questionnaire (1995)

Personality Types: Using the Enneagram for Self-Discovery (1996)

Understanding the Enneagram: The Practical Guide to Personality Types (2000)

Understanding the Enneagram

The Practical Guide to Personality Types

～

REVISED EDITION

Don Richard Riso
Russ Hudson

Houghton Mifflin Company
Boston New York

Library of Congress Cataloging-in-Publication Data
Riso, Don Richard.
Understanding the enneagram : the practical guide to personality
types / Don Richard Riso and Russ Hudson. — Rev. ed.
p.   cm.
Includes bibliographical references and index.
ISBN 0-618-00415-7
ISBN 978-0-618-00415-7
1. Enneagram. 2. Self-evaluation. I. Hudson, Ross. II. Title.
BF698.3 .R57 2000
155.26 — dc21   99-053622

The Enneagram of personality is a modern synthesis of ancient and modern psychological and spiritual teachings. The contents of this book are the result of the original work of the authors, and no body of Enneagram material has been passed down in a preexisting "oral tradition" in the public domain. Please respect the rights of the authors by not photocopying or otherwise infringing this copyrighted material. This book has been copyrighted and may not be reproduced in whole or in part by any means whatsoever without the express written permission of Houghton Mifflin Company. If you would like to obtain multiple copies of this book at a 40 percent discount, please order them from the Special Sales Department at 617-351-5919.

The Enneagram of the Passions, of the Nine Fixations, of the Nine Virtues (Serenity, Humility, Truthfulness, Equanimity, Detachment, Courage, Sobriety, Innocence, and Action), and of the Nine Holy Ideas (Holy Perfection, Holy Will, Holy Harmony, Holy Origin, Holy Omniscience, Holy Strength, Holy Wisdom, Holy Truth, and Holy Love), Psycho-catalyzer, Ten Divine Holy Ideas, and Trialectics are service marks of Arica Institute, Inc.

The authors are grateful for permission to reprint material from the following sources: *Essence: The Diamond Approach to Inner Realization* by A. H. Almaas. Copyright © 1986 by A-Hameed Ali (York Beach, Me.: Samuel Weiser, 1986).

Used by permission. *Diagnostic and Statistical Manual of Mental Disorders,* Fourth Edition, Revised. Copyright © 1987 by American Psychiatric Association. Reprinted with permission. *Personality Types: Using the Enneagram for Self-Discovery* by Don Richard Riso. Copyright © 1987 by Don Richard Riso. Reprinted by permission of Houghton Mifflin Company.

Book design by Joyce C. Weston

Printed in the United States of America

www.hmhco.com

DOC 20
4500668590

For
C. S. A., R. St. G., G. E.,
B. L. T., M. M., B. P. M., and
A. M. D. G.

*This thing we tell of can
never be found by seeking,
yet only seekers find it.*
             — *Sufi saying*

Preface and Acknowledgments

Since the appearance of the first edition of *Understanding the Enneagram* in 1990, a great deal has happened in the Enneagram world. To date, more than seventy-five books have appeared in English alone, and barely a month goes by without seeing the publication of yet another work on the subject. This mushrooming of interest in the Enneagram is a source of pride to me personally as one of the major developers of the field, and yet it also brings some degree of trepidation as well. If the Enneagram is going to continue to grow and garner the attention it deserves as an extraordinary tool for personal growth and human understanding, we must continually deepen our own knowledge of the system.

We who are working in this field need to become especially more rigorous in our writing and teaching so that clarity and precision — and ultimately, insight and transformation — are achieved. We need to bring the depth and specificity of modern psychology to the many profound, ancient sources of wisdom on which the Enneagram is based. We need to hold ourselves to the highest intellectual standards so that this remarkably useful, transformative system is not dismissed out of hand as "too New Age" or as being too vague or ill thought-out. Thus, my pride in the growth of the Enneagram field is undermined somewhat by my concern that serious thinkers and observers of human nature will not take the Enneagram seriously.

One of the basic confusions about the modern Enneagram is that *it does have ancient roots*: elements of the system go back to the Greeks (in the Enneagram symbol itself), to the Christian Desert Fathers of the fourth century, to the Kabbalists of the twelfth century, and to the Sufis of Islam. All of these ancient wisdom traditions came together in our own era, however, in the modern Enneagram of psycho-spiritual types. Thus, the Enneagram as we now know it is a new synthesis, the work of Oscar Ichazo, Claudio Naranjo, and other modern developers of the system including Russ and me. Although the Enneagram is based on ancient elements, it is necessary to recognize that its usefulness largely stems from the clarity available from modern psychology. But, unfortunately, because of its complex transmission and development, a lot of misinformation has already grown up around the Enneagram, even though it came to the United States only some thirty years ago in 1970.

For instance, the Enneagram information about the types has not been originated by "the Sufis" and transmitted to us in an "oral tradition" of any kind that is in the public domain, although some have popularized this misleading phrase. Some teachers emphasize the importance of the internal lines of the symbol, some do not. Some teach about the wings, and the nine internal Levels of Development within each type; others do not. Some teach about the Instinctual Variants (the so-called subtypes); others do not. Thus, for better or worse, there is not (and never has been) any such thing as a universally agreed-on interpretation of the Enneagram — there is only an evolving understanding of this extraordinary map of the soul. Likewise, there are only individual Enneagram teachers who approach the nine types from a wide variety of viewpoints, backgrounds, biases, and levels of understanding. Russ Hudson and I are always discovering new depths to what we have already discovered and more powerful and accurate ways of applying the Enneagram in the real world.

This book, in conjunction with our earlier ones, particularly *Personality Types* and *The Wisdom of the Enneagram*, is intended to give serious users of this system an in-depth resource for their work with the Enneagram. It will make available much new material that Russ and I have developed in our Enneagram Training

Program over the last ten years, as well as give us the opportunity to update much of the original material of the first edition. This new edition will also enable me to correct some of the errors that I made in the earlier book so that readers will have access to the most up-to-date, complete, and accurate information possible.

Of course, the work of further clarification and refinement is an ongoing matter, and perhaps this edition will not be the final one for this book, any more than the second edition of *Personality Types* may be for that book. No one can claim that understanding the Enneagram has come to a final conclusion and that everything there is to know about it has been discovered because the Enneagram is about human nature, that most mysterious and elusive of entities. There will always be more to discover, and better ways to communicate what we find.

I have been enormously supported in this work by Brian Taylor whose faith in me has always exceeded my own. Brian's support, good humor, and uncommon good sense have helped steer me in the right direction time and time again — at least whenever I took his advice! Also helping to provide the energy and stability we needed in the office were Dan Napolitano and Tomar Levine, as well as Bob and Lois Tallon, Jane Hollister, Andrea Isaacs, Brian Grodner, Mona Coates, Ed Jacobs, Sarah Aschenbach, and other senior students and colleagues of The Enneagram Institute. Thanks also go to my teachers in the Diamond Heart Approach, A. H. Almaas and Alia Johnson. Without their work and inspiring personal examples, the true spiritual context of our work with the Enneagram would not be as clear or compelling to me or to many others.

I mentioned above that Russ Hudson and I have developed a great deal of new material on the Enneagram over the last ten years of teaching together. I could not have asked for a more brilliant or dedicated teaching partner than Russ: he is a person of true genius, as well as true integrity. Russ has also brought much clear thinking and precision to the study and teaching of the Enneagram. He has helped take it from what had largely been a folk art based on anecdotal self-reportage and scattered insights to a more credible and intellectually respectable field. As important, he has brought his own deep spirituality that has helped illuminate the original meaning of the Enneagram itself.

Finally, I wish to acknowledge the Spirit that seems to be guiding the unfolding of the Enneagram in the world today. Despite so much that is superficial in the field, there is an unmistakably genuine current that is sweeping us forward, supporting us, and urging us on. If we have deeply understood the message of the Enneagram, we know that *we are not our personality* but something more — and it is this "something more" that is responding to this message and is desirous of manifesting itself more clearly in the world. May we come to know our true selves, and thus see ourselves and each other as the precious mystery that we are. If the Enneagram helps us to do this, its purpose will have been amply fulfilled after all.

> *Don Richard Riso*
> *New York City*
> *September 1999*

Like Don, I thanked many people in the revised edition of *Personality Types,* and would again like to offer my gratitude to them. They all continue to touch my life and help me to grow, if only in the fine memories of the times that we shared. I want especially to acknowledge my family — my parents, Al and Honey Hudson, and my dear sisters, Meredith Van Withrow and Lori Mauro, and their families. Many blessings to you all.

I would like also to thank Brian Taylor, Dan Napolitano, Ampara Molina, and Tomar Levine, each of whom, in his or her own way, put in many hours "behind the scenes" to support the work that Don and I are doing. Without their tireless efforts, this book would not have been possible.

Thanks go to our editors at Houghton Mifflin, Suzanne Samuel and John Radziewicz, for their hard work, and also for their generosity, support, and belief in our work. They offered gentle guidance through this process, as well as patience in working with our tight schedules. Thanks also to Susan Lescher, our friend and agent, who has done much to make this book possible.

I would like to thank again my excellent teachers, Hameed Ali, Alia Johnson, Morton Letofsky, Jeanne Hay, Rennie Moran, Kristina Baer, Scott Layton, Hameed Qabbazard, Michael Gruber, and Jerry Brewster. Each of them, by the quality of their Being, has helped me to see the magnificence of our true nature. I would also like to acknowledge our indebtedness to the pioneering genius of Oscar Ichazo. His brilliant insights and profound work are undeniably the basis of this wonderful system, and there would be no Enneagram of types teaching without him. Similarly, I want to thank Claudio Naranjo for his groundbreaking work in developing the psychology of the types. I would also like to remember the great contributions of Mr. Gurdjieff, who opened doors to real knowledge that many — whether they know it or not — have passed through.

I want to offer my love and gratitude to Nusa Maal, who in the past few months has brought much light, beauty, and sweetness into my life. Our days together have renewed the springs of creativity in my own soul and brought me great joy. She is an extraordinary human being, and I look forward to seeing the ways in which her own genius will brighten the world.

As always, I want to thank Don for his ongoing support, profound friendship, and devotion to this work. Without his genius and pioneering contributions, the Enneagram field as we now know it would not exist. While Don built on the seminal work of Ichazo and Naranjo, he has developed the descriptions of the types, discovered the Levels of Development, and made many other innovations that brought clarity, depth, and practical usefulness to the system. His commitment to truth, to integrity, and to a higher good has been a personal inspiration to me many times. Gurdjieff taught that one of the greatest gifts in life is an Essence friend — a friend who supports you in awakening — and I have certainly found an Essence friend in Don.

Last, I give thanks to the unfolding mystery of Being — the living source and destination of all existence. I pray that this work might help us to remember this.

Russ Hudson
New York City
June 1999

Contents

Basics and
New Developments

CHAPTER I

The Practical Guide to Personality Types

W̃e are like prisoners in an unguarded cell. No one confines us against our will, and we have heard that the key that will release us is also locked inside. If we could find the key, we could open the door and be free. Yet, we don't know where it has been hidden, and even if we knew, part of us is afraid to break out of our prison. Once out, where would we go, and what would we do with our newfound freedom?

This is not a meaningless metaphor: we are prisoners of our ego, enchained by our fears, restricted in our freedom, suffering from our condition. No one prevents us from searching for the key that would free us. We must, however, know where to look for it and be willing to use it once we have discovered where it is.

With the Enneagram, we have found a master key, one that will unlock many doors. It gives us access to the wisdom we need to escape from our self-imposed prison so that we can embrace a fuller life. The Enneagram helps us to let go of the limiting mechanisms of our personality so that we can more deeply experience who and what we really are. It provides insights that can help in freeing us from our fears and conflicts, from our wayward passions and compulsions, from our disordered desires and inner confusions.

No part of this process is automatic, however. Even after we have identified our personality type, it still may not be clear how to use the insights we have been given. People often ask, "Now that I know my type, what do I *do* with it? Where do I go with it now?" Understanding the inner workings of the personality types helps to some degree, but information alone is not enough to free us. Instead, we need to understand the transformative process and our role in it. The paradox is that we cannot bring about our transformation yet, without our participation, it cannot be done. So what part do we play in our own inner development, and how can the Enneagram help?

The Enneagram can help because it is an invaluable map for guiding us to the points of blockage in our particular personality structures. The fundamental premise of the Enneagram is that there are nine basic personality structures in human nature — nine points of view, nine value systems, nine ways of being in the world. They have much in common with each other, although each manifests its own set of attitudes and behaviors, reactions and defenses, motivations and habits. And each requires its own unique prescriptions for growth.

The central message of this book is that by showing us what our personality is made of, so to speak, the Enneagram indicates what is necessary for our real growth and transformation. Everyone is not cut from the same cloth, or poured into the same mold; therefore everyone's psychological and spiritual issues will be somewhat different, and the order in which they can best be addressed will be different. By helping us understand the structures of our own personality type, the Enneagram shows us how and why we have closed down and become constricted in our growth. It provides us with a panoramic view of what is happening in us and in our significant relationships. It gives us nonjudgmental, nontechnical language in which to talk about these ideas, and it demystifies much in the realms of psychology and spirituality. We see that these realities are neither foreign nor strange: they are the worlds in which we already live.

In addition to giving us insight into our day-to-day behaviors, the Enneagram offers an answer to our spiritual yearnings because it shows us with great specificity how our personality has limited us, what our path of growth is, and where real fulfillment can be found. It teaches us that the longings and structures of our personality are actually useful guides to the greatest treasures of our soul. By regarding our self-defeating patterns and even our psychological pain and limitations as indicators of our spiritual capacities, we are able to see ourselves in a different light. With this new perspective comes compassion, healing, love, and transformation.

We believe that, rightly understood, the Enneagram can have a tremendously positive effect in the world today. By touching people profoundly, mirroring their experience of themselves and helping them trace the trajectory of their lives, it reveals our common humanity. It speaks to the soul, reawakening faith, hope, and love. Many of our students and readers have told us that the Enneagram has helped them to rediscover spirituality — and even brought many of them back to the churches and traditions they once left. Their deepened appreciation of spirituality and awareness of what spirituality really means allowed them to operate more gracefully within institutional frameworks. They could see the soul of the religion they had left and were able to orient themselves to its true Spirit.

In this book, we have enriched our presentation of the Enneagram with ideas from Fourth Way* schools such as the Gurdjieff Work, the Diamond Approach of A. H. Almaas, the seminal insights of Oscar Ichazo and Claudio Naranjo, and other awareness practices. We have also drawn upon major religious traditions (principally Christianity, Buddhism, Islam, and Jewish mysticism). We hope that this book will be a useful introduction to the Enneagram for those who are unfamiliar with this system, as well as a valuable resource for those already familiar with it, as there is much new information here.

Above all, we hope this book will demonstrate the Enneagram's relevance to all forms of transformational work — and firmly place the Enneagram in its true psycho-spiritual context. The En-

---

* The term popularized by Gurdjieff to indicate a new synthesis and approach to spiritual development that combined the previously well-known three traditional ways — that of devotion, knowledge, and physical austerity. The Fourth Way includes them all, although under the condition of being "in the world, not of it." We will say more about this in a later chapter.

neagram can be applied on a superficial level, of course, and the reader may wish only to use this information to find out what type he or she is, or to find out the type of someone else. New and valuable insights are possible with even this kind of pragmatic information. But to get the full benefits of the Enneagram, one must integrate it into a genuine spiritual practice. Otherwise, the information alone tends to become an end in itself — and ironically tends to solidify the personality structures rather than liberate the person from them. But when the Enneagram is part of a spiritual practice, it more readily becomes a means for recognizing our True Nature, and hence for loosening the structures and limitations of the personality.

Of course, having a spiritual practice does not guarantee ego transcendence and liberation from egocentric structures and consequent suffering. But without a spiritual practice, it is less likely that we can become liberated from the limitations of our personality. The momentum of the ego is too great, and it cannot be transformed without bringing an even greater force to bear upon it: the awareness that comes from a spiritual perspective on ourselves and our lives.

~

The two principal areas in which to use the Enneagram are for *self-understanding* (seeing ourselves as we actually are) and for *understanding others* (so that we can have more harmonious relationships).

By far the most legitimate use of the Enneagram is to understand ourselves. It can help us understand our fears and desires, strengths and weaknesses, defenses and anxieties, how we react to frustration and disappointment — and, more positively, what our truest capacities and greatest strengths are so that we can build on them rather than on misjudgments and illusions.

We will get the most benefit from the Enneagram if we approach it with a spirit of open-ended inquiry, using it as a support for discovering things about ourselves and for seeing how our characteristic issues are played out. As we observe ourselves with the help of the system, we will see what we are up to again and again, especially how we are fleeing from ourselves — and why. And although we may discover many things that make us uncomfortable or that do not fit into the self-image that we have of ourselves, it is important not to judge or condemn ourselves for what we find. As we study our type, we will begin to understand more clearly than ever that our personality is a form of defense that we have continued to use for reasons that started in our infancy. Our personality has brought us this far, but we may not need some of its features as much as we once did. Because the Enneagram predicts the healthy, transcendent qualities that we can expect to attain, it helps us to have the courage to let go of old outmoded habits.

There are three stages to this work. First, we need to learn *self-observation* so that we can see our behavior as objectively as possible. Second, we need to increase our *self-understanding* so that we can know the true motives for our behavior. And third, we need to cultivate *awareness* or *presence*, which facilitates and deepens the process of transformation. Self-observation and self-understanding alone will merely provide us with insight to get us to the threshold of transformation, but it is only through presence and awareness that transformation actually occurs. Without developing the ability to "show up" fully, the transformative moments of our lives will have limited effect.

The Enneagram is not only about understanding and transforming *ourselves*, however; it helps us in understanding *others*, in fostering compassion for them and developing insight into how they think, what they fear and desire, what they value, and what their strengths and weaknesses are. In short, we more easily appreciate perspectives that are different from our own.

Indeed, understanding others more profoundly allows us not only to appreciate the good we find in them but also to be more objective and compassionate about things we may not like about them. Although we tend to think that other people are basically like us, it is helpful to recognize that different types think and feel and react quite differently. By understanding personality types, we can see others more objectively, connecting deeply with them yet remaining in our own center, true to ourselves. By understanding the Enneagram, we paradoxically become both more self-possessed and more capable of reaching out to others.

In fact, we often use the Enneagram in our relationships because it is as important to understand others as it is to understand ourselves. We simply cannot (and do not) go through life with no idea about "what makes others tick" — about how they are likely to react in various circumstances, about their motivations, about how genuine or truthful or good they are. Whether or not we are conscious of it, we always use some kind of "personality theory." It is therefore extremely helpful to recognize what our implicit theory is and to make sure that it is as accurate and comprehensive as possible.

Another reason for understanding the Enneagram is that it helps us recognize our unconscious tendencies before they become self-defeating habits *so that we can avoid the tragic consequences of those habits*. The Enneagram can act as an "early warning system" of potentially harmful behavior, allowing us to do something about it before we become trapped in unhealthy patterns. If our attitudes and behavior did not have potentially tragic consequences, we could think, "Well, why should I care about self-knowledge? What difference does it make to know more about myself or my personality type?"

The answer is that our attitudes and our actions *always have consequences*, some of which can affect the whole of our lives. This makes acquiring self-knowledge and insight into others an extraordinarily practical thing to do. Without self-knowledge, we can make choices that may turn out disastrously. Without knowing our own motives and not having control over our behavior, we can do harmful things to ourselves, our spouse, our children, our friends and acquaintances — even to people we may never meet.

Furthermore, without being good judges of the characters of others, we can be terribly hurt and abused. Many marriages end in bitterness and divorce because people do not know either them-selves or each other. How often have we heard somebody say, "If I had only known what my husband was really like, I would never have married him." Or, "If I had only known the Enneagram twenty years ago, my life would have been so different . . ." We can console ourselves with the thought that at least we know the En-neagram *now* — and with its help, we will be much more likely to avoid the suffering caused by our lack of self-knowledge and the unwise actions that may result. With insight, we have a much better chance to avoid tragedy and become happier.

$$\backsim$$

Each of the great spiritual traditions uses different metaphors to express many of the same discoveries about human nature and to express its insight into the way out of our predicaments. At its deepest, the Enneagram is not only profound psychology but a path toward the spiritual since true self-knowledge is the first step toward spirituality. Despite the Enneagram's origin in a variety of spiritual and metaphysical traditions, however, it is not overtly re-ligious. It can be — and has been — adapted to many different re-ligions and religious expressions because it reflects the patterns found in human nature. By helping us more clearly understand the human side of the relationship between the Divine and the human, the Enneagram can become an integral part of any spirituality.

Thus, while it can say very little about the revealed truths of re-ligion, the Enneagram can say a great deal about the forms that the human ego takes — and these are the primary obstacles to a direct experience of the Divine. It demonstrates both the need for working on ourselves and the direction we must take if we are to do so. The Enneagram is a tool that, when used properly, can help us discriminate between the more superficial aspects of ourselves — our personalities — and the deeper aspects of our true nature — our Essence. That is all it is. But considering the sublimity of this work, the Enneagram is a treasure, something more valuable than anything we could have hoped to discover.

Even in a purely psychological, nontheological frame of reference, we want to understand the Enneagram so that we can become *more free* — more liberated — from whatever is blocked, negative, and destructive — from whatever is unfree, conflicted, fearful, and wounded in ourselves. The Enneagram can aid our healing so that we can use our growing freedom in ennobling and constructive ways.

Once we begin to be liberated from our ego states and our inner conflicts — from the darkness and fear inside — with each step we take toward the light, we will gain that much more freedom and create new capacities in ourselves. Strength will build upon strength, grace upon grace, virtue upon virtue, and each new capacity will summon forth yet another as we become the persons that we are meant to be.

In the end, however, the Enneagram will be as useful and rewarding as *we* make it. The Enneagram will enrich us to the degree that we understand it correctly and use it properly in our lives. We can be confident that we will find endless insights and great riches here.

⌒

Understanding the Enneagram is a practical guide to this system, building on many of the insights first presented by Oscar Ichazo and Claudio Naranjo. We are not concerned here with the basic structure and theory of the Enneagram or with comprehensive descriptions of the nine personality types, as they have been provided in our other books.

Indeed, very little material is repeated from *Personality Types,* and what little was necessary to repeat is completely revised and expanded. This book is also cross-referenced to the Revised Edition of *Personality Types* so that you can return to that longer resource if you want to find out more about something. Furthermore, much of the new material here is completely independent of the earlier book (the Type Profiles, the Questionnaire, and the Recommendations for Personal Growth, for example) and can be used without reference to it.

THE PURPOSE OF THE ENNEAGRAM

The Enneagram reveals the patterns by which we organize and give meaning to all of our experiences. Its basic premise is that if we could see the core pattern around which we organize and interpret all of our experiences, the framework on which we hang the events of our lives, we could make much quicker progress in our spiritual and psychological growth. This core patterning is, of course, our personality type.

When we recognize our type and see it at work in ourselves, aspects of our personality that have been hidden from us are revealed, and paradoxically, start loosening up. We suddenly have considerably more psychological space in which to maneuver because we can see ourselves with more perspective.

It would not be far-fetched to say that one of the main points of the Enneagram is to show us where our personality "trips us up" the most. It highlights both what is possible for us, as well as how self-defeating and unnecessary many of our reactions and behaviors are. Our type has both positive and negative qualities, but we do ourselves no favor either by exalting it or by condemning it — not to mention using it to judge other people or their types.

No matter what our type is, and no matter what particular form our ego has taken, we all face one central problem — estrangement from our deepest nature. We may have had intimations that what lies beneath the structure of our personality is something miraculous, the very thing that we have wanted more than anything else, even though we have looked everywhere else to find it. Despite our intimations, it is difficult to let go of our personality and to trust that there is actually something more "essential" in us. It is difficult to believe that there is actually a spark of Divinity in *me*.

But there is good news as well because the structures of our personality tell us what the main blockages to our true nature are. This is why the Enneagram, properly understood, is an extraordinary tool for psychological and spiritual growth: it illuminates the unconscious parts of ourselves that stand in the way of our being more fully alive. It demonstrates that *what stands in the way between ourselves and bliss is our attachment to our personality.*

Perhaps one of the most challenging notions for us to accept at the beginning of transformational work is that the personality — the ego and its structures — is an artificial construct. But it only *seems real because up until now it has been our entire reality.* Identifying with our personality has been how we have lived and gotten by in life. Insofar as it has enabled us to do so, the personality has been a useful, even highly valuable, friend.

As our insights deepen, however, we come to accept the hard truth that our personality is largely a collection of internal defenses and reactions, deeply ingrained beliefs and habits about the self and the world that have come from the past, particularly from our childhood. To put this more simply, *our personality is a mechanism from the past,* perhaps one that has helped us survive until now, but one whose limitations can now be seen. We all suffer from a case of mistaken identity: we have forgotten our True Nature and have come to believe that we *are* the personality. The reason we must explore the defenses of the personality and the vulnerabilities it is protecting is so that we can reexperience our Essential nature — our spiritual core — and know directly who we really are.

Each of us came into the world as pure Essence, *although that Essence was still undeveloped.* Each of us has also had a mother and a father (or other caretakers) who already had their personalities very much in place. Because they had to protect themselves from experiencing their own developmental gaps and losses, it was not possible for them to fully support the unfolding of all of the aspects of our spirit, no matter how much they loved us. In short, to the degree that they could not be with the fullness of their own Essence, they could not recognize or help develop the fullness of our Essence. From this perspective, we can also see that these blockages may go back many generations.

Our parents unintentionally sent "messages" to us as children to hide ourselves. We gradually came to believe that one or more parts of us were not safe to have or to display to the world. No matter how well intentioned our parents were, to some degree, we all succumbed to the process of hiding and covering over our Essential nature. Out of the need to make unconscious adjustments to our caregivers came the need to form a personality. We began to feel that "What I am is not acceptable, so I need to be different. Maybe I need to be happier, or quieter, or less energetic." The costs of these necessary survival adjustments are great, although perhaps the greatest cost is that we gradually become terrified to be seen as we are. We have spent most of our lives not allowing ourselves to be seen, not seeing other people, and most destructively, not wanting to see ourselves.

Further, the painful events of early childhood create a particular way of interpreting our experiences so that later life events reinforce our beliefs about our self and the world. For instance, a child who has been physically abused will tend to view the world as threatening and will have problems getting close to people. Such a person will expect, and tend to find, abusive situations. As a result of this reinforcement of our earliest sense of self, our personality gets "thicker" and we begin to think, "This is me — it's just the way I am." We identify with our reactions and our habitual self-image and beliefs. We do not want to see what is beneath the personality because to go into the areas that have been blocked and covered over means that we will reexperience our deepest hurts. Furthermore, doing so reveals the insubstantiality of our personality — and that is extremely threatening both to our sense of identity and to our ideas about how to survive in the world.

This is not to say that personality is necessarily bad, but when the mechanisms of the personality are running the show, the most dire things can happen. All of us can think of dozens of times when we came within a hairsbreadth of disaster but for the fact that we had enough presence of mind to stop the momentum of events and avert a catastrophe. We can all look back to times when, if a few of the wrong words had been spoken, or if we had allowed rage, sarcasm, or pride to take over, the rest of our lives would have taken a different turn. We can all remember pivotal moments when we could have allowed ourselves to go along with the rush of our personality, but did not. Something intervened.

That something was *awareness*. Suddenly we were able to wake up to the danger, the foolishness, and the self-destructiveness of what we had been doing, and to stop it before things got worse. In retrospect, we may get cold shivers when we think about how close we came to losing a job, our best friend, our marriage, or to alienating our children. If something in us had not been awake to see what we were unconsciously doing, the rest of our lives would be very different. That we were present in those crucial moments changed the course of our own history and made all the difference.

Awareness is part of our Essential nature: it is the aspect of our Being that registers our experience. Awareness is such a fundamental capacity, that it is almost impossible to imagine what it would be like to be without it. In more mundane terms, we can also recognize awareness as our capacity to pay attention. Unfortunately, our attention is usually drawn into deep identifications with the preoccupations of our personality — into fantasies, anxieties, reactions, or subjective memories. When our awareness becomes identified with these aspects of our personality, we lose contact with the immediacy of our lived experience. Our attention shrinks away from a broader perspective and from what is actually occurring around us. It contracts into narrow concerns or reactions and we "fall asleep."

When we begin to pay attention to what is actually here, however, to become more aware of the sensations and impressions of the present moment, something very interesting happens. The simple act of returning our attention to the present causes our awareness to expand. We become aware of much more than the narrow concerns of our personality, and we reconnect with aspects of our nature we did not suspect existed.

What would it be like if we were present so often that we no longer waited until the last minute to react to impending disaster? What if we were so awake that we could see the reality of our circumstances, even as they shift and change? We would be able to notice impulses arising in us as if they were trains pulling into a railroad station. We could see destructive impulses coming while they were still at a safe distance, and decide consciously whether or not to board them, as it were. What would our lives be like if we did not automatically get on the train to be whisked away to some undesirable destination before we knew what had happened? What if we were so present that we no longer lived in a semifog of habits and diminished consciousness, going through much of our lives as if we were barely there at all? What if we were so present that we no longer felt that life was some kind of death sentence, something we must endure until we finally got through it? Rather than experience most moments as tedious and dull — and feeling the need to protect and distract ourselves from their pain and boredom — what if we experienced every moment as a gift, something indescribably precious, unique, and irreplaceable?

The good news is that *we can have a new life* if we are willing to learn and practice a few simple lessons.

The first is that there is more to us than our personality. Our true Self and our personality are not the same thing, and it is the quality of *presence* that restores the proper balance between them and allows us to embody the expansive qualities of our true nature. The personality is highly automatic: it tends to create the same problems for us again and again. *But the personality is only automatic when we are not aware of it.* When our awareness arises and we directly experience the mechanisms of our personality, they cannot function as automatically as before.

Furthermore, the habits and reactions of our personality take up far more of our energy than we can imagine. Many of us believe that letting go of the patterns of our personality will render us ineffective and dull-minded. Actually, the opposite is true. Learning to let go, to relax, to become more present and awake, liberates enormous energy in us and enables us to accomplish far more than we would have thought possible.

The second important lesson is that *presence never becomes habitual.* We will never find a formula or technique that will automatically allow us to be present all the time. Such an automatic method of being present would be a contradiction — a way of being awake while we were actually "asleep." We do not have to push ourselves, change our basic life circumstances, or use willpower for transformation to occur. A real, lasting solution lies in another direction — by coming back to ourselves with ever-deepening awareness, we see and experience the structures of our personality from a larger perspective, and our old habits begin to loosen and drop away. The miracle is that to the degree that they are *fully experienced*, our old, self-defeating structures will begin to dissolve.

By speaking to the truth of who we really are, the Enneagram reminds us of our own innate nobility and spiritual potentials. It helps us discern the more superficial, automatic self of personality from the profound riches of our Essence — our True Self.

This is the core of spirituality; real spirituality involves becoming more real. And as we become more real, we begin to become more aware of the Divine since the "really real" is the Divine. In order to come in contact with what is "really real," we must understand and disidentify with the limiting and destructive aspects of our personality. As we gradually learn to disengage from our various habits and fears, agendas and behaviors, we begin to understand the magnificence we are called to.

There is the widespread sense that humanity is at an important milestone. While the last century has seen enormous strides in science, medicine, and technology, real understanding and healing of the human psyche has not kept pace. Given our enormous technological power, and with it, our increased potential for self-destruction, we have come to a point in history where genuine self-knowledge is no longer a luxury. Whether or not human beings will learn to live together peacefully remains in doubt; whether or not we will be able to stop ourselves from stripping the earth of its resources remains in doubt; whether or not we will be able to stop fearing those who are unlike us and whose customs and religion are different from our own remains in doubt; whether or not hatred will turn out to be a stronger force than love remains in doubt.

One thing is for sure, however. Unless we humans are able to get over our identification with our egoselves — and with it, our willingness to destroy what does not support our ego and its demands — we will not survive. Unless we are able to see beyond our impoverished and desperate ego to the magnificence of the universal Self manifesting in each of us, we will be unsatisfied. Unless we truly learn to love ourselves, we will destroy ourselves.

At this momentous time in human history, something powerful and decisive has been revealed to the world: the Enneagram. Its insights puncture our defenses and lay bare the inner workings of our psyches with their mysterious mix of spiritual yearnings and destructive impulses. The Enneagram helps us rediscover our own humanity and also the humanity of all human beings. With its help, we can rediscover the ancient spiritual truth, taught by many different traditions, that *we must love one another or perish*.

What greater gift could be given to the world as we embark on a new millennium? And what deeper truth could we learn day in and day out, every moment of our lives?

The Basics of the Enneagram

This section is included so that readers can grasp the basics of the system or refresh their memories about the Enneagram. (For more details, consult *PT*, 27–55.) *

One of the most important things that distinguishes the Enneagram from other personality typologies is that it is a *dynamic system*. This means that the nine types are not static categories — they are interrelated in specific ways, as indicated by the inner lines of the symbol. The Enneagram is valuable because it sheds light on our major challenges to growth as well as on our hidden strengths. It describes nine distinct personality types — nine ways that human nature expresses itself, nine different perspectives on life, nine modes of being in the world. It has important implications not only for self-help but for intimate relationships and all other forms of interactions as well, such as therapy, education,

---

* Parenthetical references to the Revised Edition of *Personality Types* are abbreviated *PT* and include page numbers from that book.

The Peacemaker
9

The Challenger 8   1 The Reformer

The Enthusiast 7   2 The Helper

The Loyalist 6   3 The Achiever

The Investigator 5   4 The Individualist

The Enneagram

and business, to name only a few. But the primary use of this system is to help us discover our true nature and the obstacles to expressing it in the world.

The following short descriptions may help you identify your type.

Type One, *the Reformer,* is principled, purposeful, self-controlled, and perfectionistic.

Type Two, *the Helper,* is generous, demonstrative, people-pleasing, and possessive.

Type Three, *the Achiever,* is adaptable, ambitious, image-conscious, and arrogant.

Type Four, *the Individualist,* is expressive, romantic, withholding, and temperamental.

Type Five, *the Investigator,* is innovative, cerebral, detached, and provocative.

Type Six, *the Loyalist,* is reliable, committed, defensive, and suspicious.

Type Seven, *the Enthusiast,* is spontaneous, versatile, distractible, and excessive.

Type Eight, *the Challenger,* is self-confident, decisive, dominating, and confrontational.

Type Nine, *the Peacemaker,* is reassuring, agreeable, disengaged, and stubborn.

We have given the personality types these names, just as other authors have given the types different names. The names we have chosen reflect traits of each type that are relatively *healthy.* In the Arica presentation, by contrast, the types are given names based on their "ego fixations"; for example, the One is given the name "Ego Resentment." (See Lilly and Hart or Wagner for the other correlations.*)

The names that we have assigned to each type were also chosen to help focus on the type's most prominent role. From another perspective, each type's most important *weakness* is related to (but not the same as) its most important strength. You may find a little of yourself in each type, although *one* type should stand out as most typical of yourself. That is your *basic personality type.*

To understand personality types is to understand general patterns. This understanding is enormously useful, but we must keep in mind that the types are generalizations and that no person is precisely like the description of his or her type. General descriptions must walk a fine line between being specific enough to convey precise information about each type while being general enough so that all the individuals who belong to each type can find themselves in it. The rule, then, is this: the types are general patterns; individuals are unique variations on those patterns.

An analogy might help. Just as we all know what we mean when we say that something is the color "red," once we have understood the personality types, we are given similarly specific in-

---

* Works contained in the Bibliography are referred to in the text by their authors' last names, and page numbers are given where appropriate.

formation when we say that someone is a "Five." In both cases, the words "red" and "Five" give us only a general idea of the particular class under consideration; in both cases, there are hundreds of possible individual variations. For example, crimson, brick, scarlet, maroon, burgundy — and many more hues — are variations on red, and yet we know very clearly what someone means when he or she says that something is "red." Even if we cannot be certain of the precise shade of red the person is referring to, we still know enough to distinguish a red object from a black one or a yellow one. Red is clearly not black, and yellow is certainly not red — just as a Five is not an Eight or an Eight a One. Categories such as these are different and distinct. To further the analogy, just as we can distinguish between types, we can distinguish between individuals within a type. I might be a cobalt blue while someone else is an aquamarine blue: we are both still in the "blue family" and therefore have a number of traits in common. And yet we are still different, still ourselves, and still unique. Once we know the Enneagram, we know that we are talking about general patterns when we refer to different types.

Seen from this point of view, the personality types of the Enneagram are as diverse and distinct as the colors of the rainbow, only much more complicated. Each one of us is an individual, unique person, and yet a moment's reflection will reveal some of the many ways in which we are alike. In fact, we should expect to find that human beings are alike in many ways. After all, we share the same biological basis for our common human nature. We all have blood and bones, the same basic male or female anatomy, we all use language and are able to deal with abstract ideas, we have all had parental figures, and we have all had to learn to relate to ourselves, the world, and other people. Even though cultural differences influence us a great deal, certain underlying qualities are common to all human beings.

Nor is uniqueness denied by the Enneagram. Uniqueness is to be found in the different facts of our lives: no two individuals in the history of the human race have been born at the same instant, to the same parents, into the same family and culture, with the same genetic endowments, educated in the same way, and the subject of precisely the same influences. What makes us unique is our unique history. But what makes us part of a personality type is the fact that we also share certain traits with other human beings. Although we are unique, we are not totally different. It would be an impossible world if everyone were literally *completely unique,* that is, if everyone were a totally dissimilar entity unto himself or herself. Language, literature, the arts, commerce, communication — all of society and culture — would be impossible if people did not have a great many qualities in common.

From the point of view of psychology, if people were totally unique, they would also have totally different neuroses, and no general theories or techniques could be devised to help them. The fact that we are like each other (and are especially similar to those of our personality type) is shown most clearly by how much alike people with common personality disorders are. Depressives are like other depressives — thinking and saying things very similar to other depressives. Hysterics resemble other hysterics; those who dissociate from reality are like others who do the same, even in their appearance and their responses to the world around them.

All this being said, finding one's personality type can still be challenging. Those new to the Enneagram frequently encounter three common problems. First, people tend to pick the personality type they would like to be rather than the one they actually are. Learning to be objective about ourselves and about our core motivations is, of course, very difficult — nevertheless, objectivity is one of the very things we are ultimately trying to achieve with the Enneagram. (More guidelines for identifying your type are given in Chapter 5.)

Second, people tend to make an identification based on a single trait. For example, someone might say, "Twos are kind, and I'm kind, so therefore I must be a Two." While it is true that Twos are kind, so are Nines and Fours — and sometimes Ones, Threes, Fives, and all of the types. It is almost impossible to determine your type based on one trait: it is important to see the larger pattern of traits as well as the motivations behind them. Once you have discovered your personality type, you will find that it really does describe you better than any of the other types. Of course, it will also contain traits that you may not have recognized in yourself before as well as traits that are as familiar as old clothes. (For more guidelines about distinguishing between similar types, see Chapter 6.)

A third common problem is that people are tempted to pick and choose among the traits as if the descriptions were a smorgasbord. This approach does not work because the personality types are not arbitrary. The traits that constitute each of the types have not been haphazardly thrown together by human nature. On the contrary, they grow out of each other, proceeding from each other like the colors of the rainbow. They are expressions of our basic fears and desires, our fundamental needs and values and reactions to ourselves and the world around us. While there may well be strange and contradictory traits found among the types, they are all of a piece.

Nor are the nine types of the Enneagram arbitrary: they fall into three groups of three, each group being one of the Triads of the Enneagram. (Each of these three Triads is also associated with a "center" or function of human intelligence — the Thinking Center, the Feeling Center, and the Instinctive Center. These have also been called the head, heart, and gut centers, respectively.) The three types in each Triad share a number of significant issues and features. Primary among these is that each of the three types in a Triad shares that Triad's center as the basis of their personality structure. For example, types Two, Three, and Four are the three types found in the Feeling Triad — and their common assets and liabilities involve issues related to the heart. These types are most centrally concerned with finding a sense of value and identity, as well as with expressing the other authentic qualities of the heart. Types Five, Six, and Seven constitute the Thinking Triad — and their strengths and weaknesses involve their ability (or inability) to find a sense of inner guidance and support — functions traditionally associated with the Thinking Center. These types have difficulty making decisions and determining how to move into the future. Finally, types Eight, Nine, and One are the types in the Instinctive Triad — and their assets and liabilities involve their ability to relate in a more or less balanced manner with their own instinctual energy — with their vitality and life force. These Triads can be understood more clearly on the Enneagram itself.

Each Triad has an inner structure based on a dialectical relationship among the three types in it (*PT,* 28–30). In each Triad, one type *overexpresses* the characteristic faculty of the Triad, another type *underexpresses* the faculty, and the third type is *most out of touch* with the faculty (this is the "primary type" of each Triad and is the type on the equilateral triangle).

If we move around the Enneagram Triad by Triad, beginning with personality type Two in the Feeling Triad, we will see these dialectical relationships more clearly. The Two is the type that tends to overexpress its feelings. Twos become effusive and overly friendly, expressing only their positive feelings for others while repressing any awareness of their own needs or ulterior motives. The Three is the primary type of the Feeling Triad. Because Threes are most out of touch with their feelings, they focus on tasks and

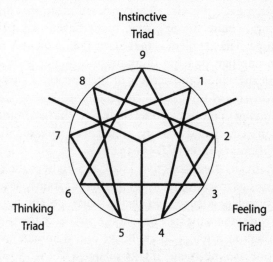

The Triads of the Enneagram

performance while unconsciously being motivated by their feelings — principally their desire to be valued and accepted. The Four is the dialectical opposite of the Two; Fours are painfully self-conscious and underexpress their feelings, revealing themselves instead through various forms of art or creativity, or simply by withholding the direct expression of their feelings. All three types have common problems with their identities and with hostility, both of which are expressed differently and have different causes (PT, 34–37).

In the Thinking Triad, the Five is the type that, in a sense, overexpresses thinking: Fives are the most cerebral and mentally intense of all of the types. They live for their ideas, their concepts, and their imagination while neglecting many of the practical aspects of life. The Six is the primary type of this Triad. Sixes are most out of touch with the inner guidance that an open Thinking center can provide. Sixes think plenty; in fact, they overthink — anxiously figuring things out and second-guessing themselves so much that they are unable to recognize their own inner guidance. Sixes look to beliefs or to trusted others to reassure them and to give them the confidence to act decisively. The Seven is the type that underexpresses thinking. This does not mean that Sevens are unintelligent — quite the opposite, many Sevens are bright and quick-minded. The problem is that Sevens jump quickly from one thought to another, or from thinking into doing, without really thinking through the ramifications of their actions. This can lead them to do too many things at once, becoming hyperactive and addicted to staying in motion. These three types have common problems with insecurity and anxiety, which are expressed differently and have different causes (PT, 37–39).

And, finally, in the Instinctive Triad, the Eight is the type that overexpresses its instinctual energy. Eights constantly assert themselves, their independence, and their vitality, potentially wearing out themselves and others. Their desire to assert themselves can also lead them to attempt to challenge and dominate everything and everyone around them. Eights relate to the world by seeing themselves as stronger and more realistic than everyone else. The

Nine is the primary type of the Instinctive Triad. Nines are most out of touch with their instinctual energy — their passion, anger, and zest for life. Nines would like to transcend this energy or "mellow it" in order to maintain their peace of mind and ease in life. This lack of identification with their own instinctive energy can lead Nines to identify more strongly with others, living through someone else. Nines also try to maintain their independence, but not by asserting it like Eights. Nines feel autonomous by withdrawing their active attention from others. The One is the type that underexpresses its instinctual energy, but primarily by trying to control it. Ones try to resist acting on their instincts, believing that they need to feel justified by being right before they act. Ones constantly measure themselves against ideals of various sorts that they strive to attain. All three types have in common aggression and repression (*PT*, 39–41). Of course, these issues are expressed differently and have different causes. (More about the Triads can be found in *PT*, 28–30, 34–43, and 433–36, and in the Overview of the description of each type.)

⌐

In the Enneagram, as in life, there are no pure types. Everyone is a unique mixture of his or her basic type and one of the two types adjacent to it, called a "wing." Second in importance to the basic type, the auxiliary type, or wing, provides the basic type with other psychological functions, sometimes complementing the basic type, sometimes working in opposition to it. Of all the theoretical aspects of the Enneagram, the so-called wing theory is the most controversial because some writers feel that there is no wing, some (including the authors) feel that there is usually one dominant wing, and others feel that there are two wings, one on each side of the basic type.

The truth, with regard to this dispute (as with others regarding the theory of the Enneagram), can be discovered only by looking to human nature: what are human beings really like?

We initially saw that the vast majority of people we encountered in our workshops seemed to have a dominant wing, but there were also a number of individuals who seemed to have either both wings or no wings. We have resolved this apparent conflict by thinking of the wings in relation to the circle part of the Enneagram symbol. If you look at the symbol itself, you can easily see that the circle could be divided into nine segments or arcs corresponding to the nine types. Thus, a type is not a single point where the inner lines of the Enneagram touch the circle, but a range of points along the circle's circumference. Our personalities, we could say, fixate or crystallize somewhere along that segment. For instance, a Three's personality might crystallize on the segment of "Threeness" closer to type Two. This, of course, would be a Three with a Two-wing. Another Three might crystallize on the opposite end of the segment, closer to Four. This person would be a Three with a Four wing. Naturally, the farther away from the central point, and the closer to one of the other points, the stronger the person's wing would be. But a person who crystallized close to the center point of the range of Threeness could be said to have both wings, or no wings, depending on whether you see the glass as half full or half empty. This is an example of creating a map or theoretical framework to account for what we actually encountered in real people.

Also remember that, in truth, we possess the entire Enneagram in our psyches. Seen from this point of view, it would be true to say that we have "two wings" since (to return to our example) a Three with a Two-wing would also automatically have something of the Four by virtue of possessing all of the human potentials symbolized by the Enneagram.

⌣

There has also been some question about whether it is possible to change your basic personality type, especially as you become older. Some people feel that they were one type when they were children but became another type as adults owing to various factors in their lives.

We remain convinced that people do not change from one basic personality type to another. We develop from childhood as an example of a certain personality type — as a unique individual within a larger group — and we essentially remain that type for the rest of our lives. We grow or deteriorate from that beginning point, our basic type, which reflects who we have become as the result of genetics and our childhood experiences, especially the relationships we have had with our parents. Which type we have become is profoundly who we are, and this does not change to a radically different type.

But of course, in reality, people do change, and the Enneagram accounts for psychological change of various sorts. We may shift in our emotional states many times a day, but usually in recognizable patterns. These patterns can be predicted by the inner lines on the Enneagram. Everyone "moves" in specific Directions of Integration and Disintegration as indicated by the lines of the Enneagram from the basic type.

The Direction of Disintegration or Stress (which signals that the person is under increased stress and that the normal coping mechanisms of the basic personality type are being overtaxed) is indicated on the Enneagram by the sequence of numbers 1-4-2-8-5-7-1 and 9-6-3-9. The Direction of Integration (which signals that we are more secure and can mark the further integration of your basic type) is indicated by the reverse of these two sequences; thus, 1-7-5-8-2-4-1 and 9-3-6-9. For example, a One under stress will move to Four, the type in its Direction of Disintegration, while a One who is more relaxed can move to Seven, the type in its Direction of Integration; a Nine will go to Three when more secure, or to Six under greater stress.

While it is helpful to have separate Enneagrams for each of these sequences, it is really not necessary once you know what the two lines from each basic personality type mean — one indicates that type's Direction of Integration; the other indicates its Direction of Disintegration (*PT*, 47–51) — and the arrows can be eliminated.

Thus, *four* of the personality types are pertinent for a full analysis of any individual — the basic type, the wing, the type in the Direction of Integration, and the type in the Direction of Disintegra-

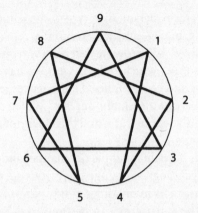

The Direction of Integration   The Direction of Disintegration
1-7-5-8-2-4-1   1-4-2-8-5-7-1
9-3-6-9   9-6-3-9

The Directions of Integration and Disintegration

tion. We must attempt to see how these four types (at their various Levels), along with other important personality factors (such as intelligence, which the Enneagram does not categorize), combine in us to help make us the unique persons we are. Thus, as we continue our quest for self-understanding, not only the basic personality type but also the wing and the types in our Directions of Integration and Disintegration must be taken into consideration.

It is also important to have a sense of the movement within our own personality. The many hundreds of traits that make up our type are part of a larger pattern — our type as a whole. The traits found in each type are not arbitrary: they are interrelated in extremely complex and subtle ways. Moreover, people fluctuate among the traits that constitute their type along a Continuum of nine Levels of Development, ranging from high-functioning states to painful, potentially pathological ones.

Because people are constantly changing and are functioning in different Levels of Development, not everything in the descriptions will apply to them equally. When you are healthy, the unhealthy traits will not apply to you as you are right now. Nevertheless, you should be able to recognize all of the traits of your basic type as genuine *tendencies* inherent in yourself.

Our unhealthy traits should strike us as accurate reflections of what would happen to us — of how we would become — if we were to become emotionally unhealthy or neurotic. Likewise, we should recognize the traits of the types in the Directions of Integration and Disintegration as accurate descriptions of behavior we have observed in ourselves. The Continuum (with the nine Levels of Development it comprises) can be pictured as follows:

Level 1	X
Level 2	X Healthy
Level 3	X
—	—
Level 4	X
Level 5	X Average
Level 6	X
—	—
Level 7	X
Level 8	X Unhealthy
Level 9	X

The Levels of Development

As you get to know the personality types — and yourself — in more depth, you will find that on a profound level, the Enneagram lays out the full range of psychological possibilities, revealing the many different potential parts of yourself *in all of the types*. While it remains true that everyone emerges from childhood as a unique member of only one basic personality type, it is equally true that as we develop over our lifetime, it is possible to integrate the healthy psychological aspects of the other types as we activate new capacities. We can move beyond the type in our Direction of Integration to the next type and then to the next, around the Enneagram in an endless upward spiral of integration (*PT*, 54–55, 418).

The Enneagram is not imposing a narrow theory on human beings. Rather, it is a framework within which we can understand the subtle dynamics that make each of us who we are. Everyone constantly changes, and the very structure of the Enneagram reflects the fact that human nature is in process, always coming into being.

CHAPTER 2

The Traditional Enneagram

~

The Enneagram of Personality Types is a modern synthesis of a number of ancient wisdom traditions, and the person who originally put the system together was Oscar Ichazo. Ichazo was born in Bolivia and raised there and in Peru, but as a young man, he moved to Buenos Aires to learn from a school of Inner Work he had encountered. Thereafter, he journeyed in Asia gathering other knowledge before returning to South America to begin putting together a systematic approach to all he had learned.

After many years of developing his ideas, he created the Arica School as a vehicle for transmitting the knowledge that he had received, teaching in Chile in the late 1960s and early '70s, before moving to the United States where he still resides. In 1970, when Ichazo was still living in South America, a group of Americans, including noted psychologists and writers Claudio Naranjo and John Lilly, went to Arica, Chile, to study with Ichazo and experience firsthand the methods for attaining self-realization that he had developed.

This group spent several weeks with Ichazo, learning the basics of his system and engaged in the practices he taught them. The Arica School, like any serious system of inner work, is a vast, interwoven, and complex body of teachings on psychology, cosmology, metaphysics, spirituality, and so forth, combined with various

practices to bring about transformations of human consciousness.
(The authors are not affiliated with this school, and therefore cannot describe it with any justice, but those seeking to learn more
about it can do so through Arica publications.*)

Among the highlights for many of the participants was a system
of teachings based on the ancient symbol of the Enneagram. The
Enneagram symbol has roots in antiquity and can be traced back
at least as far as Pythagoras.† The symbol was reintroduced to
the modern world by George Gurdjieff, the founder of a highly
influential inner work school. Gurdjieff taught the symbol primarily through a series of sacred dances or movements, designed to
give the participant a direct, felt sense of the meaning of the symbol and the processes it represents. What Gurdjieff clearly did *not*
teach was a system of types associated with the symbol. Gurdjieff
did reveal to advanced students what he called their "chief feature." The chief feature is the linchpin of a person's ego structure
— the basic characteristic that defines them. Gurdjieff generally
used colorful language to describe a person's chief feature, often
using the Sufi tradition of telling the person what kind of "idiot"
they were. People could be round idiots, square idiots, subjective
hopeless idiots, squirming idiots, and so forth. But Gurdjieff never
taught anything about a system of understanding character related to the Enneagram symbol.

For these and other reasons, many early Enneagram enthusi-
asts have mistakenly attributed the system of the nine types to
Gurdjieff or to the Sufis because of Gurdjieff's use of some Sufi
techniques. This has led to the widespread and erroneous belief
that the Enneagram system has been handed down from the Sufis
or from some other ancient school as an ongoing "oral tradition."
While it is true that Ichazo drew on his knowledge of a number of

---

* We particularly recommend *Interviews with Oscar Ichazo* (Arica Press, 1982). It
gives readers a feel for Ichazo's overall philosophy and explains in simple language his
orientation and use of Enneagrams, or Enneagons, as he calls them.

† Ichazo has called the Enneagram the Ninth Seal of Pythagoras; see Goldberg, 1993.

such traditions, the actual combination of those traditions connected with the Enneagram symbol is purely his creation. Thus, the "traditional Enneagram" only goes back to the 1960s when Ichazo was first teaching it, although the philosophy behind the Enneagram contains components from mystical Judaism, Christianity, Islam, Taoism, Buddhism, and ancient Greek philosophy (particularly Socrates, Plato, and the Neo-Platonists) — all traditions that stretch back into antiquity.

In *Personality Types* (11–26), we offered a more extensive history of the system, but here we want to look at the basics of the Enneagram system developed by Ichazo.* Ichazo actually taught Aricans a system of 108 Enneagrams (or Enneagons, in his terminology), but the Enneagram movement in America has been based on the first few, and primarily on four of them. These are called the Enneagram of the Passions, the Enneagram of the Virtues, the Enneagram of the Fixations, and the Enneagram of the Holy Ideas.

To grasp the significance of these diagrams and the relationship between them, we must remember that the system was designed primarily to help elucidate the relationship between Essence and personality, or ego (See Chapter 1 of *Personality Types*, "The Purpose of the System"). In Ichazo's words:

> We have to distinguish between a man as he is in essence, and as he is in ego or personality. In essence, every person is perfect, fearless, and in a loving unity with the entire cosmos; there is no conflict within the person between head, heart, and stomach or between the person and others. Then something happens: the ego begins to develop, karma accumulates, there is a transition from objectivity to subjectivity; man falls from essence into personality.†

---

* We do not claim to be representatives of Ichazo's teachings, but rather wish to offer our own interpretation of a few of them based on our own work with the system over the last few decades.

† John Bleibreu, ed., *Interviews with Oscar Ichazo* (New Rochelle, N.Y.: Arica Institute Press, 1982), 9.

Thus, Ichazo saw the Enneagram as a means to examine specifics about the ways in which actual soul qualities of Essence become distorted, or contracted, into states of ego. In developing his Enneagram theories, he drew upon a recurrent theme in Western mystical and philosophical tradition — the idea of nine Divine Forms. This idea was discussed by Plato as the Divine Forms or Platonic Solids — qualities of existence that are essential, that cannot be broken down into constituent parts. This idea was further developed in the third century by the Neo-Platonic philosophers; Plotinus specifically discussed it in his central work, *The Enneads*.

These ideas found their way from Greece and Asia Minor southward through Syria and eventually to Egypt. There, it was embraced by early Christian mystics known as the Desert Fathers who focused on studying the *loss* of the Divine Forms in ego consciousness. The particular ways in which these Divine Forms became distorted came to be known as the Seven Deadly Sins: anger, pride, envy, avarice, gluttony, lust, and sloth. How the original *nine* forms, in the course of their travels from Greece to Egypt over the course of a century, became reduced to *seven* deadly sins remains a mystery.

Another key influence Ichazo employed in developing these ideas comes from mystical Judaism, and particularly from the teachings of the Kabbala. Central to the Kabbala is a diagram called the Tree of Life (*Etz Hayim* in Hebrew). The Tree of Life is said to be a map showing the particular patterns and laws by which God created the manifest universe. The diagram is composed of ten spheres (*Sefirot*) connected by twenty-two paths in particular ways. Most significantly, Ichazo must have been aware of the Kabbalistic teaching that all human souls are "sparks" that arise out of these spheres or emanations from the Kabbalistic Tree. (The first sphere, *Keter*, is reserved for the Messiah, leaving nine other spheres for the rest of us.) In the traditional teachings of the Kabbala, for instance, each of the great patriarchs of the Bible was said to be an embodiment of the different spheres of the

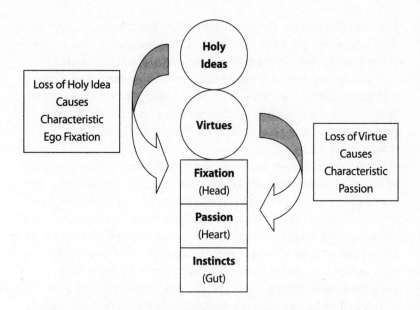

Relationship between Higher Essence Qualities and Ego Distortions

Tree.* This teaching suggests that there are different kinds of souls — different emanations or facets of the Divine Unity.

Ichazo's brilliant work was in discovering how these Divine Forms and their corresponding distortions connected with the Enneagram symbol and with the three Centers of human intelligence: Thinking, Feeling, and Instinct. He called the higher, essential qualities of the human mind the Holy Ideas, in accordance with Western mystical tradition. Each Holy Idea also has a corresponding virtue. The Virtues are essential qualities of the heart experienced by human beings when they are abiding in Essence. As a person loses awareness and presence, falling away from Essence

---

* See *Adam and the Kabbalistic Tree,* by Z'ev ben Shimon Halevi (Weiser, 1974). On page 192 he provides the relationship between the sefirot and the patriarchs. See also Howard Addison's *The Enneagram and Kabbala* (Jewish Lights Press, 1998).

into the trance of the personality, the loss of awareness of the Holy Idea becomes a person's ego fixation, and the loss of contact with the Virtue causes the person's characteristic Passion. While everyone has the capacity to embody all of the Holy Ideas and Virtues, one pair of them is central to the soul's identity, so the loss of the pair is felt most acutely, and the person's ego is most preoccupied with recreating it, although in a futile, self-defeating way. (See the diagram on page 35.)

Thus, the Passions and ego fixations represent the ways that spiritual qualities become contracted into ego states. There are, according to Ichazo's theory, nine main ways that we lose our center and become distorted in our thinking, feeling, and doing; thus there are nine ways that we forget our connection with the Divine. (The Passions can also be thought of as our untamed animal nature before it is transformed by contact from higher influences — awareness and Grace.)

Because of this particular relationship between the higher qualities of the soul and their corresponding ego distortions, a person could, by using presence and awareness to recognize the pattern of their distortion — their characteristic passion and ego fixation — come to recognize the quality of Essence that had been obscured. By remembering or contemplating the higher quality, balance could be restored, thus accelerating the person's awareness of himself or herself as Essence. Knowing one's "type" was a way to direct one's inner work to facilitate the transformative process.

The Virtues, Passions, Holy Ideas, and Fixations

The Virtues describe the expansive, nondual qualities of Essence experienced in a direct, felt way by a person abiding in their true nature. The Virtues are the natural expression of the awakened heart. We do not try to force ourselves to be "virtuous" — rather, as we relax and become more present and awake, seeing through the fear and desire of the ego self, these qualities naturally manifest themselves in the human soul.

An essential individual will be in contact with these [virtues] constantly, simply by living in his body. But the subjective individual, the ego, loses touch with these virtues. Then the personality tries to compensate by developing passions.*

The Passions represent an underlying emotional reaction to the loss of contact with our Essential nature. As we saw in Chapter 1, we all inevitably lose contact with the ground of our Being, with our true identity as Spirit or Essence. The underlying hurt, shame, and grief that this loss entails are enormous, and our ego is compelled to come up with a particular way of emotionally coping with the loss. This temporarily effective, but ultimately misguided coping strategy is the Passion. But because the Passion is a distortion of an inherent, essential Virtue, recognizing the Passion can help us to restore the Virtue.†

In a related way, the Virtue of each type can also be seen as an antidote to its Passion and as a focal point for the type's positive traits. By recalling the Virtue in a state of presence, the Passion can be gradually transformed. The restoration of the Virtue and the transformation of the Passion is an extremely important part of the spiritual use of the Enneagram.

The Holy Ideas represent *specific nondual perspectives of Essence* — particular ways of knowing and recognizing the unity of Being. They are what naturally arises in a clear, quiet mind when a person is present and awake, seeing reality as it actually is. The loss of a Holy Idea leads to a particular ego delusion about the self or reality, called the type's ego fixation. Through the ego fixation, the person is trying to restore the balance and freedom of the Holy Idea, but from the dualistic perspective of ego, he or she cannot. Again, understanding the perspective of our type's Holy Idea func-

---

*John Bleibreu, ed., *Interviews with Oscar Ichazo* (New Rochelle, N.Y.: Arica Institute Press, 1982), 19.

† For a more extensive discussion of the Passions, see *Character and Neurosis*, by Claudio Naranjo (Gateways, 1994).

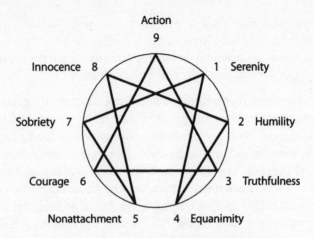

Oscar Ichazo's Enneagram of the Virtues

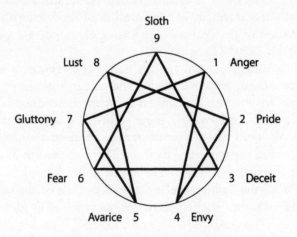

Oscar Ichazo's Enneagram of the Passions

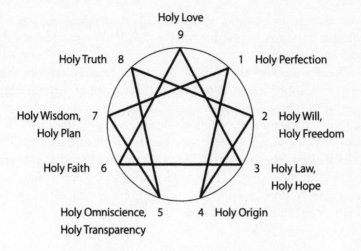

Oscar Ichazo's Enneagram of the Holy Ideas

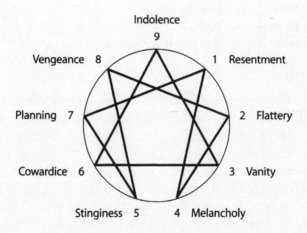

Oscar Ichazo's Enneagram of the Ego Fixations

tions as an antidote to the ego fixation. The nondual perspective of our true nature is restored as we see through the particular delusions of our type.*

The descriptions that follow provide a brief commentary on each of the nine Virtues, Passions, Holy Ideas, and Fixations of the nine types. These descriptions are intended to be short and introductory, and represent *our own understanding of these qualities*. In some cases, we offer alternative names for the different qualities to help clarify the original name's meaning. Please also note that the descriptions of the Holy Ideas and Virtues are of necessity somewhat impressionistic. This is because it is difficult to convey in words the sense of the nondual perspectives of Essence.

TYPE TWO

Passion:	*Pride, Vainglory*
Virtue:	*Humility*
Fixation:	*Flattery*
Holy Idea:	*Holy Will, Holy Freedom*

PASSION:

Pride (vainglory). Pride is caused by the loss of the Virtue of humility. To distinguish it further, we can also call this Vainglory, a pride in one's own goodness, taking a special satisfaction in one's own Virtue, seeing oneself only as a loving, well-intentioned person. The Passion of Pride causes us to see our ego selves as the most important source of love and goodness in the lives of others. ("Where would they be without me?") Further, this is "goodness" that calls attention to itself so that the person will be admired for being

---

* For a full treatment of the Holy Ideas, see *Facets of Unity,* by A. H. Almaas (Diamond Books, 1998).

selfless, praised for being humble, rewarded for being self-sacrificial, repaid for being generous, and so forth.

Another more subtle element to pride is the inability to admit that we are hurting, the unwillingness to acknowledge our own suffering and neediness. This part in each of us says, "*You've* got problems, not me! I'm okay and I'm here to help you." But in fact, all of us, and particularly Twos, are terrified that people will see how sad and lonely we are much of the time. Not only does pride prevent us from allowing people to see that we are in pain, it also prevents us from letting people see that we need anything, or that we are really trying to get something from others. Pride can also be seen as a fundamental denial of the loss of contact with Essence — particularly the loss of contact with qualities of real love.

VIRTUE:

Humility. When we are abiding in our true nature, our identity does not require support from the approval of others or from our own self-regard. Humility is simply Being without self-reflecting. It is not self-disparagement as some of us have been taught, nor is it resisting satisfaction in our work or relationships. When we are really present and awake, issues about our identity and self-worth do not arise. Without attempting to be, we are humble.

This quality gives very healthy Twos the ability to love others disinterestedly, without any thought of self, of being thanked or repaid, or of even having the good regard and appreciation of the people they do things for. They strive to do good unselfishly, helping others for others' sake, without even thoughts of self-congratulations for the effort. They simply see a need and respond (or not) spontaneously and freely.

FIXATION:

Ego flattery. When we lose contact with the Holy Idea of Holy Will, the ego compensates by trying to make good things happen. Twos flatter people, serve others' needs, and make others feel good about themselves so that they will get approval and appreciation.

Like everybody else, Twos need to feel good about themselves, but because of the way that their egos are structured, they cannot feel good about themselves without getting gratitude and love from others. As a result, Twos go out of their way to do good things for others in order to get positive feedback (flattery) about themselves. As a result, the minds of Twos become preoccupied with finding nice things to say or do so that they can feel good about themselves, convince themselves of their loving goodness, and have others confirm it. ("Mary Ann just couldn't live without me.") The ego activity of flattery thus sustains the emotional stance of pride.

Thus, the Two's general pattern becomes "giving in order to get." They give to others with the secret hope that someone will notice how much they have done and give positive attention back to them in return. They meet others' needs with the hope that their needs will also be fulfilled.

HOLY IDEA:

Holy Will, Holy Freedom. The ego mind of the Two believes that its personal efforts are required to make good things happen. Without Twos' goodwill and tireless interventions, goodness will not flower. Thus, others need their help, support, praise, flattery, encouragement, and so forth. When we have the nondual perspective of Holy Will, we recognize that there is only one Will, one unfolding reality, and that the ego only thinks that it is making things happen. We see that everything really is "in God's hands," not as a comforting belief, but as a palpable reality. The recognition of this truth releases the Two's awareness from the compulsive need to help and support: they see that they can help or not help, but that their identity, their Beingness, does not depend on sustaining this activity. This brings Holy Freedom, freedom from the ego and from the compulsive need to prop the ego up by being "good." We could also say that Holy Freedom describes the sense of exhilaration and openness that arise when we experience ourselves as part of the unfolding Divine Will.

TYPE THREE

Passion:	*Deceit, Untruthfulness*
Virtue:	*Truthfulness, Authenticity*
Fixation:	*Vanity*
Holy Idea:	*Holy Law, Holy Hope*

PASSION:

Deceit (untruthfulness). Deceit results from the loss of the Virtue of Truthfulness and can be seen as the tendency to believe that one is the assumed self of personality and not Essence. Deceit entails presenting "images" of ourselves both to ourselves and to others to cover our loss of contact with Being. The sin of the Three is one of the more difficult ones to understand in our culture since it is so pervasive. The passion of deceit does not necessarily refer to people lying all the time in an overt way. In everyday terms, we are talking about being inauthentic instead of being completely honest and real with someone. The more we examine deceit, the more we see how seldom we authentically express what we feel, what we think, or what our true intentions are. To do so requires presence and connectedness with our hearts. If we are caught in the trance of our personalities, this is not possible. More often, we tend to behave in ways that we think will be acceptable to others.

Over time, adjusting ourselves to professional, social, and personal demands becomes so automatic that we lose touch with our true nature. We become identified with a particular self-image that we believe would be more acceptable than our authentic selves, and then must deceive ourselves about who we are and what we really want. Do we identify ourselves with our job? our peer group? our gender? There are all sorts of things that define who we are, but who are we really? Who is this person that is reading the words on this page right now?

Average Threes learned to develop their image and the perfection of their "package" rather than their authentic feelings and identity. Often, average Threes have become so accustomed to identifying with their performance, that they actually do not know who they really are or what they really want from life. They learn to reject their authentic identity and start to deceive themselves that the "improved and polished" picture of themselves is actually who they are. They develop a self-image that they believe will be more acceptable and worthwhile, identify with it, and then expect others to support and applaud it. While Threes are usually rewarded for this self-abandonment, their real growth depends on their reconnecting with their deeper self — their true heart's desire.

VIRTUE:

Truthfulness (authenticity). When we are abiding in our true nature, we speak and act with complete truthfulness: we see that any *untruthfulness* causes us to detach from our true nature. We experience our heart's desire, and realize that the most important thing in life is to be ourselves, deeply and completely. We understand that nothing else will satisfy us, no matter how many accomplishments we pile up. Further, a person embodying real authenticity sees no reason for deception, feeling that the profound connection with others, indeed, with all of reality, makes anything other than simple truth seem absurd.

When healthy Threes understand that their value is not based on any particular achievement, they are able to experience the depths of their own hearts in ways that liberate them from the roles they believe they must play in order to be acceptable. They are able *to be,* but they do not lose their ability to make the most of themselves. Their identity is based on a direct experience of themselves in the living moment, not on a narcissistic, inflated notion of themselves. Truly being themselves enables Threes to love others simply and genuinely. The preciousness of truth and of their true identity are also recognized as the preciousness of everyone and everything.

FIXATION:

Vanity. When we are not in contact with a more authentic experience of ourselves, we must invest our energies in cultivating our persona — making it valuable to compensate for our loss of Essential value and identity. Thus, vanity is the ego activity of trying to make the personality feel real and valuable. Clearly, if we deceive ourselves into believing that we are the personality, then we must apply all of our efforts to doing whatever we believe will make the personality more important, attractive, brilliant, and worthwhile. We will tend to regard meditating and doing deep psychological work to reveal the falseness of the ego and its agenda as a waste of time, or even threatening.

Vanity causes us to invest our energies in building up our self-image. We become concerned with doing and being whatever we believe will make us feel more worthwhile, such as having a successful career, presenting ourselves favorably, attending good schools, achieving goals, building up our résumé, or winning awards. We become lost in the roles that we play in life, and then must make the role valuable instead of recognizing the real value of our true nature.

HOLY IDEA:

Holy Law, Holy Hope. This Holy Idea has to do with correcting the ego's false perception that it is the source of doing and functioning — that the ego is accomplishing something. From the nondual perspective of Essence, everything is one: there is only one complete and total reality that is here in each moment. Right now, if we sense our experience of this moment, we can perceive that all that we can experience is a unity, a oneness. Only our mental activity defines objects and divides our experience into different categories.

If we stay present, however, observing this unity of experience, we will come to see that it *changes* from moment to moment — it *unfolds*. Thus, Essential reality is not static, but a dynamic unfolding of reality moment by moment. The ego mind thinks that we are animate objects interacting with other animate and inanimate objects in a background of space. The perception of Holy Law is quite different: it is perceiving the dynamic, living unity of everything as an unfolding process. There can be no independent doing or accomplishment because everything is happening together. The whole flow of reality is one enormous creative dance, so who is it that is doing? Furthermore, in presence, we understand that the unfolding of the universe is benign, always developing and optimizing. This perception gives us confidence to rest in being (Holy Hope) and allows our ego minds to cease their endless agendas and projects. In a profound, direct way, we understand that God is doing a good job.

TYPE FOUR

Passion:	*Envy*
Virtue:	*Equanimity, Emotional Balance*
Fixation:	*Melancholy*
Holy Idea:	*Holy Origin*

PASSION:

Envy. Envy results from the loss of contact with the Virtue of Equanimity, and leads to the feeling that something is missing in us. We are not sure what it is, but other people seem to be happier, better off than us. Rather than investigate the source of our unease, in the throes of envy, we focus on comparing ourselves with others, believing that they possess qualities that we do not have, that others have had better childhoods, parents, or luck than us. Other people are somehow more alive and more whole. Other people seem to be having more productive lives and careers and wonderful marriages, and envy leads us to believe that these things are not possible for us. ("No one suffers the way I do.") In short, envy sees in others qualities that we would like to have for our own self-completion, but perpetuates the sense of inner lack without dealing with the root problem.

The problem is that Fours identify with their woundedness, with their sense of inner deficiency, and then make a lifestyle out of their suffering. In fact, Fours are perceiving something true: the ego is false, based on suffering, and ultimately deficient. But rather than stay with this direct awareness in a way that would transform them, Fours get caught up in emotional reactions and beliefs about this deficiency, and construct their identity out of it. Thus, the ego self is sustained by identifying with the feeling of inner lack, and by holding on to stories and interpretations about its origin. Envy also alienates us from others and from life. It causes us to feel like outsiders who never belong anywhere, while imagining that others do — and disliking them for it. The result is a constant emotional storminess and reactivity that obscures our ability to perceive our true identity or value, or that of anything else.

VIRTUE:

Equanimity (emotional balance). When we abide in presence, it is natural for us as human beings to feel expansive and open in our hearts. We are touched and affected by our experiences, often in profound ways, but we are not lost or swept away by emotional reactions. Experiencing our true value and identity releases us from the ego's endless frustration and craving — we are calm and abide in our essential dignity. Thus, equanimity gives us tremendous support to remain present even to potentially painful experiences or realizations. We are able to embrace life without being so "storm-tossed" by every feeling. Even negative experiences can be made into something positive, and we find peace in knowing that the soul is able to transform every experience into something worthwhile and valuable.

FIXATION:

Melancholy. We might also call this fixation *Fantasizing*. Fixated Fours become lost in fantasy, using their imaginations to support their intense, envious feelings. Average Fours fixate on thoughts that stir up feelings of longing, of bittersweet romance, of loss, and other melancholy feelings. Unfortunately, this mental activity also blinds Fours to many aspects of objective reality and obscures their true nature. In its more extreme form, this fixation plays itself out as a constant inner commentary on one's one inadequacies and on how others have let one down. It causes Fours to create and sustain elaborate personal histories that reinforce the notion that they have been particularly victimized. ("Not only am I hurt — I'm hurt worse than anyone else! No one has suffered as much as I have!") This fixation causes us to become extremely self-conscious, attached to past hurts, and profoundly cut off from the source of our identity.

HOLY IDEA:

Holy Origin. Because our ego mind is profoundly cut off from the ground of Being, it needs constant support and reinforcement, otherwise its inherent unreality will be revealed. The Four's ego agenda is to sustain a particular identity, to be an individual, and the ego achieves this by focusing on all the ways in which we are unlike others. But when the ego activity slows down and rests, we become aware of Being itself as the source and origin of our true identity. This is not a concept or a belief, but a direct experience of our identity as Essence. We do not, and cannot, do anything to be ourselves. The more we try to become a particular image or idea of ourselves, the more we lose immediate contact with the rich, delightful contact with our true self as Being. We see that we are not separate from anything, that our true nature partakes of the whole of reality. We know directly that all parts of the universe are manifesting a tremendous creative intelligence, and that the self is an aspect of that creative flow and cannot be otherwise. We understand that the source of everything is also the core of our true identity — that it is creating and sustaining the self always. The recognition of this brings a feeling of exquisite delight in simply resting in and being one's true identity.

TYPE FIVE

Passion:	*Avarice*
Virtue:	*Detachment (Nonattachment)*
Fixation:	*Stinginess*
Holy Idea:	*Holy Omniscience, Holy Transparency*

PASSION:

Avarice. The meaning of the word "avarice" is often misunderstood as it applies to type Five. Avarice is usually associated with greed, or the desire to accumulate worldly possessions; however, avarice does not necessarily express itself in materialistic ways. Avarice began to manifest in us when, as small children, we lost contact with our essential natures, and consequently felt small, tiny, and helpless in a vast, uncaring universe. This left all of us, and Fives especially, terrified of life and doubting our ability to function in the world. Thus, Avarice leads Fives to feel that they must retreat from reality or defend against it, while trying to restore the feeling that they are capable and competent to deal with this overwhelming situation. It leads to an emotional attitude of rejection and detachment — a turning away from the world as if one were not part of it. Avarice causes us to feel as though the universe has rejected us, so we better find a way to make do with our wits and with minimal support and resources.

Avarice is often confused with Gluttony, the Passion of type Seven. Gluttony seeks to fill the emptiness of the false self up with experiences and ideas from "outside." Avarice is also based on a sense of inner impoverishment, but it copes by withholding the self, by shrinking back from contact, and by clutching at the little we think we already have because we are afraid of losing it. The ego self feels empty, rejected, and without nourishing sustenance, so it hoards whatever it feels it has. Avarice is trying to retain in the self the resources and knowledge the ego believes it needs to function in the world.

Thus, Avarice in Fives is most often expressed as a kind of collector mentality, collecting more and more knowledge, reading more and more books, continually preparing so that Fives will be able to go out into the world with confidence.

VIRTUE:

Nonattachment. Although Ichazo's original name for the Virtue at point Five is *Detachment,* we prefer the term "nonattachment" to distinguish it from the emotional detachment caused by schizoid withdrawal — the rejection of one's feelings and need for nurturing. Nonattachment contains no hint of rejection; in fact, it requires a radical acceptance of reality. It is the quality described by the familiar spiritual injunction to "be in the world but not of it." When we are present and abiding in our true natures, we do not cling to anything, inner or outer.

Particularly, we no longer need to cling to the endless activity of the mind as a source of identity and orientation to the world. We feel at one with the unfolding universe and as if we contain it within us at the same time. Everything touches and transforms us, yet there is nothing that we need to attach our identity to; our existence is not based on anything, not our thoughts, not our feelings, not our body, not our perceptions. Everything arises and disappears in a state of profound stillness and peace.

This state of nonattachment also gives us a profound compassion for all living things because we see their transient nature. When there is no need to attach ourselves to any view, it is easy to be compassionate and forgiving (*"Tout comprendre, c'est tout pardonner"* — "To understand all is to forgive all").

FIXATION:

Stinginess. Stinginess refers to the ego mind's tendency to hold on to experiences and information in an effort to build up knowledge and power and to maintain a familiar orientation with reality. It is as if the mind were stockpiling resources to prepare for some future catastrophe. Thus, Fives spend their time gathering information, skills, and resources to "build themselves up," as if they were creating a separate space in which to prepare themselves to reenter reality.

The problem is that identifying with the mind this way detaches us from the support of our Being and from feeling connected with the world. Further, when Fives become trapped in constantly thinking that they need more and more information or skill before they can really live, it becomes increasingly difficult to get their lives started. It also becomes frightening to give, to be generous with one's self. It's as if Fives were thinking, "There is not enough of me even for me. If others want things from me, there won't be anything left. I need time to learn how to live." However, no amount of studying, learning, or hoarding makes them feel any more ready to deal with their lives.

HOLY IDEA:

Holy Omniscience, Holy Transparency. Holy Omniscience is a direct apprehension of the knowing-ness, the awake-ness of Essence. Essence experiences reality through our organism, through our senses and perceptions. Looked at from this perspective, the human being is like a sense organ for the Divine awareness. The universe knows *itself* through us. When we are present and abiding in our true nature, our minds become clear, and we know the immense, brilliant intelligence of Essence.

This clarification of the mind also results in the clarification of ego boundaries and mental categories: we "see through" boundaries, recognizing them as arbitrary inventions of the mind. Reality is a unity, but contains an infinite number of distinguishable characteristics. We can distinguish color, texture, form, and movement, but we do not see these phenomena as separate objects. Rather, we see both the endlessly transforming manifestation of reality as well as its underlying depths. We ourselves feel as if we are completely transparent — everything passes through us; nothing "sticks" in our consciousness. We perceive and understand reality with a penetrating, brilliant clarity that does not require the exertions of the ego mind.

TYPE SIX

Passion:	*Fear*
Virtue:	*Courage*
Fixation:	*Cowardice*
Holy Idea:	*Holy Faith*

PASSION:

Fear. Fear is the feeling that arises when we feel unsupported and without guidance. When we feel unsupported, we feel unable to move into the next moment with assurance and confidence. We believe that something terrible that happened in the past might happen again in the future. In a sense, fear is always based on some kind of imagined future — we are not afraid of something that concluded yesterday because we know the outcome. And this reveals a second point: fear is also a response to not knowing what is going to happen. Whenever we are unsure of our fate and feel unsupported, we become fearful.

The truth is, however, that we are never certain of what will happen next. "Not knowing" is a fundamental condition of our individual existence. We can plan and try to predict and prepare, as type Six does, but in the end, a single twist of fate can undo all of our defenses against the future.

While "not knowing" is fundamental, feeling unsupported and without guidance is not, and this is really the basis of the Six's fear. Lack of contact with inner guidance leaves Sixes anxious and unsure of how to make decisions, avoid danger, and move forward in life. Further, many of type Six's fears are not based on reality, but on things that *might* happen. This constant background of anxiety drives Sixes to organize and systematize their environment as much as possible so that it will be predictable and thus less threatening, but such activity does not ultimately reduce their fear.

VIRTUE:

Courage. The Virtue of Courage might also be called Fearlessness because it truly is the absence of fear. This is absolutely different than defying fear or behaving aggressively to toughen oneself up (counterphobia). True courage arises in the heart when a person is present and deeply grounded in the moment. When we are abiding in our true nature, tremendous support and inner strength naturally arise every time they are needed. Courage draws upon the Essential qualities of Strength and Will, such that we feel like we are held up by a tremendous, supportive solidity. We experience directly the enormous capacities of our Essential nature such that we can totally accept not-knowing the outcome of things. Here and now, we are more than fine — we are solid, real, vital, and embedded in the unfolding Will of the Divine.

FIXATION:

Cowardice. We have found the term "Cowardice" for the fixation of type Six one of the less satisfying ones, because cowardice can be seen as a simple caving in to fear. But if we examine the way that the activity of the ego mind supports fear and anxiety, then the broader meaning of this term is revealed. Basically, cowardice is a failure of confidence in our ability to know, to receive inner guidance. In Enneagram terms, it is the loss of the Holy Idea of Faith. Thus, we might also call the fixation *doubt*.

Sixes (and the Six in us) respond to this lack by trying to hedge their bets against life: they want to create stability and "social security." Unfortunately, cowardice also causes Sixes to undermine whatever sense of security they have by second-guessing themselves and doubting their own decisions. "Where can I get support? Where will I find security? What is a safe bet in life? Is that person *really* my friend? I know they said they are, but will they be there to help me out when the chips are down? Is this job going to be there in six months? If I invest in this, will I lose all my money?"

HOLY IDEA:

Holy Faith. Real faith has nothing to do with beliefs, or with trying to convince oneself that a certain belief is true. The faith we are discussing is a recognition of the actual support of presence and Being that is available right now. It is the recognition that Essence, our true nature, is real and cannot be lost. Essence really exists. Reality is supporting us and we are part of it. We do not have to make support happen because it is already here. From this viewpoint, we see that it doesn't matter whether we believe in this support any more than it matters whether or not we believe in the sky. Essence is a felt, experienced reality.

Thus, Holy Faith gives us an unshakable confidence in the inherent goodness of life and of the universe. Even when things seem to be going wrong to the ego's perspective, in presence, we recognize that we are supported and that our true nature cannot be harmed. Holy Faith gives us the inner freedom to respond spontaneously to whatever emerges in the moment because we are not bound by beliefs, doubts, and learned procedures. We are guided in each moment to optimal action.

TYPE SEVEN

Passion:	*Gluttony*
Virtue:	*Sobriety*
Fixation:	*Planning*
Holy Idea:	*Holy Wisdom, Holy Work, Holy Plan*

PASSION:

Gluttony. Gluttony results from the loss of the Virtue of Sobriety. The original meaning of the sin of gluttony is stuffing one's self, overeating and overindulging in food and drink. On a psychological and spiritual level, it is the belief that all good and desirable things exist outside of myself in the world, and that I need to get those things for myself. It arises from a deep feeling of inner emptiness that the ego tries to suppress. Gluttony denies the inner deficiency of the ego self, creating a false sense of abundance and excitement that masks the underlying frustration and pain driving this Passion.

The gluttony of the Seven is based on the belief that one can fill up the emptiness with exciting experiences. "If I can just keep having good experiences, I will not feel bad or be anxious." Sevens fear that they are not going to get what they need to feel secure and happy. "No one is going to take care of my needs, so I have to go out and get what I want myself." Gluttony in Sevens also refers to the tendency to take all experiences too far, to become *excessive* in every area of life. At such times, Sevens do not make a sufficient distinction between "wants" and "needs" and attempt to fulfill all of their wants as if they were legitimate needs. The tragedy is that the more they attempt to fill themselves with things and experiences (some sort of external sustenance for the self), the more Sevens become incapable of finding the fulfillment they seek.

VIRTUE:

Sobriety. When we are present and abiding in our true nature, we feel awake, sober, and in clear contact with our immediate experience. The effect is bracing, like a crisp morning or a refreshing breeze. We see the real world in exquisite detail, and feel a quiet satisfaction, quite distinct from the giddy excitement of gluttony. Everything is satisfying and profoundly moving, but we are not swept away in our enthusiasms: we are fully here and grounded in the moment. Further, the pleasure we take in existence is not dependent on any particular external source, much less the anticipation of a particular experience. We feel clear and open, such that every movement of reality registers in our consciousness with subtle delight.

Sobriety also brings with it a sense of gratitude, a deep and abiding joy in the miracle of life. Very healthy Sevens are grateful for everything they have. Life is a gift, full of wonders, and they realize that they have more than their share of blessings and are grateful for them. Every experience that falls on a sober, receptive consciousness can fill us with joy.

FIXATION:

Planning. Ichazo called this type ego plan, referring to Sevens' tendency to fill their minds with exciting future projects. When we lose contact with the Holy Idea of the Holy Plan, the ego mind starts trying to make sure that our future experiences will be optimal. In this respect, we can see how the fixation is related to the loss of Faith in type Six. Because we have lost contact with the support of Being, we do not trust that our needs will be provided for. Until we really feel the truth of this, the ego will continue to scheme and strategize to make sure that we get what we think we need, while missing the actual treasures that are here.

Another appropriate name for this type might be ego anticipation, for Sevens are always anticipating, always eagerly awaiting the next moment. They are future-oriented, thinking two steps ahead, and as a result have difficulty staying focused on the here and now. Spiritually, this tendency can manifest as looking forward to mysterious, exotic experiences. Sevens often feel that they have some sacred purpose in life, but they are afraid they will miss it. They fear that they will not be at the right place at the right time. ("Maybe in that coffee shop, a Spiritual Master is waiting to reveal to me that I am the student he has been waiting for. Maybe I am the chosen one . . .") Of course, a great deal of New Age literature does little to help people discern the problem with this fantasy. As long as we are waiting for the magic to begin, we inevitably miss the magic that is right here, right now.

HOLY IDEA:

Holy Wisdom, Holy Plan. Recognizing that, in this very moment, the Divine Plan is unfolding perfectly is Holy Wisdom. When we are present, we see that there really is a Divine Plan, and that it is happening right now. The ego's desire to steer reality in preferred directions is seen through: we know that in this moment, we are having the optimal experience for our souls.

We start to understand that consciously participating in the miraculous unfolding of reality is the Holy Work, and it is the greatest source of satisfaction that we can have. Satisfaction is not to be found in having a particular experience. Rather, it is the quality of our awareness and presence in any experience that gives it its satisfying quality. Knowing in our souls that we are part of the Holy Plan fills the heart with joy. We do not need to plan or anticipate or figure out where we are going or how we are getting there. The pleasure is in the journey itself. We do not necessarily know our destination, but we know that the closer we get, the more our heart is illuminated.

TYPE EIGHT

Passion:	*Lust*
Virtue:	*Innocence*
Fixation:	*Vengeance*
Holy Idea:	*Holy Truth*

PASSION:

Lust. The Passion of Lust is not primarily sexual lust, but it might better be understood as an addiction to intensity. This lustful intensity arises in response to the loss of the Virtue of Innocence. When we are relaxed, open, and present, we feel a natural vitality and experience our "realness" and freedom directly. When we are gripped by the passion of lust, however, we attempt to gain this sense of aliveness and freedom through the intensity of our interactions with the environment and with others. We do not want to have a discussion: we want to have a *discussion,* or even an argument. Becoming agitated gives us a false feeling of being strong and real. But to the extent that Eights are blocked from relaxation and presence, they will need to be worked up all the time.

Thus, lustful Eights are not interested in lukewarm responses to life and particularly do not want weak responses to themselves. "If you are going to go for it, go for it." The more insecure Eights become, the greater their need for intensity, excess, struggle, and control. The need to assert themselves can turn into the desire to dominate their environment and the people in it. Ironically, when we have succumbed to the Passion of Lust, we are quite out of control. The objects of our lust, positive or negative, dominate and control us.

VIRTUE:

Innocence. We think of innocence in connection with children, and indeed, there is something about the open wonder at existence we can see in children that characterizes this Virtue. Innocence is being fully, deeply human: it is simplicity itself. When we are present and awake, we behave without artifice or manipulation. Our responses to life and to other people are completely sincere, direct, and heartfelt. We are completely unselfconscious because we experience a profound communion with the natural world. The universe feels intimate, like it was made for us.

Innocence awakens in Eights a largeness of heart that allows them to feel deeply benevolent toward themselves, others, and the world. Their magnanimity is seen in their gentleness, self-restraint, forbearance, mercy, benevolence, and protection of others.

FIXATION:

Vengeance. Vengeance is the ego's response to the loss of the Holy Idea of Holy Truth. Like Fours, Eights are aware that something is missing, something has been lost. But also like Fours, Eights' egos react to the loss rather than really understanding the deeper truth of it. Eights react by feeling that someone must be responsible for this catastrophe. They feel cut off, hurt, as if they had been rejected by God — thrown out of paradise for a crime they did not know that they had committed — and they are angry about it. Thus, Eights come to feel subconsciously that the world is somehow against them, and that they must fight to have the space to exist. Once caught in this fixation, they tend to see everything as a struggle, as something to be overcome. Nothing will be easy, and they are going to have to push to get what they need.

Of course, the vengeance is often directed at other people. Eights want to fight for what they see as justice, but from the fixated perspective, justice often means retribution. ("If you hurt me, I'll hurt you back." "An eye for an eye and a tooth for a tooth.") It isn't difficult to see how the ego's desire for retribution plays itself out in popular culture, and more disturbingly, in the events that fill the news every day.

HOLY IDEA:

Holy Truth. Holy Truth is the simplest of the Holy Ideas, but perhaps the most difficult to grasp without a direct experience of it. The Holy Truth is simply that All is One. There is only one reality, one existence that is here, happening right now. All of the different levels of existence, all of the endless manifestations, light and darkness, surface and depth, Being and non-Being, are part of one unfathomable reality that collectively is the Holy Truth. Everything is exactly what it is and everything is an aspect of the one, indivisible Reality.

When we perceive Holy Truth, we no longer perceive of ourselves or others as objects, as things moving around against a background. In this living moment, the objects and the background, the dancer and the dance, the stars and the space that holds them, are all of one substance, one ultimate truth, one ultimate reality. The experience of this is powerful, immediate, and nonconceptual. We feel the truth in our very cells. When we know the Holy Truth, all sense of separateness, alienation, fear, and desire ends. We feel our unity with the One and realize that it has never been otherwise. In this knowledge is liberation and profound inner peace.

TYPE NINE

Passion:	*Sloth*
Virtue:	*Action*
Fixation:	*Indolence*
Holy Idea:	*Holy Love*

PASSION:

Sloth. In this context, the Passion of Sloth results from the loss of the Virtue of Action. It is a resistance to being deeply affected by or engaged with the world, to being present and putting out the energy to be fully here, fully feeling and responding. While Sloth may manifest as laziness and lack of energy, the deeper meaning refers to the Nine's habit of giving little attention to his or her own development. It takes a great deal of energy to resist being affected by aspects of reality, and this often causes us to lack energy for self-awareness or self-remembering. Ultimately, Sloth refers to the wish to "go to sleep" to one's life, to not arise as an independent person, taking one's rightful place in the scheme of things. It causes us to want to stay in an internal zone where we feel safe, peaceful, comfortable, and will not be disturbed by anything. We want to avoid anything that might upset our inner tranquillity. Some Nines are fond of saying that they "go with the flow," but in truth, they are hoping that everything will flow around them and let them be.

Ironically, many Nines are actually interested in spiritual work because on some level they remember the blissful feeling of unity that lies beyond ego consciousness. The problem is that Sloth causes them to dream of that unity, to fantasize about it, or to live by some kind of philosophy related to a belief in it. But all of this is quite different from doing the inner work necessary to make the unity a real, embodied experience in the world. Sloth keeps us visualizing white light, contemplating high-minded philosophies and yogas, and going through the paces of our spiritual practices, but definitely *not* contacting the deficiency at the core of our egos

— the emptiness from which our true nature can reemerge into full manifestation.

VIRTUE:

Action. The Virtue of Action does not refer to doing things physically; rather it is an embrace of the *dynamism* of reality. To live in presence is to be affected and transformed constantly. Everything in reality grows and changes, and our soul is no different. Self-realization is not some cushy, pleasant stasis that we retire to — a significant part of it entails surrendering our familiar identity to the dynamism of True Nature. Somehow, we all believe that we can improve and become transformed without affecting the comfortable and familiar parts of ourselves. But a person who is present and awake sees that the self is being reshaped and transformed every moment.

As a result, the Virtue of Action empowers us to participate dynamically in our lives. We are moved to help others achieve peace, harmony, and an awareness of the dynamic unity of existence. Nines who have awakened to the Virtue of Action play a powerful, active role in creating a healing and harmonious environment for themselves and others. Simply put, this virtue gives us the capacity to live fully and dynamically in each moment of our lives.

FIXATION:

Indolence. The loss of the Holy Idea of Holy Love results in the ego fixation of Indolence. It is a style of attention that causes us to avoid deep contact with our interior being. We might be aware of others or of the environment, but we are not aware of what is happening in our presence. Even if we are able to be present to some degree, indolence causes us to *be present without content.* Of course, as we become more entranced by this fixation, we also lose any meaningful awareness of others too.

Because of the loss of Holy Love, the self feels lost and centerless, but Indolence causes us to cover over the wound of that loss by withdrawing from it into the "safety" of our imaginations. We may also deal with it by adopting comforting philosophies, or by focusing on and idealizing others. Indolence leads us to disengage our attention from the core of ourselves so we will not feel the suffering caused by our loss of contact with Essential love, the very fabric of our souls.

Thus, Nines become the masters of dissociation, of mentally "checking out" when situations threaten to uncover the primal loss of contact with Holy Love. In their imaginations Nines create an imitation of the real feelings of wholeness and benevolence that arise in presence and real contact with experience. This inner feeling of peace is then defended against the actual dynamic processes of reality. Thus, indolence serves to perpetuate Sloth. On the surface, Nines can seem quite easygoing, agreeable, and adaptable. They are friendly and do not seem to mind going along with the wishes of others. On a deeper level, however, Nines do not want to be made to change, or to be other than who and what they are comfortable with.

HOLY IDEA:

Holy Love. Holy Love is the recognition that all is one *and* that the oneness is ultimately benevolent and supportive. From this perspective we truly experience the well-known spiritual assertion that everything actually is made from Divine Love. When we truly know this, we relax our ego activity and trust Being to support us. It is almost unfathomable to the ego mind that not only could we be loved by the Divine, but that we are actually made of that love. The knowledge of Holy Love lets us move through our lives with deep compassion, nobility, and unshakable inner peace.

We can also see how Holy Love relates to the Virtue of Action, because love itself has a dynamic effect on our souls. What transforms our lives more powerfully than love? What transforms our sense of ourselves more profoundly? Love is not static: it is a living, dynamic force that melts down all barriers and boundaries, constantly working to restore our awareness to its pristine unity with Truth. In Holy Love, our sense of separateness dissolves, and we know ourselves as arising from the brilliant light of Divine Love that creates and sustains the universe.

TYPE ONE

Passion:	*Anger, Resentment*
Virtue:	*Serenity*
Fixation:	*Resentment, Judging*
Holy Idea:	*Holy Perfection*

PASSION:

Anger (resentment). The Passion of Anger results from the loss of the Virtue of Serenity. In understanding this passion, it is important to remember that the response of anger itself is not the problem. Anger occurs spontaneously when we feel that someone or something is threatening our integrity. It rises in our presence, lasts for a few moments, then passes. But when we are not present to our anger, we resist its natural unfolding and become tense, frustrated, and resentful. Over time, this simmering frustration becomes an underlying feeling that is always with us.

Because Ones fully resist expressing their anger, they are often unaware of its presence as a continual backdrop of smoldering resentment. Of course, not even the average One's deeply ingrained habits of self-control can keep the anger down indefinitely. Sooner or later it is expressed, often inappropriately, and often with negative consequences for Ones' relationships.

This resentful attitude toward life is also directly related to the One's *resistance* to reality. The passion of anger causes chronic dissatisfaction with oneself and with reality. It causes us to feel that reality is not the way it ought to be. ("I don't like the way things are. Things should be better. This should be done in a different way.") Ones do not generally see themselves as angry; rather they see themselves as "under control," as always striving to get things right.

VIRTUE:

Serenity. When we are awake and present, it is natural for human beings to accept reality exactly as it is. We may be moved to action, we may help and support others as we see the need, but we accept the conditions that we are working with. This openness allows us to interact with the world more effectively and more compassionately. We do not feel separate from others, let alone better or worse than them. Such distinctions and evaluations are seen as meaningless. We are open and receptive, trusting that whatever wisdom we may need will arise in the moment.

Serenity does not only entail being open to others, of course: it is also being open and accepting of ourselves, exactly as we are. We are comfortable with ourselves, with our bodies, and with our feelings. We are deeply relaxed and allow the energies of life to flow through us without resisting them or trying to control them. In the Virtue of Serenity, there is no feeling of effort or of striving. We are soothed and soothing. We flow from one experience into the next, feeling calm and balanced, regardless of the ups and downs of life.

FIXATION:

Resentment (judging). Resentment and Judgment result from the loss of the Holy Idea of Holy Perfection. Ones seem to have a vague memory of Holy Perfection: they recall the feeling of knowing that reality is perfectly unfolding according to a Divine Plan. Early in their lives, though, they became cut off from that feeling and became angry about it. On the deepest level, their response to life is "Why is everything all messed up? It wasn't always like this! It doesn't have to be this way!" Ones' egos then become caught up in trying to recreate the sense of perfection that is actually a part of their Essence.

As a result, Ones become convinced that aspects of themselves and the world are somehow flawed, and they have deep convictions about how to restore a proper order to everything. Resentment causes them to strive to be perfect, but when they fail to find the perfection they seek, they become more angry about their own apparent imperfection — thus sustaining their passion.

The key to unlocking this dilemma is recognizing how the ego activity of *judging* divides the self into judging and judged parts, thus destroying the unity of the self. It is only from unity, from a whole and complete contact with all of the self, that we are able to embody and recognize perfection.

HOLY IDEA:

Holy Perfection. Whenever we show up fully in the here and now, the present moment is always perfect. We could be looking at a sunset, paying bills, speaking with our spouse, or watching a friend pass away — it does not matter what the specific experience is. When we are present and awake to the living reality of the here and now, the experience always has an inherent rightness. We experience the unfolding of reality as perfection. We feel in our depths that the Divine Plan is unfolding exactly the way it needs to. There is nothing we can add to it or subtract from it.

In our ego minds, we can imagine all sorts of terrible things, past and future, and ask, "What is so perfect about that? What is good about that tragedy happening?" From a certain perspective, the mass extinctions that have occurred on our planet could be seen as enormous tragedies, and yet scientists tell us that if they had not occurred, it is unlikely that we as a species would have evolved. Even if we could have been alive at the time to complain about the unfairness of the dinosaurs dying out, we could not have foreseen the ultimate results of their disappearance. Of course, Holy Perfection does not mean that we ignore suffering or refuse to help when we can. As we have seen, the present and awake person of Essence is truly able to support others with compassion, wisdom, and strength. But Holy Perfection allows us to see that we cannot discern the big picture from our limited ego perspective. Only in presence can we perceive the unity, goodness, and perfection of this moment — of right now. And since right now is where we actually are, this realization is all we need.

CHAPTER 3

The Nine
Personality Types

B asic descriptions of the nine personality types are presented in this chapter — although with a difference from *Personality Types*. The descriptions given here are condensed and are presented with several new features that approach the types thematically rather than analytically. Those already familiar with the full descriptions in *Personality Types* can use this chapter to augment the essentials since much new material is presented here for the first time. For those not familiar with the types, this chapter can be used as a more concise introduction.

Each type description begins with a profile of the type's main traits. These profiles are, in effect, the "core traits" — the complex cluster of related traits that is the essence of each type — in the healthy, average, and unhealthy Levels of Development. The development of the Enneagram as a typology depends a great deal on arriving at some agreement about which traits constitute the core of each personality type. One of the fundamental problems with many descriptions has been that traits have often been misattributed from type to type. Without an adequate understanding of the *vertical* dimension of the types — the nine Levels of Development — it is extremely difficult to understand which trait goes with which type and why. While the profiles presented here are not encyclopedic, they present the core traits of each type. We hope that this chapter, and the following one on the Levels of Development, will provide some much-needed clarity about what traits constitute each type.

Following the profiles of each type are very brief sketches of that type's Direction of Disintegration and the Direction of Integration. The longer explanations in *Personality Types* are much more complete, but for readers who want to understand the basic movements toward integration or disintegration, these short entries should be helpful. Also, this revised edition of *Understanding the Enneagram* provides brief descriptions of each type's Security Point. The Security Point describes the movement in the Direction of Integration, *but in the average Levels.* We have found that each type can act out behaviors from the average range of its Direction of Integration, but only in situations and with people that the person feels secure with. We generally do not employ these behaviors with strangers, acquaintances, or at any time in which the relationship's solidity is in doubt.

We provided the Childhood Patterns for each type in the Overview to each type in *Personality Types.* Here, we present a very brief restatement of the fundamental unconscious relationship that each child has had with his or her parents, although with some new insights included. (For a longer discussion of the Childhood Pattern of each type, refer to the cross-referenced pages in *Personality Types.*)

A word of explanation about how the Childhood Pattern came about is also probably in order. The ideas about the Childhood Patterns have evolved over the last decade, although many of their original elements remain. Don Riso recalls his initial thought process in arriving at these patterns:

> During the years that I was researching the Enneagram, I was always on the lookout for "three times three" patterns that could be applied to the nine personality types. Two of the most basic categories of parent-child relationships in early formation are child-to-mother and child-to-father relationships. Yet, to my knowledge, no one had perceived that children could be related

to mother and father taken together. Thus, children could be related primarily to their mothers or primarily to their fathers or to their mothers and fathers equally. That third category was a major breakthrough, as obvious as it now seems.

Then I realized that while children could have a connected or disconnected relationship with their parents, there can also be an "ambivalent" relationship, even at an early age — and this yielded another group of three. The result was three groups of three whose permutations yielded nine combinations for the Childhood Patterns of the nine Enneagram types.

The next step was to discover if these nine theoretical categories actually occurred in real life: did the theoretical origins match the childhood development of real people? While not proving anything scientifically, the anecdotal evidence presented by people in workshops, trainings, and in counseling has borne out the basic theory. For example, Sixes have had strong connections and issues with their father figures, Threes with their mother figures, and so forth, as they have been given in *Personality Types,* and as recapitulated briefly in this chapter.

While we explored these issues with workshop participants over the years we were able to refine the theory in a number of ways. First, we came to understand that some people did not initially recognize these patterns because the patterns are developed early in the first three years of life. Different relationships could occur later, for instance, in adolescence. Nevertheless, the personality was still largely structured by earlier patterns, just as modern psychology suggests.

Second, we realized that the relationship was actually not always with a specific person such as the father, but with the whole category of experience that "the father" represents. Thus, we saw that Sixes were strongly related to the fathering aspects of the early childhood environment. This would include the functions of guidance, protection, structure, and support in coping with the outer world. The mothering functions provide nurturing, mirroring, a sense of value and identity, and many other things. Modern psychology has referred to the whole quality of the childhood environment, including both of these parenting functions, as the "holding environment." Often, small children associate these functions with the parent in question (or sometimes the lack of that parent), although, in reality, different individuals may play a role in creating the holding environment for the child.

The third insight was drawn from further observations of our students and from object relation theories (another aspect of modern ego psychology). We saw that the types with a connected orientation had strong *attachments* with the parenting function in question, the disconnected types were *frustrated* with the parenting function, and the ambivalent types felt *rejected* by the parent. We will return to this pattern in Chapter 9.

Formal research has yet to be done on these categories but, at least informally, they are being confirmed and will give researchers a fertile, clear set of hypotheses with which to work. Importantly, the Childhood Pattern of each type correlates with the findings of other psychological systems; while this in itself does not prove anything, it is an encouraging indication that theories are converging on objective facts about the development of the personality types.

Several more clarifications must be made about the Childhood Pattern. First, it is likely that the prenatal and genetic basis for personality — what psychologists refer to as *temperament* — is the primary determinant of our personality type. Thus the Childhood Patterns do not *cause* our personality type. Nonetheless, for reasons we cannot yet explain, we see these patterns consistently repeating in the vast majority of people of a given type. These patterns are important because they powerfully affect all of our significant adult relationships. We tend to play out these Childhood Patterns over and over again.

We do not recommend that you determine your personality type by using the Childhood Patterns alone: they are but one factor among many and should not be given undue weight. Also, because these patterns were established so early in life, many people do not know what their true relationship with their parents was.

Memories may be distorted, for one reason or another. For example, we have stated that Sevens are disconnected with (frustrated with) their nurturer or mother figure. In later life, Sevens may have become friends with their mothers, but the earlier difficulties remain imprinted in the Seven's psyche. Additionally, the defense mechanism of denial often present in average to unhealthy Sevens can lead to difficulty facing childhood troubles. Often it is only after years of therapy that the true picture emerges, and so it is not surprising that a person for whom denial is a defense mechanism simply would not be able to admit the truth about himself or herself. Thus, because these memories were established so early in life, or because of inner resistance, our initial reaction to the theory of Childhood Pattern may not reflect the reality of our past.

One of the many implications of the Childhood Pattern is that it gives rise to our fundamental motivations, to our sense of self, and, in a way, to the entire orientation of our lives, or "life script." Our ordinary conscious motivations have their roots in an unconscious Basic Fear and Basic Desire that have arisen from childhood experiences, particularly in our responses to the inadequacies of the holding environment created by our parents. The inspiration for this insight came from Karen Horney's work on the concept of "basic anxiety." Don Riso initially took it a step further by discovering that an underlying Basic Fear and Basic Desire are unique to each personality type and that this twin source of negative and positive motivation is responsible for the subsequent secondary (derivative) motivations and behaviors (traits) that constitute each type at each Level of Development.

The Basic Fear and Basic Desire produce the secondary, or derivative, fears and desires that appear at each Level in each type. An expanded list of Secondary Motivations has therefore been provided. These motivations are especially noteworthy since traits alone do not help us to understand each type: *we must comprehend the range of related motivations that underlie the traits we observe.* Failure to understand the different motivations for similar behavior in different types has been a persistent source of confusion for readers as well as for those who have written about personality types, whether from the viewpoint of the Enneagram or of other systems. Without understanding each type's underlying motivations, it is difficult to discriminate between types: their behavior may seem arbitrary or unmotivated or otherwise difficult to account for.

Another new feature of this chapter is how each personality type sees itself — that is, its healthy sense of self. Each type has a different sense of self, and maintaining a stable sense of self is an underlying, unconscious goal for everyone; it constitutes one of the most important areas for understanding ourselves and others. The healthy sense of self arises from our Basic Fear and Basic Desire, as well as from our cognitive functions and defense mechanisms. (The sense of self is discussed further in Chapter 4.)

Although only the healthy sense of self of each type is given here, our sense of self shifts as we move up or down the Levels of Development. Many of our intrapsychic conflicts result from a disparity between the sense of self that we consciously maintain and the sense of self that our actual behavior and attitudes warrant — just as many of our interpersonal conflicts result from the discrepancy between the sense of self that we have and the perception of us that others have. Sometimes our sense of self is inflated, while at other times it is too negative; in either case, it must become more realistic if we are to develop a healthier, more integrated personality. When it is not realistic, anxiety results, triggering defense mechanisms and the complex interplay of more secondary fears and desires. In short, our sense of self, how we defend it (and many other related issues) are important factors not only for understanding our personality but for actualizing our true nature.

Besides the characteristic healthy sense of self that has been listed for each type, there is a related typical Hidden Complaint that points to a frustrated or unfulfilled claim made about the self, particularly as the person begins to deteriorate down the Levels of Development toward greater fixation and unhealth. The Hidden Complaint is an unstated source of many of the underlying attitudes a person holds toward others; as a result, the Hidden

Complaint is the unacknowledged source of many of the type's interpersonal conflicts. It is useful to be aware of the Hidden Complaint (and other "hidden complaints" you may become aware of) as another key both to self-understanding and to change.

The traditional teaching of the Enneagram lists *one* defense mechanism for each type, attributed to Claudio Naranjo. Our investigations indicate that there are at least three key Defense Mechanisms for each type — and there are probably more. In addition, even though all nine types employ many of the same Defense Mechanisms, the specific defenses they employ produce a different pattern for each type. Thus, two similar types can have one or two Defense Mechanisms in common, providing yet another explanation about their similarities and differences.

The Defense Mechanisms give us insight into the motivation and behavior of each type, into how the sense of self is characteristically defended, into interpersonal relations, and into other important matters. Furthermore, the Defense Mechanisms help explain why each type is the way it is; the traits are not arbitrary because the underlying structures of the personality are not arbitrary. Traits grow out of the unique pattern of motivations and defenses.

A Characteristic Temptation arises at the beginning of the average Levels of each type, at Level 4. The Characteristic Temptation is a way of thinking or behaving (or both) that initiates the type's fixation in the personality patterns of the type. When a person succumbs to his Characteristic Temptation, he gradually becomes entrapped in attitudes and behaviors of his type, like getting caught in quicksand, and loses the freedom and awareness of the healthier Levels. The Characteristic Temptation can therefore function as an early warning signal of potentially more neurotic behavior — while there is still time and psychological perspective left to avoid it.

Each type's Saving Grace is the kernel of strength that remains in the person after he or she has deteriorated fairly far (to Level 6) and is in danger of deteriorating into the unhealthy Levels of Development. The Saving Grace is the positive quality that still remains and can be drawn on to help the person out of his or her predicament. The neurotic condition itself does not have the potential to save a person from being neurotic; rather, a remaining source of strength that is active despite deterioration becomes the anchor that not only prevents the person from deteriorating further but can help restore the person to healthier functioning. If the deteriorating person is aware of the Saving Grace and is able to act on it, he or she can begin to reverse the downward movement toward neurosis.

The type's Structural Patterns make explicit its psychological patterns of intrapsychic and interpersonal conflicts. It is essential to understand larger patterns if we are to understand each type as a whole; therefore, it is helpful to understand each type's internal and external conflicts more explicitly.

The Cognitive Error is an assumption about the self or reality that leads the type deeper into ego fixation and away from the immediacy of presence. This way of looking at things is usually unconscious, but it has many implications for the type's ego-based attitudes and behaviors.

Last, Inevitable Consequences describe the inexorable results of the person's fixation in the particular pattern of their personality type, and how this pattern is ultimately self-defeating. By becoming more enmeshed in the egoic attitudes and behaviors of one's type, a person actually loses the ability to fulfill his or her Basic Desire, and increasingly brings on himself his Basic Fear. This section makes explicit the "self-fulfilling prophecy" that is each type's tragic element — how the person loses the very thing he or she most desires (Basic Desire) while bringing on himself or herself the thing most feared (Basic Fear). This process began when the person succumbed to his or her Characteristic Temptation and continued to gather momentum if the person did not act on the Saving Grace (among other, more complicated reasons).

We will begin the Expanded Profiles and other new features of each type with personality type Two, the first type in the Feeling

Triad (*PT*, 24–26 and 30ff). By our convention, we often start with type Two: doing so allows us to see the types within their Triads and thus to understand the larger patterns both with the Enneagram and within each type.

PERSONALITY TYPE TWO: *THE HELPER*

The Demonstrative, Generous, People-Pleasing, Possessive Person

Healthy. Healthy Twos are empathetic, compassionate, full of feeling for others. They put themselves in the place of others and are caring and concerned about others' needs. Sincere, warmhearted, appreciative, and encouraging, seeing the good in others when they may not see it in themselves. Service is important: they are extremely generous, giving, and helpful. "Good Samaritans." Loving and thoughtful, they give people what they really need, even if it means going out of their way to do so. Healthy Twos maintain good boundaries and also take care of their own needs. *At their best:* Become profoundly disinterested, unselfish, and altruistic; are able to give unconditional love with no expectation of reward because they have found the love they seek within themselves. Joyfully nurturing self and others, gracious and patient. Deeply charitable, truly humble.

Average. Want to be closer to others, so they start "people-pleasing," becoming overly friendly, emotionally demonstrative, and full of "good intentions" about everything. Attempt to win others over by giving seductive attention: approval, "strokes," flattery. Frequently talk about "the relationship." Increasingly needy, but unable to admit it, average Twos can become overly intimate and intrusive: they want to be reassured that others need them, so they hover and meddle in the name of love. Become the self-sacrificial person who cannot do enough for others — wearing themselves out for everyone, creating needs for themselves to fulfill. Want others to depend on them, to keep them informed about everything, to come for permission and advice. Can be enveloping and possessive of those they have "invested" in. Increasingly self-important and self-satisfied, they begin to feel indispensable (while overrating what they do for others) and that others owe them for what they have been given. Patronizing, overbearing, imperious, highhanded. Begin to expect to be constantly thanked and honored for their goodness. May become hypochondriacs or play the role of martyrs who have suffered because of their good works on behalf of everyone else.

Unhealthy. Feeling unwanted and unappreciated, unhealthy Twos become resentful and complain bitterly. Begin to be extremely self-deceptive about their motives and how aggressive and egocentric they can be, becoming manipulative and self-serving. Fearful of losing others, they may undermine their confidence and play on their guilt and weaknesses. May abuse food and medication to "stuff feelings" and get sympathy. Obsessive love and stalking can occur. Begin to make belittling, disparaging remarks; gradually become coercive and domineering, feeling entitled to get anything they want: old favors must be repaid, money given as tokens of thanks, special favors granted. Able to rationalize and excuse whatever they do since they feel victimized and abused by the ingratitude of others. Repressed anger becomes evident in psychosomatic problems ("conversion reactions").

Triad Issues. In the Feeling Triad, their overdeveloped empathy for others causes Twos to feel that they must put the needs of others first. Thus their ability to nurture themselves is underactive, and Twos rely on others to give them positive attention in return for their service, love, warmth, and encouragement. Their identity requires that they maintain conscious positive feelings toward others and see themselves as the main source of goodness in others' lives. As with all three types in this Triad, there are problems with narcissistic wounding, and questions of value and worthlessness. We also see problems with *identity* (the authenticity of their self-presentation) and *hostility* (narcissistic rage) when their identity is questioned or undermined in some way.

Direction of Disintegration. Average Twos have difficulty stating their needs directly, feeling that to do so would be selfish. They attempt to fulfill their needs by doing good things for others and hoping that others will care for them in return. When this strategy fails or when Twos fall into increased stress, however, they may suddenly assert themselves and their needs more forcefully, like average Eights. Twos may lose their tempers or let others know in unsubtle ways that they cannot be trifled with or taken for granted. Like Eights, they can become defiant and argumentative, and may make threats. Others can be surprised at the Two's belligerence. Under extreme stress, Twos may also attempt to control others by creating dependencies.

Unhealthy Twos can become resentful and enraged at the ungrateful treatment they feel they have received from others. Like unhealthy Eights, they may strike out at those who have not responded to them as they wanted. Extremely deteriorated Twos can become physically violent, even murderous, usually to those closest to them, the very people for whom they think they have had nothing but the kindest, most tender feelings.

Direction of Integration. When healthy Twos go to Four, they get in touch with the full range of their genuine feelings and become aware of themselves as they really are. They become emotionally honest, acknowledging their aggressions and mixed motives as fully as they have accepted their positive view of themselves. By unconditionally loving themselves for their real value, they recognize that they do not have to be all good to be loved. They can be themselves and reveal themselves more fully; thus, their relationships become more honest, human, reciprocal, and satisfying.

Security Point. Average Twos can also "act out" the average behaviors of type Four, but usually with trusted friends and intimates. At such times, the true degree of the Two's loneliness and neediness is revealed. They can become temperamental and may get into moody, self-absorbed, self-pitying parts of themselves that they would not want to reveal to more casual acquaintances.

Childhood Pattern. Ambivalently identified with the father or a father figure (*PT,* 65). The key element is that as children, Twos learned to fit into the family by serving or pleasing others, thus winning their love and praise. On a deep (possibly unconscious) level, Twos felt *rejected* by the person or people responsible for guidance, structure, and discipline in the household. This is often, but not always, the father. To defend against feelings of rejection, Twos learn to play the complementary role of the "little nurturer" to the parents or other siblings. Later, they can become trapped in this role in their adult relationships.

Basic Fear. Of being unloved and unwanted for themselves alone.

Basic Desire. To feel loved.

Secondary Motivations. Twos want to express their feelings for others, to help people, to be appreciated for what they have done, to be an important influence on others, to be intimate with others, to be necessary to others, to control people, and to justify the demands they make on others.

In Search of: Intimacy. The Two's search is not simply for the feeling of being close with people, but to find a way to establish a relationship in which they are truly welcomed, close, and deeply wanted. In short, they want their value to be validated by being wanted by others. If Twos deteriorate down the Levels, however, the intensity of their drive for intimacy actually drives people away.

Healthy Sense of Self. "I am a caring, loving person."

Hidden Complaint. "I am always loving, although people don't love me as much as I love them." "I am taken for granted and unappreciated."

Key Defense Mechanisms. Identification, reaction formation, denial.

Characteristic Temptation. To believe that they are without needs and always well intentioned. Average Twos begin to think of themselves as entirely well meaning and always completely loving toward others, totally without any ulterior motives or emotional needs of their own. When they are unable to acknowledge their own needs, they must find ways to maneuver others into fulfilling them.

Saving Grace. Despite their sense of pride and self-importance, average Twos may still have enough genuine empathy for others to prevent themselves from deteriorating any further into outright manipulation or coercive behavior. Their healthy capacity to identify with others can act as a catalyst to help them return to healthier attitudes and behavior.

Suggestions for Personal Growth. See Chapter 10.

Structural Patterns. The keynote here is *indirection*. Personal needs and desires are expressed indirectly, through service to others. Twos feel that they cannot go after what they want directly: it must be given to them by others as a sign that they are really loved and appreciated. Therefore, whatever Twos want must be elicited from others through "hints" and other forms of indirection so that the rewards they seek seem to have come spontaneously from the other as a sign of love for the Two. In other words, average to unhealthy Twos communicate what they want from others without saying so openly. Unacknowledged needs, covert claims, and ulterior motives can cause tensions and conflicts between their loving, empathetic, positive feelings and their unconscious resentments and aggressions — often toward the same people. In unhealthy Twos, these internal conflicts may become expressed in aggressive acts against others (expressed as overbearing, coercive behavior) as well as in aggressions turned against the self (in self-sacrifice and moral masochism). Although their inner conflicts are consciously repressed, their aggressive impulses take their toll at an unconscious level and in their relationships. Therefore, the pattern is one of interpersonal and intrapsychic tension, often producing conscious suffering and physical ailments.

Cognitive Error. Believing that their value depends on the positive responses of others, and that only by getting others to respond to them in certain specific ways will they feel loved and worthwhile.

Inevitable Consequences. As with everyone who deteriorates down the Levels, less healthy Twos undermine their Basic Desire (to be loved) while increasingly bringing on themselves their Basic Fear (that they are unloved and unwanted for themselves alone; *PT,* 94). The more intrusive, manipulative, and coercive they become, and the more domineering and inflated with self-importance they are, the more they drive others away. (Ironically, the reactions of others can help Twos see how loving or how ego inflated they actually are, rather than see their self-deceptive claims about themselves. If Twos are consistently having interpersonal conflicts, it is a strong indication that they are falling into the trap of prideful self-deception.)

The single most important thing for Twos to remember is that their desire to be loving and supportive of others can only be realized if Twos are honest about their own needs and limitations. Twos need to find a balance between their empathetic focus on others' needs, and an honest acknowledgment of their own needs. Further, Twos need to learn to nurture themselves as well as they would like to nurture others. In fact, it is not the Two's generosity that is the problem, but the hidden expectation that his or her generosity will be rewarded with appreciation and reciprocal caring. Others may or may not be able to respond to the Two's overtures in the way that the Two would like, yet the more rejected Twos feel, the greater their expectation for what they see as a loving response from others. The instant they begin to call attention to themselves or expect praise for whatever they give to others, they are going in the wrong direction and will only be frustrated and suffer as a result.

PERSONALITY TYPE THREE: *THE ACHIEVER*

The Adaptable, Excelling, Driven, Image-Conscious Person

Healthy. Healthy Threes are self-assured, feel desirable, and enjoy high self-esteem, believing in themselves and their own value. High-spirited, energetic, often attractive, charming, and popular. Ambitious to improve themselves, to be the best they can be: often become outstanding in some way, truly admirable, a human ideal, embodying widely admired qualities. Others want to be like them, to imitate their achievements. Highly competent, focused, and diligent in achieving goals — they meet challenges by being extremely adaptable. Can be excellent communicators, motivators, and promoters, know how to present something in an acceptable and compelling way. *At their best:* Self-accepting, inner-directed, genuine and authentic: everything they seem to be. Fully accept themselves, not feeling that they must become more successful in order to be worthwhile. Live modestly, within their own "center," and treat others with gentle graciousness. Communicate with heartfelt simplicity. Can be profoundly moving and inspiring to others.

Average. Average Threes become driven to excel — increasingly all activities are in service of their bid for success. They become "human doings" instead of human beings. Focus on their performance: seek recognition for their accomplishments. Need to be "the best" at whatever they do. Can become anxious comparing themselves and their achievements with others. Begin to emphasize personal status and prestige: social climbers for whom exclusivity, career, and being a "winner" is important. Use charm and diplomacy when questioned or challenged. Pragmatic, goal-oriented, and efficient, but can also be calculating and affectless beneath the cool, polished façade. Become image-conscious, highly concerned with how they are perceived by others; concerned with credibility, with projecting an acceptable image, saying the right thing, adjusting their behavior and affect according to expectations. Increasingly expedient, they begin to lose touch with their own hearts: depend on smooth "professionalism," jargon, and style. Fear that others will "see through them," so problems with commitment and intimacy emerge. As underlying feelings of worthlessness worsen, less healthy Threes feel compelled to impress others with their achievements. They constantly promote themselves and inflate their talents and accomplishments. Increasingly narcissistic, they hold grandiose expectations of themselves and their potential. Seductive and exhibitionistic, as if saying "Look at me!" Arrogance and contempt for others surface as defenses against narcissistic vulnerability.

Unhealthy. Fearing failure and humiliation, unhealthy Threes become desperate to convince themselves and others that they really are still superior people. They do not want to deal with their increasing emotional turmoil, burying it beneath a functional façade. "I don't have any problems." This orientation often results in burnout and chronic depression. If Threes do not seek help, their ability to function deteriorates, so they must increasingly rely on self-deception and the deception of others to preserve illusions about self: false résumés, plagiarism, and other forms of dishonesty can occur. Once caught in this pattern Threes can become exploitative and opportunistic, covetous of the success of others, and willing to do "whatever it takes" to succeed. Pathological liars, they become more devious and deceptive so that their mistakes and wrongdoings will not be exposed. In extreme cases, can become dangerous, maliciously betraying or sabotaging people to triumph over them. Finally, become delusionally jealous of others: can be vindictive, striking out at those who know the truth about them. Relentless, obsessive about destroying whatever reminds them of their own shortcomings and failures. Psychopathic tendencies, murder.

Triad Issues. As the primary type in the Feeling Triad, Three is most out of touch with its own real feelings. Underlying feelings of hurt and shame are suppressed in order to adapt to the expectations of significant others. The feelings of Threes are compartmentalized ("put in a box"), producing a personality pattern that is concerned with competency, achievement, performance, and results. Threes also have problems with maintaining a particular *identity* (to themselves and others), and with *hostility* that results when their identity is questioned or threatened.

Direction of Disintegration. Average Threes strive to be effective and efficient in all their activities, and are reluctant to slow down their efforts, lest they be overtaken by others. When Threes have pushed themselves beyond their limit, however, stress may cause them to act out the average behaviors of type Nine. At such times, Threes become disengaged from their activities, running on "auto-pilot," while becoming more vague and unfocused. They may lower their profile to avoid potential conflicts with others, but can be extremely stubborn and uncommunicative when confronted. If their stress is not relieved, they become increasingly passive, resigned, and uninterested in their work — basically going through the motions to get through their days.

Unhealthy Threes may reach a point where they simply cannot maintain the effort to meet their unrealistic expectations of themselves. They become depressed and unresponsive. Others can scarcely believe that the Three is the same person who had previously been an overachiever. They show a complete lack of interest in themselves or anything else. If unhealthy Threes have committed wrongdoings, the anxiety that results may cause them to dissociate from themselves in profound ways. Rather than feel the full brunt of their anxiety or guilt, any feelings they have suddenly "turn off" completely. When they go to Nine, deeply unhealthy Threes dissociate even from their hostile feelings, with the result that they feel nothing. They "go dead," and become depersonalized and catatonic.

Direction of Integration. When healthy Threes go to Six, they become committed to others and in doing so find more of value to affirm in themselves. Their love for another, paradoxically, creates more value within themselves. Integrating Threes begin to become real — more genuine and more developed as persons — by sustaining a mutual relationship. They no longer are competitive but cooperative; no longer falsely superior but equal; no longer tending to exploit people but committed to others and their welfare. Integrating Threes find deep satisfaction and joy in working with others for purposes beyond their own need for recognition. In their devotion to others, to their craft, and to a higher purpose, they find the sense of value they have been seeking.

Security Point. Average Threes can also "act out" the average behaviors of type Six, but usually with trusted friends and intimates. At such times, the true degree of the Three's self-doubt, pessimism, and anxiety is revealed. With loved ones, Threes may download a litany of complaints, fears, and frustrations about their work projects that they would not want to reveal to more casual acquaintances.

Childhood Pattern. Connected with the mother or with a mother figure (*PT,* 101–103). The essential element is that as children Threes came to believe that they were loved and valued primarily for their performance and accomplishment. At a deep, sometimes unconscious level, Threes became emotionally *attached* to the person or people responsible for nurturing, mirroring, and emotional holding in their family of origin. This is often, but not always, the mother. To hang onto whatever love was available, young Threes learned to adapt in order to become whatever the nurturing figure found most pleasing. Thus, Threes became unconsciously directed to redeem the shame of their families through achievement — being the family hero. Later, they can become trapped in this role in their adult relationships.

Basic Fear. Of being worthless.

Basic Desire. To feel valuable.

Secondary Motivations. Threes want to develop and improve themselves, to feel competent, to distinguish themselves, to get attention, to be valued and admired, to create a favorable impression of themselves, to impress others, to convince themselves and others of the reality of their image.

In Search of: Acceptance and validation. Threes are typically blocked from experiencing the Essential quality of Personal Value, and so must look to others for validation of themselves in terms of the values created by personality and their culture. Fearing that they are worthless, Threes want to assure themselves of a steady supply of admiring attention in order to "be somebody," thus reinforcing their sense of self and counteracting their Basic Fear of being worthless. Threes are also in search of acceptance from others by becoming a kind of "human ideal" against which others must judge themselves and their achievements. By being outstanding, however, Threes often unwittingly provoke jealousy and competitions.

Healthy Sense of Self. "I am an outstanding, effective person."

Hidden Complaint. "I am a superior person, but other people are jealous of me."

Key Defense Mechanisms. Repression, projection, displacement.

Characteristic Temptation. To constantly push themselves to be "the best." Average Threes want to distinguish themselves in some way to defend against underlying fears of worthlessness. They can become caught up in a relentless drive for success as well as the need to demonstrate their superiority to others. They also begin to compare themselves with others, looking over their shoulders and redoubling their efforts to stay ahead of the competition.

Saving Grace. Despite increasing narcissism and obsession with success, the desire of average Threes to feel valuable and worthwhile may prevent them from engaging in deceptive or dishonest activities that could cause them shame and humiliation. Also, their healthy desire to be accepted by others may guide Threes away from acknowledged and unacknowledged competitions and back to balanced, healthier behavior.

Suggestions for Personal Growth. See Chapter 10.

Structural Patterns. The keynote is *adaptability*. Threes form their identities and interact with others by adapting to people, by responding to others' expectations, and by adjusting to the "feedback" they are given. Beneath what appears to be a highly functional, independent façade, average to unhealthy Threes are covertly dependent on the acceptance of others and are continually adjusting themselves to make sure that they will be accepted and receive as much attention and affirmation as possible. The inner pattern for average Threes, therefore, is of emotional vulnerability or even emptiness, concealed by a superb capacity for social interaction and adaptability. Outwardly, their interpersonal image changes constantly depending on whom they interact with and what social expectations are placed on them.

Cognitive Error. Thinking that their value comes from their "performance" or their external image — how successful they are in terms of wealth, social standing, or professional accomplishment.

Inevitable Consequences. The inevitable result of ego inflation is that Threes undermine their Basic Desire (to feel valuable and worthwhile) while invariably bringing on themselves their Basic Fear (of feeling worthless; *PT,* 132–33). This occurs because, in truth, the ego self *is* inherently without value. It requires constant attention and outer support to prop up its sense of importance. No matter how much success and admiration Threes achieve, they are still left with the fundamental problem of being detached from their true self, their Essence, which is the only real source of value and identity. The more Threes invest their life energy in polishing their image, in trying to make the ego feel valuable, the more they must inevitably remain detached from the source of their Being with all of the attendant feelings of emptiness and worthlessness that this self-abandonment produces.

Threes need to remember that if they wish to enjoy the admiration of others they must remain *authentic*. This means being present, in the moment, connected deeply with one's heart, and acting from that presence and connection. To be authentic is actually an enormous human accomplishment, no matter what a person's Enneagram type may be. While authenticity brings enormous rewards of its own, it also gives Threes their Basic Desire. People value and esteem those who can embody these qualities. Threes may gain fleeting fame or recognition for other accomplishments, but without this heart connection, Threes will remain untouched by it. Ultimately, the lower road leads to loneliness, empty victories, and emotional disconnection.

PERSONALITY TYPE FOUR: *THE INDIVIDUALIST*

The Expressive, Dramatic, Self-Absorbed, Temperamental Person

Healthy. Healthy Fours are introspective, self-aware, in touch with feelings and inner impulses, in a search for self. Sensitive and intuitive both to self and others: compassionate, tactful, discreet, and respectful of others. Self-expressive, highly personal, individualistic. Highly impressionable, healthy Fours enjoy being alone, taking time for their unconscious impulses to surface into consciousness. Self-revealing, emotionally honest, authentic, and true to self. Passionate about their relationships as well as their inner lives: willing to explore any feeling without judging it, they are the "deep-sea divers" of the psyche. They emphasize beauty and enjoy expressing their feelings aesthetically. Have an ironic view of life and self: can be serious and funny, easily touched, and yet emotionally strong. *At their best:* Profoundly creative, expressing the personal and the universal, possibly in an inspired work of art. On the personal level, they become regenerative and self-renewing — possessing a self-creating, redemptive quality, able to transform all their experiences into something valuable.

Average. Begin to take an artistic and romantic orientation to life, creating a beautiful, aesthetic environment to cultivate and prolong personal feelings. Intensify reality through fantasy, imagination, and by heightening passionate feelings. To stay in touch with feelings, they interiorize everything, taking everything personally, getting emotionally vulnerable and hypersensitive, feeling they are "different," "outsiders." Average Fours may withdraw to protect their self-image and to buy time to sort out feelings. Get into pattern of becoming alternately infatuated and disenchanted with objects of their affection. Become temperamental, difficult, make others "walk on eggshells" around their stormy feelings. Increasingly self-absorbed, moody, and self-conscious, unable to be spontaneous or to "get out of themselves." Feel increasingly different from others and therefore exempt from living as others do. They become melancholy dreamers, disdainful, decadent, and sensual, while becoming hostile to anyone who questions their lifestyle. Feelings of intense desire and hatred coexist and interfere with simple day-to-day functioning. Self-pity and envy of others lead to different kinds of self-indulgence, to wallowing in a world of dreams, illusions, and unrealistic expectations, and to becoming increasingly impractical, unproductive, effete, and precious.

Unhealthy. As their ideas about themselves become more unrealistic, Fours reject anyone or anything in their life that does not support their self-image, and become increasingly dependent on a few people to maintain their way of life.

When their dreams (fantasies and expectations) fail, they can become furious at themselves for their failures and at others for not supporting them enough. ("Everybody lets me down.") Trying to suppress the intensity of their hatreds and rage, Fours become alienated from others and severely depressed, full of self-inhibitions and emotional paralysis. Profoundly fatigued, mentally confused, emotionally "blocked," and unable to work or function, they develop a deep sense of futility and meaninglessness. Racked with delusional self-contempt, irrational hatred of others who Fours believe have let them down, self-reproaches, morbid thoughts, and tormented by their failures and unfulfilled desires:

everything becomes a source of withering self-accusations. Feeling worthless and hopeless, they despair and become self-destructive, possibly abusing alcohol or drugs to escape their crushingly negative self-hatred. In the extreme, emotional breakdown, crimes of passion, or suicide is likely.

Triad Issues. The blockage of the Feeling Center leads Fours to use their imagination to stimulate and prolong emotional reactions on which they base their sense of self. They identify with their emotions, which are reinforced by continual introspection on their changing emotional states. Constantly attending to their feelings, especially their negative ones, leads to interpersonal and practical problems. Problems common to the types of this Triad include issues with *identity* and with *hostility*. Fours' hostility is expressed in envy, in rancorous sarcasm, and in cutting off connections with others when their own identity is questioned or threatened in any way.

Direction of Disintegration. Average Fours can become self-absorbed and moody, distancing themselves from the important people in their lives. The stress that this causes for Fours, especially in their significant relationships, can cause them to take on the behaviors of average Twos. They seek to reassure themselves that they have not alienated others — that others will not abandon them despite their emotional storms. To this end, they people-please, try to find needs to fulfill, and call attention to the good things they have done for their loved ones.

Unhealthy Fours despair of ever actualizing themselves; when they move to Two, it may well be as the result of an emotional breakdown. Since they can no longer function very well, in effect they coerce someone else to take care of them. They may live with their parents or with a friend, or become entirely dependent on a spouse, while resenting these people for not understanding them or caring for them adequately. Severe problems result, however, because deteriorated Fours hate themselves and may ruin even the relationships on which they have become dependent. They may allow themselves to become completely broken down as a way of eliciting care from others.

Direction of Integration. When healthy Fours go to One, by overcoming their self-consciousness and self-absorption, they are no longer controlled by their ever-changing feelings. They act on objective principles rather than subjective moods; rather than becoming self-indulgent, they are self-disciplined. They no longer see themselves as different and no longer feel exempt from the need to work; thus, they make a place for themselves in the real world. By learning balanced self-discipline and discernment, they are able to bring their emotional riches to others more often, with a creativity they themselves can depend on.

Security Point. Average Fours can also "act out" the average behaviors of type One, but usually with trusted friends and intimates. Fours can adopt a superior attitude, feeling that they alone can do things well, while criticizing or scolding others. They can become fussy about particulars, even perfectionistic. At such times, the true degree of the Four's frustration and lack of empathy is revealed. Fours may take out on key intimates their dissatisfaction with themselves and with their lot in life.

Childhood Pattern. Disconnected from both parents, feeling abandoned or misunderstood by them in some way (*PT*, 140–42). The key element in their early formation is that, because of their lack of suitable role models, Fours were forced to create their own identities by looking inward to their feelings and imaginations. This leaves them feeling frustrated with the quality of mirroring and support they received. Fours may recreate these frustrations in their adult relationships.

Basic Fear. Of having no identity or personal significance.

Basic Desire. To be themselves.

Secondary Motivations. Fours want to express themselves, to create something beautiful that will allow them to communicate themselves to others, to have others appreciate their unique identity and contribution, to withdraw from people so that they can sort out and protect their feelings, to cope with their emotions before dealing with anything else, to indulge themselves to make up for what they are missing in the real world.

In Search of: Identity. Fours want to know who they are, but more than that, they want to have a solid and dependable sense of themselves that they can call on. They have a sense that "something is missing" in the self that they would like to find and fix. Fours often look to others who seem to them to embody all that they feel they lack in themselves. They search for a "rescuer" who not only embodies all of these qualities, but who will also see and validate the Four. Fours also seek validation of their identity and worth in their creative work, feeling that it is a stand-in for themselves.

Healthy Sense of Self. "I am an intuitive, sensitive person."

Hidden Complaint. "I am different from others, and I feel I don't really fit in."

Key Defense Mechanisms. Introjection, displacement, splitting, turning against the self.

Characteristic Temptation. To overuse their imaginations in the search for self. Average to unhealthy Fours think that they will find themselves and the meaning of their feelings by retreating into fantasies. But they only lose themselves in their imaginations. Rather than deal with reality, they become engrossed in fantasies, retreating into an imaginary world where they give themselves permission to feel and be anything, thus wasting their time and energies on illusions.

Saving Grace. Despite their growing self-indulgence, their withdrawal from people, and the many bad habits they have gotten into, average Fours may still have enough self-awareness to know what they are doing to themselves. Their honesty with themselves may prevent them from deteriorating further.

Suggestions for Personal Growth. See Chapter 10.

Structural Patterns. The keynote is *subjectivity*. In order to keep their sense of self alive, Fours need to have a personal and emotional resonance with their experiences. They therefore "take everything personally," and for better or worse, often invest meaning or find intention where there is none. Their need to personalize experience can lead to profound insights into the self, or more negatively, to being dramatic, stormy, and temperamental. The overall pattern is of conflicts between subjective feelings and impulses — and between the need to express them and to hold them back. The self-inhibitions of Fours are due to the dark, hostile feelings they have toward their parents for inadequately seeing them, as well as those directed toward themselves for the guilt they experience for having such feelings about their parents. As Fours deteriorate, the pattern is of spiraling inward down the Levels of Development into increasingly self-enclosed, self-referential negative states until they become completely alienated from others and, ironically, from themselves. In the end, if they are unable to break the pattern of introversion and self-absorption, they will ultimately become worn down by seething hatred of themselves and of the people that have disappointed them. Their hostility toward self and others does not allow anything positive to offset it.

Cognitive Error. To identify themselves with their changing feelings and emotional states, especially negative ones. Since their feelings constantly change, their identity does as well, undermining many of their psychological needs.

Inevitable Consequences. The inevitable consequence of their ego inflation (in fantasies and subjective withdrawal) is that Fours undermine their Basic Desire (to actualize themselves) while increasingly bringing on themselves their Basic Fear, that they have no clear identity or sense of personal significance (*PT*, 171–72). The more solipsistic Fours become in their endless "search for self," the more they lose touch with the realities of their actual lived life. Their identities remain undeveloped and their sense of personal significance stunted by lack of involvement in the world. Once they withdraw into fantasies and avoid engaging themselves in realistic ways, Fours need to recognize they are going in the wrong direction.

Fours will find themselves only by grounding themselves firmly in the realities of the here and now, thus becoming less prey to their shifting moods. They can get beyond self-consciousness by taking the "leap of faith" that they will actualize themselves if they involve themselves with the real world. Rather than indulge in useless dreams, they must start taking an active, realistic interest in their own lives — as paradoxical and strange as that may seem. However, Fours know what it means: they must stop imagining life and start living it.

PERSONALITY TYPE FIVE: *THE INVESTIGATOR*

The Perceptive, Innovative, Secretive, Isolated Person

Healthy. Healthy Fives are able to observe everything with extraordinary perceptiveness and insight. Most mentally alert, curious, with an acutely searching intelligence — asking the right questions while using extraordinarily fine perceptions. Able to concentrate, to become engrossed in what has caught their attention, and to "tinker" with their interests until they discover or create something entirely new. Love learning, excited by acquiring knowledge, and often become experts in some field. Independent thinkers, innovative, inventive, and highly imaginative, producing extremely valuable, original ideas and boldly creative works. Mental or creative brilliance are balanced with compassion and feeling. *At their best:* Become intrepid discoverers and explorers, broadly comprehending the world while penetrating it profoundly. Deeply grounded in themselves and reality, and feel emotionally connected to the world rather than cut off from it. Visionaries, open-minded, taking in things whole, in their true context, seeing things as they actually are. May make pioneering discoveries of something entirely new or create new forms of artistic expression. Experience *gnosis,* direct knowing unmediated by mental constructs.

Average. Average Fives begin conceptualizing everything before acting — working things out in their minds: model building, preparing, practicing, and gathering more resources. They retreat from the world into their own inner world of concepts and imagination. Studious, acquiring technique. Become specialized, and often "intellectual," focusing on research, scholarship, and developing ideas. Much time spent on a few key interests while other areas of life are neglected. Increasingly detached as Fives become more involved with complicated ideas or imaginary worlds. Highly speculative ("What if this were to happen?"). Become preoccupied with their visions and interpretations rather than with reality. Immerse themselves in details, beginning to "lose the forest for the trees," not seeing the true broader context. Are fascinated by offbeat, esoteric subjects, even those involving dark and disturbing elements. Detached from the practical world, a "disembodied mind," although very high-strung and intense. Begin to take an antagonistic stance toward anything that would interfere with their inner world and personal vision. Can be aggressive as a defense against being emotionally involved or overwhelmed. Become provocative and abrasive, with intentionally extreme and radical views. Cynical and argumentative: others are too stupid to understand. Their extreme, iconoclastic interpretations may contain valuable insights, but also far-fetched half-truths.

Unhealthy. Rejecting and repulsing all social attachments, unhealthy Fives become reclusive and isolated from people and reality; increasingly secretive, strange, eccentric, and mentally unstable. Severe depressions and nihilism are common. Highly antagonistic and vituperative, yet fearful of aggressions from others, they become increasingly suspicious and emotionally overwrought. Get obsessed with, yet frightened by, (their own) terrifying ideas, becoming horrified by themselves and by reality, and prey to gross distortions, phobias, and hallucinations. Feel like existence is torture. Seeking oblivion, Fives may commit suicide or have a psychotic break with reality. Deranged, explosively self-destructive, with schizophrenic overtones.

Triad Issues. Identified with the Thinking Center, the Five's mind is overactive, overwhelming other functions, with the result that there is little connection with the physical body. Awareness of the emotional and interpersonal dimensions is generally undervalued and undeveloped. Thinking gets stuck in "preparation mode" — readying the self for postponed action. In this Triad, we also see themes concerning *anxiety* and *security.* Fives are anxious about their inability to cope with the potentially overwhelming outside world and so retreat into their minds, which they see as safer and more secure.

Direction of Disintegration. Average Fives can become isolated and socially withdrawn to focus on pursuing whatever they believe will give them a sense of competence and mastery. To this end, they also cut off from basic needs for comfort, contact, and connection. This inevitably leads to stress, causing Fives to act out some of the average behaviors of type Seven. At such times, Fives become more scattered in their thinking, and impulsive in their actions. They may entertain themselves compulsively or suddenly try to connect with others socially, although their impulsivity often causes such efforts to backfire, leading to more withdrawal and social isolation. They may also seek to escape from painful feelings through manic activity or substance abuse.

Unhealthy Fives can become extremely isolated and incapable of acting effectively in their environment; when they go to Seven, they become even more impulsive, acting erratically and hysterically. Thinking too much has gotten them into many problems, so they no longer think but act compulsively. Deteriorated Fives become unstable and reckless, lunging out at an apparent solution to their problems, although often doing only more harm to themselves than good.

Direction of Integration. When healthy Fives go to Eight, they become grounded in their own body, feeling the power of their instinctual energy. Thus they are able to act from a realization of their own mastery; their grounding gives them a solid support for their knowledge such that they can act and lead others with confidence. (They also realize that while they do not know everything, they still probably know more than most.) Fives no longer feel cut off from the world; rather, they experience the depth of their connection with everything and their ability to engage fully in life and with other people. As a result, they feel more capable and secure than they did from observing reality while trying to detach themselves from it. This empowers them to use their wisdom compassionately for the good of the world.

Security Point. Average Fives can also "act·out" the average behaviors of type Eight, but usually with trusted friends and intimates. They can become extremely assertive and defiant, pushing people's boundaries while aggressively defending their own. Disagreements or fears of control by others can cause Fives to lose their tempers. At such times, the extent of a Five's underlying anger and feelings of rejection and powerlessness is revealed.

Childhood Pattern. Fives are ambivalently identified with both parents or parent figures (*PT*, 178–79). At a deep, sometimes unconscious level, Fives felt *rejected by both parents*. The other two ambivalent types, Two and Eight, coped with feelings of rejection and fit into the family by attempting to play a complementary role to the "rejecting parent." Thus, Twos learn to play the role of the nurturer, and Eights play the role of protector. In Fives, however, the two roles cancel each other out, leading young Fives to feel overwhelmed by the needs of their caretakers and uncertain as to what they might be able to contribute to the family. As a result, Fives begin to look for a role that has not been taken, a niche they can fulfill that will give them a sense of place and belonging. But because they feel they do not have a niche, they focus on searching for one. Fives do not believe they can engage deeply in sustainable relationships until they have adequately mastered their niche.

Basic Fear. Of being helpless, useless, and incapable.

Basic Desire. To be capable and competent. (To be able to do.)

Secondary Motivations. Fives want to understand reality, to observe everything, to master something to gain confidence (find a niche), to create an inner reality that feels more controllable than the real world, to shut out our intrusions, to challenge or scare off anyone who threatens their inner world or niche, to isolate themselves from the outside world.

In Search of: Mastery. Fives want to master something so that they can feel more confident and ready to meet life's challenges. To the degree that they have been damaged in childhood and their confidence (especially in their physical powers) has been compromised, they begin to create a private mental world (or an "alternative reality" of some kind) and master that. Average to unhealthy Fives might attempt to master anything from math to piano playing to chess or computer games in order to gain a feeling of confidence — and not to be intruded on in their private space.

Healthy Sense of Self. "I am an intelligent, perceptive person."

Hidden Complaint. "I am so smart that no one else can understand the things I understand or appreciate the things I know."

Key Defense Mechanisms. Displacement, projection, isolation.

Characteristic Temptation. To replace direct experience with concepts. Average to unhealthy Fives literally "think too much," in inappropriate categories and circumstances. They are convinced that by pondering everything they will attain insight and thus be able to build competence and confidence. If Fives understand their environment, they can master it — and therefore will be able to defend themselves against it, if necessary. However, as they abstract from reality, average to unhealthy Fives become increasingly lost in their own thought processes until they lose all perspective. Their intense focus on their inner worlds leads them further and further from grounded contact with themselves and with reality. Excessive conceptualizing is therefore the potential prelude to distortions of perception and increasing failure of confidence.

Saving Grace. Despite their intense preoccupations and increasingly dark interpretations of reality, average Fives may realize that they have begun to introduce distortions into their thinking rather than coming closer to any real understanding. Awareness of their own thought processes may prevent them from deteriorating further and getting out of touch with reality. Their healthy capacity for observation may help them reassess their ideas; their perceptiveness may help them return to a more balanced, healthier state.

Suggestions for Personal Growth. See Chapter 10.

Structural Patterns. The keynote is *concentration*. The objective world of reality is the focus of their attention; however, the more subjective world of thought is the arena that Fives inhabit. Therefore, the inner pattern is of thinking oriented to comprehending reality but impelled by subjective impulses (including aggressions). (Conflicts arise if and when their subjective impulses overpower and distort their perceptions.) Their minds are highly active, intensely driven, and yet defensive — and as their minds become increasingly overheated, Fives unconsciously project subjective ideas into their perceptions. Fives tend to go into so much depth and detail with what has caught their attention that they "disappear" socially and physically. This can make Fives characteristically awkward or even completely unaware of social conventions and graces. Outwardly, the pattern is of increasing distance from reality as Fives reject attachments with the world, particularly with other people. The overall pattern is of paradoxical curiosity and withdrawal, involvement and detachment, immersion and defense, aggression and fear of aggression, attraction and repulsion, and so forth.

Cognitive Error. To think that they can understand the world by seeing themselves as a disconnected, "outside observer." Whether or not they like it, Fives participate in the world and affect the subject of their observations.

Inevitable Consequences. The inevitable consequence of detachment and withdrawal (into mental constructs, ideas, theories, and imagined alternative realities) is that Fives undermine their Basic Desire (to be competent and capable) while increasingly bringing on themselves their Basic Fear, that they are helpless, useless, or incapable (*PT,* 214–15). If Fives cease engaging with reality and do not check their ideas against objective facts, they are in danger of becoming completely lost in their own inner world, and of getting out of touch with reality. Further, their disengagement from their own physicality and needs undermines their ability to feel confident to function in the world. Their increased loss of contact with their physicality, their groundedness, make it inevitable that they will feel threatened and overwhelmed either by someone else or by reality. Rather than be more safely defended by their powerful mental focus, they are literally driven mad by it.

PERSONALITY TYPE SIX: *THE LOYALIST*

The Engaging, Responsible, Anxious, Suspicious Person

Healthy. Healthy Sixes are able to elicit strong emotional responses from others: they are engaging, friendly, playful, and ingratiating. Others feel warmly toward them and want to support them. Trust is important, although it is not given blindly. They are highly reliable and trustworthy themselves, making sure that they follow through with their commitments. Questioning people and circumstances is also part of even the healthy Six's vigilant outlook, however, as are careful foresight, prediction, and troubleshooting. They are hardworking, thrifty, dependable, and cooperative, and help to build an egalitarian spirit with others. Become committed and loyal to those with whom they have identified: family and friends important, as is the feeling that they "belong" somewhere. Healthy Sixes are highly practical and maintain a balanced self-discipline: they are committed to meticulous craftsmanship and quality in their work. People of action, they are also persevering and steady in the face of challenges. *At their best:* Become self-reliant, trusting their own inner guidance, independent yet fully supportive and cooperative with others as an equal. Real faith in life leads to a heroic, positive attitude, as well as manifesting courage, intrepid leadership, and richness in creativity and self-expression.

Average. Average Sixes begin to doubt themselves, so they start investing their time and energy in whatever they believe will be reliable and stable. Organizing and structuring, they look to alliances, beliefs, and authorities for guidance and support. Seek insurance and reassurance. Anxiety about the future causes them to be constantly vigilant, anticipating problems. Try to "cover all the bases," yet still feel like they are not doing enough to be secure. The more anxious they are, the more commitments they make, and the more they feel obligated to follow through with different commitments. Feel pressured — others expect too much. Vacillate between being convinced about a belief or of others' support and doubting them. Become increasingly ambivalent and skeptical, as well as more defensive about self and whatever beliefs or structures are "working." Begin to get suspicious, and react against their supporters or authorities through indirect passive-aggressive behavior, giving contradictory, mixed signals. Inner confusion makes Sixes react unpredictably: they procrastinate, become indecisive, cautious, and evasive — they "clam up," becoming unwilling to express their inner anxieties readily. Fear that others will "jump down their throats." As tensions increase, they get grumpy, pessimistic, and obstructionistic. To overcome doubts and tensions, they become more stubborn and reactionary, taking a tough, rebellious stance to overcompensate for growing insecurities. Can become sarcastic, belligerent, and short-tempered, aggressively reacting to apparent threats to their security. Begin to divide people into friends and enemies, overzealously defending whatever gives them security with a "them against us" siege mentality, while blaming others for their anxieties. Increasingly authoritarian and closed-minded.

Unhealthy. Fearing that they have ruined their security either by impulsive acts of defiance or by lack of initiative, they become extremely panicky and highly insecure. Can become clingingly dependent and self-disparaging, *or* compulsively "tough" while denying need for help or support. In both cases, acute inferiority feelings and panic attacks are common. Have a low self-image and become depressed, feeling worthless and incompetent; plagued by fears. Overreact to everything, exaggerating problems: Sixes' irrational actions may actually bring about the very thing they fear. Seeing themselves as defenseless, they seek out a stronger authority or belief to resolve all problems. May look to others for rescue or become a loner who seeks relief from anxieties in fanatical beliefs or in substance abuse. Increasingly paranoid, feel persecuted and attacked by others, imagining that people are "out to get them." In some cases, can get mean-spirited and bigoted, scapegoating others and lashing out at anyone who seems to threaten them, as a way to silence their fears and insecurities. Overwhelming anxiety and fears of abandonment may cause Sixes to abase and humiliate themselves to an authority figure to be rescued. Hysterical and seeking to escape punishment, they become self-punishing, self-destructive and suicidal. Advanced alcoholism, drug overdoses, "skid row" lifestyle, extreme paranoia, and masochistic behavior as pathology.

Triad Issues. As the primary type in the Thinking Triad, Six is most out of touch with its ability to quiet the mind and to contact "inner knowing." Sixes lack clear inner guidance, so they look outside of themselves (to others, belief systems, authorities, etc.) for direction and reassurance. For this reason, Sixes are often plagued by doubt, but when they find a plausible belief system they can become emotionally attached to it. Sixes also have problems with *anxiety* and *insecurity*, which manifest themselves in many different ways.

Direction of Disintegration. Average Sixes are often visibly anxious and self-doubting, but they do their best to persevere and meet all of the important commitments and responsibilities in their lives. As a result, stress becomes almost a way of life. But when it begins to overwhelm their usual defenses, Sixes may go to Three, hiding out in their work and putting on a brave face as if to tell others, "You don't have to worry about me. I'm doing great!" Fears of abandonment or of inadequacy may also cause them to become more emotionally distant and fearful of intimacy, not wanting those close to them to see the degree of their distress. Threats to their security may lead Sixes into covert competitions in the manner of lower average Threes. They become more expedient, political, and calculated.

Unhealthy Sixes feel extremely anxious and become masochistic, filled with feelings of inferiority and worthlessness. When they go to Three, they may become unscrupulous in their efforts to preserve their position or security — becoming dishonest and unprincipled. Very unhealthy Sixes can slip into the psychopathology of very unhealthy Threes: they may strike out violently at others both to overcome their feelings of inferiority and to hurt anyone who has hurt them. Often, their targets are authorities or people who symbolize for the Six a great betrayal. (This is the lone office worker who finally cracks and goes on a killing spree at his place of employment.) Male Sixes are more likely to engage in irrational acts of violence: female Sixes more often take on a false, charming persona while punishing or striking out at perceived oppressors in more focused, personal ways.

Direction of Integration. When healthy Sixes go to Nine, they find a stable sense of support within themselves that enables them to relax and feel more open to the world and to others. Sixes learn that they can become grounded by finding a deeper connection with their physical presence in the here and now. This does not mean becoming more athletic or active; rather, it means being open to the sensations of life in the present moment. This offers them some respite from their restless minds: both their ambivalence toward others and their tendency to overreact to anxiety diminish. They are much more emotionally stable as well as receptive and trusting of others. They become supportive and reassuring, beacons of stability and maturity. Their problems with anxiety have largely been resolved, and as a result they are more peaceful, secure, generous, and relaxed than ever.

Security Point. Average Sixes can also "act out" the average behaviors of type Nine, but usually with trusted friends and intimates. They can become disengaged and unreceptive to others — basically shutting down. The feeling is "I've been frantically working to hold things together and to take care of everything for too long, and now I don't want to have to do anything. I don't want to have to respond to you." With trusted others, Sixes give themselves permission to "numb out" and avoid addressing further responsibilities.

Childhood Pattern. Sixes are connected with the protective figure, an idealized other who is often the father or a father figure (*PT*, 224–26). The key element in their development is that they look outside themselves, to an authoritative figure, for guidance, support, security, approval, and to learn how to be an independent person in the world. When we are children, the father figure ideally helps us move away from our dependence on our mothers by bolstering our confidence, teaching us about the world, and mirroring our strength and capacity. When this need is not met adequately, or if the father is completely or largely absent, the person is left with deep anxiety about the world and doubts about his or her ability to function independently. Thus, Sixes, who are particularly vulnerable to this developmental challenge, look for trusted guides and supports to help them gain the autonomy they seek.

Basic Fear. Of being without support and guidance.

Basic Desire. To have support and guidance.

Secondary Motivations. Sixes want to be liked, to have approval, to test the attitudes of others toward themselves, to assert themselves to overcome their fears, to gain reassurances if they are afraid, to have the authority figure come to their aid.

In Search of: Security and safety. Sixes are looking for someone or something in which to believe. In the absence of a palpable feeling of being supported by life (or their own Essence) and of having contact with Inner Guidance, Sixes must look elsewhere for feelings of safety and security, including how to make decisions and move forward in their lives. Average Sixes are therefore in search of an authority they can trust. Only healthy Sixes discover their own inner authority and believe not so much in themselves but in the voice of Inner Guidance, which comes from a mind clear of fear, anxiety, and projection.

Healthy Sense of Self. "I am a committed, dependable person."

Hidden Complaint. "I am dependable and do what I'm supposed to, although other people don't."

Key Defense Mechanisms. Identification, displacement, projection.

Characteristic Temptation. To rely on others to help the Six become independent. Sixes fundamentally want to become independent, but their increasing self-doubt leads them to feel that they need more support. Caught in cycles of indecision and second-guessing, Sixes increasingly rely on friends, allies, spouses, or pronouncements from books or trusted authorities to reassure them that they are making the right decision. Despite occasional overcompensations, average to unhealthy Sixes become increasingly dependent on others or on familiar beliefs and procedures for emotional security. But by constantly looking to other sources for support, however reassuring in the short run, Sixes undermine their self-confidence in the long run.

Saving Grace. Despite increasing tensions and overcompensations, average Sixes may still want to build genuinely secure and cooperative relationships with others. Their healthy capacity for maintaining committed relationships may prevent them from deteriorating further or from doing something that would bring about rejection and potential abandonment.

Suggestions for Personal Growth. See Chapter 10.

Structural Patterns. The keynote is *reactivity*. The Six has a complex and ever-changing psychological pattern because of constant emotional and interpersonal shifts from Level to Level. Outwardly, they oscillate from one state to another as they interact with people and react to their own feelings and anxieties. To find security, Sixes feel they must engage others emotionally. But to maintain their self-esteem, Sixes also become defensive and resist the influence of others, tending to overcompensate in the opposite direction by acting forcefully to prove that they are not dependent on anyone. They can be tough and belligerent to prove that they are their own masters, while still wanting to feel that they are approved and that others care for them. Internally, Sixes experience constant reactions between their aggressive and compliant feelings, between their fears and their aggressions, between their desire to be close to people and their desire to be on their own. The overall pattern is one of ever-changing double circles — an external circle of interpersonal interactions and an internal circle of emotional reactions, both of which constantly react with each other as well as with the external world, particularly other people.

Cognitive Error. To look for guidance and security outside themselves in received knowledge, social structures, and relationships. Sixes then must constantly focus on evaluating the truth or falsehood of external sources of information rather than letting their minds become quiet so that their own inner guidance can arise.

Inevitable Consequences. The inevitable consequence of constant anxiety-based hyperthinking and chronic self-doubt is that Sixes undermine their Basic Desire (to find support, guidance, and security) while increasingly bringing on themselves their Basic Fear, that they are abandoned and without support and guidance (*PT,* 258–59). Fear and anxiety are the twin monsters that threaten

Sixes, and unless Sixes learn to deal with them at their true sources, they will be eaten alive. They must remember that some anxiety is inescapable: if they cannot cope with it and resolve its causes — if they attempt to flee from it in some way — they will likely bring more of it on themselves. However, rather than reacting to anxiety, Sixes can *learn to experience the actual sensation of anxiety* in the here and now. If they can do this, they can see the sensation as an invigorating force. Anxiety that is consciously used can become the "shock" that Sixes need to help boost them to a higher level of accomplishment and independence.

PERSONALITY TYPE SEVEN: *THE ENTHUSIAST*

The Spontaneous, Versatile, Acquisitive, Scattered Person

Healthy. Highly responsive, free-spirited, and enthusiastic about their experiences, healthy Sevens are powerfully oriented to the real world of things and sensations. They are spontaneous, adventurous, and exhilarated by every experience. Every stimulus brings an immediate response, and they find everything exciting and invigorating. Happy, vivacious, stimulating people: resilient and lively. They are curious about the world and often possess quick, agile minds. Become accomplished achievers and generalists who do many different things well: multitalented, Renaissance people, frequently gifted with virtuosic talents and prodigious skills. Healthy Sevens are practical, productive, and prolific — people of action and energy. Their active minds also lead them to explore many different areas of life: they become versatile, cross-fertilizing their many areas of interest. *At their best:* They assimilate experiences in depth, becoming appreciative and grateful, enthralled (awed) by the wonders of life. Life-affirming, joyful, and ecstatic. Begin to have intimations of a spiritual reality, and a deep sense of the boundless goodness of life. At the same time, Sevens are aware that physical reality *is* spiritual, and they take great delight in even common day-to-day experiences.

Average. As restlessness increases, average Sevens want to have more options and choices available to them. They become adventurous and "worldly wise," but grow less focused, constantly seeking a variety of new things and experiences, becoming avid consumers, sophisticates, connoisseurs, trend-setters, and sensation seekers. They are good at initiating projects, but begin to have trouble following through with them. Become hesitant to commit to a specific course of action because of fear of missing out on better options.

Average Sevens are increasingly unable to prioritize or to deny themselves anything: they grow hyperactive, throwing themselves into constant activity, doing and saying whatever comes to mind. They become scattered and distracted: their minds move so quickly that they have difficulty staying focused. Anxieties escalate, and because they fear boredom, they try to heighten their stimulation and excitement — and defend against painful feelings — by staying in perpetual motion, distracting themselves with whatever promises to be "fun" at the time.

Schedules, previous plans, and appointments may get discarded as more interesting options present themselves. Indiscriminate activities can lead them to becoming superficial, glib dilettantes merely dabbling around: they seem unable to discriminate what is really good for them. Uninhibited, flamboyant, outspoken, and attention-grabbing — constantly talking, exaggerating, wisecracking, joking, and "performing" to stay in high spirits. Begin to easily feel trapped or deprived, so they become more flighty and unreliable, as well as excessive and extravagant, engaging in conspicuous consumption to compensate for repressed emotional problems. Having even more variety and money to afford new amusements becomes important. Sevens do not intentionally cause others pain, but they also do not want to see their harmful effects on others: can be self-centered, insensitive, demanding, and impatient, while being unwilling to do much to support others reciprocally. Deny guilt or responsibility for problems they create.

Unhealthy. Desperate to quell their anxieties, unhealthy Sevens are very easily and quickly frustrated, becoming rude and abusive as they demand whatever it is they believe they need to keep their growing panic under control. Become infantile escapists, impulsively discharging their anxieties in manic talking or activity: they do not know when to stop. Unhealthy Sevens can become jaded and callous toward others, insulting, flying into rages and tantrums; have extreme difficulty controlling themselves. Danger of addictions to alcohol, drugs, or of reckless overspending or gambling: a profligate lifestyle takes its toll as they become dissipated, dissolute, debauched, and depraved. Increasingly hardened by their lavishness and excesses, yet unsatisfied, Sevens begin to lose the capacity for pleasure, or to feel anything. Terrified by their growing inner chaos, they act out impulses rather than dealing with anxiety, going out of control, prey to wildly erratic, volatile mood swings and compulsive, manic actions (the "manic-depressive" defense). They engage in wild sprees of various sorts, grandiose and delusionally unrealistic, as if there could be no limits on them. Eventually Sevens' defenses collapse and their energy and health are poor, leaving them in severe depressions with bouts of hysteria and feelings of physical and emotional paralysis. Physical disabilities from excessive lifestyle are also common. They often give up on themselves and life: deep despair, self-destructive overdoses, impulsive suicide.

Triad Issues. The Thinking Center is identified with, but instinctive impulses (doing) are used to stimulate the mind and keep their thinking processes active. Because they are out of touch with Inner Guidance, Sevens do not know what will fulfill them, so they tend to try everything — going in too many directions and scattering their energy. In type Seven, we also see themes of *anxiety* (which is suppressed) and concerns about *security*. Their flight from their inner world to the external world leads to a search for exciting and pleasurable experiences, possessions, and gratifications.

Direction of Disintegration. Average Sevens value being spontaneous — they like to go with whatever strikes them as the most interesting or potentially fulfilling option at the time. When this goes too far, however, Sevens begin to feel uneasy about their lack of focus and structure. As real obligations and growing backlogs of problems pile up, the increased stress causes Sevens to take on some of the average behaviors of type One. They try to order their affairs, but can become rigid and compulsive about doing so. At such times, they can become self-critical and impatient with themselves and their accomplishments, while being curt and impersonal with others. Because these efforts stem from a punitive superego and not from real inner guidance, Sevens usually balk at staying with their discipline or plan, and soon resume their impulsive escape from anxiety, albeit with greater guilt to suppress.

Unhealthy Sevens can become highly impulsive and out of control (manic). They know that they are losing the possibility of finding any real fulfillment and that they need to put brakes on many of their activities. When they take on unhealthy One behaviors, they try to impose a strict, arbitrary order, becoming obsessive, punitive, and vindictive toward themselves or toward anyone who threatens the fragile structure they have created. Like unhealthy Ones, they can also become obsessively fixated with someone or something that seems to them to be the solution to their unhappiness.

Direction of Integration. When healthy Sevens go to Five, they become more involved with their experiences in depth, learning to concentrate, and to stay focused such that they are contributing to the environment rather than merely consuming it. Integrating Sevens no longer fear that they will be deprived of happiness unless they are constantly seeking positive experiences for themselves. They delve into their experiences more profoundly, getting to the heart of things, comprehending more, and therefore enjoying reality on a deeper level than ever before. Further, they are able to do this because they no longer avoid the darker side of life or of their own psyches. They realize that any happiness in life is fleeting and ultimately meaningless if it does not take life's difficulties into account. Sevens can take in the totality of experience without denying any of it. This allows their minds to become more open and quiet such that the guidance and deeper satisfaction they have been seeking rise into awareness.

Security Point. Average Sevens can also "act out" the average behaviors of type Five, but most often with trusted friends and intimates. Sevens become accustomed to being the entertainers and energizers in their social circles and often in their workplaces, enjoying contact, conversation, and good times. But with intimates or close friends, they can become strangely detached and preoccupied — in effect, demanding space and independence from those closest to them. They may withdraw from contact with intimates, become secretive and compartmentalize relationships, or lose themselves in work projects as a way of defending their autonomy like average Fives.

Childhood Pattern. Type Seven is disconnected from the nurturing figure, which is often the mother or a mother figure (*PT*, 265–66). The key element in Sevens' early development revolves around their fear of being deprived by their nurturers, leading to chronic feelings of frustration. The deprivation may have been material or emotional, and it could have been caused in any number of ways, but it left the Seven feeling that his or her needs would not be adequately met. Sevens then make it their business to nurture themselves, and to ensure that their needs will always be met. The deprivation may have been more feared than actual, and yet the determination never to feel insecure or in need became a major force in their development.

Basic Fear. Of being trapped in pain and deprivation.

Basic Desire. To be satisfied and content, to have their needs fulfilled.

Secondary Motivations. Sevens want to maintain their freedom and happiness, to enjoy themselves, to avoid missing out on worthwhile experiences, to keep themselves excited and occupied, to be amused and to have fun, to get whatever they want, to stay "up" and in motion regardless of the consequences, to flee from or discharge anxiety and pain.

In Search of: Satisfaction and fulfillment. Sevens are searching for the thing that will make them happy and satisfied. In the absence of feeling nurtured and supported by their own Essence, Sevens look to the world of experience to feel safe and secure. They are also searching for their life's purpose, for the one thing that they believe will completely fulfill them. They search for their Grail by acquiring the experiences that will make them happy, while suppressing fear, anxiety, self-doubt, and awareness of "the dark side" of life.

Healthy Sense of Self. "I am a happy, enthusiastic person."

Hidden Complaint. "I am happy, although I would be a lot happier if I got everything I wanted."

Key Defense Mechanisms. Repression, externalization, acting out.

Characteristic Temptation. To think that fulfillment is somewhere else. Sevens are tempted to think that while what they are doing is good, something just around the corner might be better. This can lead to the belief that *more* of a good thing is better. However, as they attempt to pursue options and acquire more experiences or possessions, they only increase the strength of their appetites without really satisfying them. To be satisfied requires that we be present to the experience we are having. But the restless search for variety, and for bigger, better, and more leads Sevens away from presence, literally guaranteeing that they will remain unsatisfied.

Saving Grace. Despite their increasing distractions and excesses, average Sevens may still have enough genuine enthusiasm for things that their very love of the world will prevent them from deteriorating further into mere escapism or manic hyperactivity.

Their healthy capacity to appreciate life and the beauty of the world may act as a brake on their desire for mere stimulation, helping them to return to healthier levels of functioning.

Suggestions for Personal Growth. See Chapter 10.

Structural Patterns. The keynote is *responsiveness*. The Seven's psyche is extraordinarily externalized since most of its energies are invested in being stimulated by the external world. Sevens move outward toward ever-new, different, and more exciting experiences. They are energized by interacting powerfully with people and with the real world of material objects. As Sevens deteriorate, they get caught in a flight from self, anxiety, unconscious impulses, aloneness, and insecurities while demanding that the material world (including other people) fulfill their every need. The overall pattern, therefore, is of a buzzing, humming vibrancy, full of energy and vitality, but in danger of becoming shallow and impulsive. When that energy is in service of avoiding pain and anxiety, average to unhealthy Sevens consume their experiences with little or no personal internalization of them, feeling continually frustrated and sometimes lashing out at the very hand that feeds them.

Cognitive Error. To think that they will achieve satisfaction and happiness by anticipating the future rather than maintaining contact with themselves and with what is happening in the moment. Anticipation of the future takes Sevens out of the immediacy of their own experiences, thereby undermining the possibility of being satisfied by them.

Inevitable Consequences. If Sevens continue to jump impulsively from one activity to another, trying to avoid pain and anxiety, they increasingly bring about their Basic Fear (of being trapped in pain and deprivation), while undermining their Basic Desire (satisfaction and fulfillment; PT, 296). Yet, who will have denied them happiness? The truth is that average to unhealthy Sevens bring much of their unhappiness on themselves by allowing their whims and misplaced sense of freedom to run away with them. Once they become unwilling to say no to their whims and impulses — to stay

with a course of action or a commitment to themselves or others
— they cross a boundary that can have serious consequences. The
way for Sevens to become healthier is to become still enough inside to grieve their losses and to recognize that inner quiet where
true fulfillment can be found. The answer to that question is always here and now.

PERSONALITY TYPE EIGHT: *THE CHALLENGER*

The Self-Confident, Decisive, Willful, Confrontational Person

Healthy. Self-assertive, self-confident, and strong, healthy Eights
have learned to stand up for themselves for what they need and
want. Action-oriented, with a can-do attitude and inner drive.
They love a challenge and are resourceful self-starters, taking the
initiative and making things happen. Tenacious and robust, they
value independence and foster it in others. Strong-willed, impas-
sioned people of action, they communicate simply and directly —
"what you see is what you get." Eights are natural leaders that
others respect and turn to for direction: decisive, authoritative,
and commanding. Earn respect by being honorable, by using
power constructively, by championing and protecting people, by
acting as providers, sponsors, mentors, and promoters of worthwhile causes and valuable enterprises. Seek justice and fair play,
and have a positive vision for their world. *At their best:* Become
compassionate and magnanimous, merciful and forbearing, mas-
tering themselves, carrying others and fulfilling others' needs with
their strength. Empowering, gentle, and inspiring, have the courage to be openhearted. Truly fearless, they are willing to put themselves in jeopardy to achieve vision: possibly heroic and historically great.

Average. Average Eights want to be as independent and autonomous as possible: they fear becoming too dependent on others,

so they toughen themselves up. ("I don't need anyone.") Self-sufficiency, financial independence, and the prospect of having adequate resources are important concerns: Eights become enterprising, pragmatic, "rugged individualists," wheeler-dealers. They are hard-working, businesslike, and shrewd, competitively seeking advantages for themselves and their loved ones. Eights also like to play hard: they can be audacious, full of gusto, loving adventure and risk-taking for the excitement and to test and prove themselves. As stress mounts, they become more self-protective and emotionally defended. They doubt that others support their efforts. Attempt to let others know that they are important, becoming boastful and proud, making big promises and big plans. As Eights' trust in their situation deteriorates, they want to dominate the environment (including others) by becoming more assertive, forceful, aggressive, and expansive: their word is law. Use more energy and force than is necessary for almost every activity. Exhausting self, but still willful and egocentric, demanding loyalty and imposing "their way" on everything. Do not see others as equals or treat them with respect. Can become bossy, ordering others around while openly defying anyone who attempts to tell them what to do. Begin to feel rejected and unsupported by others, but react by becoming confrontational, belligerent, and bad tempered, creating adversarial relationships. They make everything into a test of will and do not back down. They push others' boundaries and are willing to go "toe-to-toe." Use threats, intimidation, and fear of reprisals to extort compliance from others, to keep them off balance and feeling powerless. ("You *don't* want to get me angry!") Unjust treatment makes others fear and resent bullying Eights, possibly causing others to band together against them.

Unhealthy. Unhealthy Eights feel deeply betrayed, but also feel that they have crossed some limit and cannot go back. Defying any attempt to control them, they develop an outlaw mentality, respecting no law or limit on their behavior. Some become criminals, renegades, and con-artists. They want to hold on to whatever power they have and prevail no matter what the cost: become completely hardhearted, ruthless, immoral, and potentially violent, defying guilt, fear, tenderness, and any other vulnerable human feelings. Of course, this attitude inevitably creates real enemies, and Eights must "up the ante" to protect themselves and quell their suppressed terrors. Raging and tyrannical, espousing the "might makes right," "law of the jungle" philosophy, they terrorize others to feel empowered. Begin to develop delusional ideas about themselves (megalomania), feeling omnipotent, invincible, and invulnerable; become increasingly reckless, overextending themselves and their resources. Finally, if in danger, Eights may vengefully and brutally attempt to destroy everything that has not conformed to their will. Sociopathic tendencies: barbaric and murderous.

Triad Issues. Identification with their Instinctive Center gives Eights tremendous vitality but also causes them to "act out" instinctive impulses rather than containing them or feeling them. When instinctive energy arises, Eights feel compelled to take action, although sometimes without fully considering the consequences of their actions. This pattern also causes Eights to constantly seek out intensity: their sense of identity is sustained by intensifying their reactions to whatever they do (related to their Capital Sin or "passion" of lust). They maintain their identity by forcefully asserting themselves, while seeking not to be affected or controlled by anything in the environment. Their instinctual energy is used to maintain boundaries and to test the boundaries of others. Issues with *aggression* (rage) and *repression* (of vulnerability) are also seen.

Direction of Disintegration. Average Eights are people of action. They assert themselves openly, take strong positions, work and play hard, and sometimes jump into power struggles with others as they seek justice or simply desire to protect their self-interest. Of course, this stance can be extremely stressful, and when Eights feel overwhelmed by the challenges that they have taken on, they may develop many of the behaviors of average Fives. They become more reclusive and emotionally withdrawn, pulling back in order to strategize and better assess an appropriate course of action. At such times, they can be secretive and remote, but also more cynical and pessimistic about the world and other people. Going to Five buys average Eights time but can add fuel to their suspicions and feelings of rejection.

Unhealthy Eights feel as if they are at war with the world, and they try to dominate or control their environment so completely that they often make real enemies. The stress is enormous, and eventually, the Eight's bravado and inflated self-confidence collapse. When they go to unhealthy Five, their terrors about the world and about their helplessness erupt into consciousness, and they retreat into nihilistic isolation. They feel hopeless and unable to connect with anyone, often developing strange phobias or distorted perceptions. At such times, they trust no one, seeing everything and everyone as a threat to their existence. Doubts about themselves and horror about the life they have become trapped in can also come into consciousness, but as soon as possible, unhealthy Eights attempt to repress their doubts and return to their aggressive defenses.

Direction of Integration. When healthy Eights go to Two, they discover long-suppressed feelings of compassion for people, and use their power and strength to support and uplift others. They become caring, generous, and personally concerned for the welfare of others, using whatever influence they have to improve conditions and raise standards. They understand the power of love rather than succumbing to the love of power, becoming servants of something higher than their own willfulness. Further, integrating Eights find that they are able to express their feelings more freely for others in simple, sincere ways. They are better able to nurture others and to accept real nurturing for themselves without feeling that doing so will leave them weak. They learn that they can truly love without losing themselves.

Security Point. Eights can also "act out" the average behaviors of type Two, but most often with trusted friends and intimates. At such times, Eights may try to get others to acknowledge how much they need the Eight — Eights want to be reassured that they are wanted, so they go out of their way to provide good things for the people they care about. ("Nothing's too good for you.") Similarly, in secure settings, Eights may display an unembarrassed sentimentality, being especially touched by the innocence of children or pets, and wanting to care for them.

These behaviors make explicit Eights' underlying feelings of rejection and suppressed needs for closeness and nurturing, as well as sadness about their own lost innocence.

Childhood Pattern. Type Eight is ambivalent to the nurturer, who is usually the mother or a mother figure (*PT*, 304–06). For whatever reason, Eights grow up with largely unconscious feelings of *rejection* by their nurturers. The source of these feelings may arise from the toddler stage when Eights, like all children, test wills against their mothers, essentially asserting their independence. But since Eights are endowed with more powerful wills and instinctual drives than most, they often produce stronger emotional reactions in adult caretakers, which their young selves are likely to interpret as rejection. At the same time, young Eights learn the message that the way to get whatever nurturance is available in the family is by playing a complementary role. They become the "little protector," the strong one, who is tough and independent and can take care of others. As a result, many Eights develop a sense of adult responsibility or burden at an early age. They learn to suppress the fear, vulnerability, and emotional need of their child self in order to take on this role.

Basic Fear. Of being harmed or controlled, of violation.

Basic Desire. To protect themselves and their independence.

Secondary Motivations. Eights want to assert themselves, to prove themselves and their abilities, to be respected, to have the resources they need to "run things," to convince themselves of their importance, to dominate the environment, to get their way, to fight for their survival, to be invulnerable.

In Search of: Survival. Eights are in search of physical survival, as well as the survival of whatever "legacy" they have built. Eights have a vision of how they want their environment to be and how it should reflect them personally. However, they feel that the conditions of live are difficult and threatening and must be resisted, that they must protect themselves and those they care about. They are tough on themselves and others to prevent the environment from hurting them or destroying what they have achieved.

Healthy Sense of Self. "I am a strong, assertive person."

Hidden Complaint. "I am fighting for my own survival, and others would take advantage of me if I let them."

Key Defense Mechanisms. Repression, displacement, denial.

Characteristic Temptation. To think that they are completely independent and self-sufficient. Average to unhealthy Eights want to be utterly autonomous and independent of others so that they will need no one, although, ironically, they want to become so powerful and capable that everyone else will be dependent on them.

Of course, Eights really do need people, but that need is resisted to the degree that they believe they have to be strong and in control of their situation. Need is equated with weakness, and this view sets the stage for increasing emotional isolation, resentment of others, and compensating efforts to control everything.

Saving Grace. Despite increasing confrontations and their ability to intimidate everyone, average Eights may realize that their own survival is increasingly threatened because of the very confrontations they are creating. Their desire to protect themselves may act as a catalyst for returning to a healthier state by asserting themselves in a more balanced way. Furthermore, Eights' desire for self-protection and self-reliance may cause them to be concerned that others become similarly empowered and may lead them to help others achieve that end constructively.

Suggestions for Personal Growth. See Chapter 10.

Structural Patterns. The keynote is *expansiveness.* The psyche of Eights is "volcanic," as if a massive force were constantly moving outward to impact or dominate the environment. The primary force is aggression (mixed with sexual elements) that is directed toward the external world by the Eight's formidably strong ego. Eights generally experience little internal conflict since the structure of their psyches allows them to discharge their aggressions outwardly rather than to repress them or turn them against themselves. However, while conflicts seldom exist in Eights, interpersonal conflicts frequently arise when Eights pit themselves against others in confrontations and displays of will, ego, or sexual dominance. (Such a conflict may produce momentary feelings of anxiety and fear, although Eights will deny and defy them.) Thus, the overall pattern is of relentless expansion into the environment (including other people) to affect it, influence it, or dominate it completely.

Cognitive Error. To identify themselves with their ability to assert themselves independently of others. This subtly leads Eights to feel that they are constantly working *against* something, whether it is nature, God, other people, or a jar that will not open easily. It also leads them to see their own welfare as fundamentally unrelated to the welfare of others.

Inevitable Consequences. Although Eights fear being harmed or controlled by others (their Basic Fear), they increase the likelihood of this happening by their raging confrontational attitude. They bluff and provoke others, and eventually, others call their bluff — placing them and their interests in danger. Moreover, this chip on the shoulder undermines their Basic Desire — to protect themselves and their independence (*PT,* 336). But by acting rashly out of rage or belligerence, they invite retaliation and inevitably curtail their freedom and ability to act. Ironically, as they deteriorate, they are not self-sufficient or self-reliant — they become ever more dependent on others to protect them and do their bidding. Far from being the masters of their worlds, they live like prisoners, in constant fear of retribution.

What less healthy Eights have difficulty remembering is their own fear, vulnerability, and neediness. Their aggressive rejection of these qualities in themselves erodes their souls and also makes them insensitive or even aggressive toward these qualities in others. Unless this cycle of self-rejection and oppression is stopped, the consequences for Eights and the people in their lives are likely to be tragic. Sometimes recognizing this — seeing how they are perpetuating the very kinds of abuses that were once visited on themselves — helps Eights to use their great strength and passion to turn around this vicious cycle.

PERSONALITY TYPE NINE: *THE PEACEMAKER*

The Receptive, Reassuring, Agreeable, and Complacent Person

Healthy. Healthy Nines are deeply receptive, open, unselfconscious, emotionally stable, and serene. Accepting, trusting of self and others, easygoing, at ease with self and with life. Patient and gentle, but also direct and unpretentious, they have an innocence and simplicity about them, and are genuinely kind people. Their attitude is optimistic, reassuring, and supportive; they make people feel comfortable and have a calming, healing influence, harmonizing groups and bringing people together. When healthy, Nines are also powerful and dynamic when they need to be. Their steadiness, common sense, and quiet strength are reassuring to others. They easily can see other people's points of view, making good mediators, negotiators, and counselors. Their sense of well-being comforts and sustains others. Have enormous dignity, deep serenity, and real peace that come from acceptance of their human condition. *At their best:* Become self-possessed and have great equanimity and genuine contentment. Feel autonomous and fulfilled, paradoxically at one with themselves yet able to form more profound relationships because of their union with themselves. Become powerfully alive, awake, grounded, alert to self and others.

Develop an indomitable spirit, like a force of nature — dynamic, connected, truly at one with life. They are exuberant, vital, and self-possessed.

Average. Average Nines begin to fear conflicts, so they become self-effacing, accommodating themselves and going along with others, saying yes to things they really do not want to do. Become agreeable and conciliatory on the surface, while maintaining an inner resistance. Start to use beliefs and stock sayings to deflect others or "airtight philosophies" designed to defend against change. Increasingly feel that they do not want to rouse themselves, and may accept conventional roles and expectations naively and unquestioningly — often idealizing and living vicariously through the other. Try to maintain relationships while resisting being affected by them. Do not want change, upset, or pressure of any kind. Can become passive, phlegmatic, unresponsive, and complacent, walking away from conflicts and sweeping problems under the rug. Claim to have few needs. Increasingly suppress desires. May be physically active but inwardly slothful, emotionally indolent, unwilling to exert the self. Nines exhibit indifference and lazy procrastination, stalling until problems go away on their own. Fill days with familiar routines and busywork, or perform tasks while feeling little connection with what they are doing. Confuse numbness with relaxation — start to seek numbness through television, potboiler novels, and substance abuse. Begin to "tune out" reality, becoming oblivious to what they do not want to see. Much daydreaming, ruminating, dwelling in comforting fantasies, and "being mellow" — often spiritualizing these states as higher virtues. Disengaged, inattentive, and unreflective: thinking becomes hazy, unfocused, and ruminative, mostly about idealized notions of how harmonious and pleasant everything should be. Increasingly stubborn, uncommunicative, and resistant to being affected, although still able to be pleasant. If problems do not go away, Nines begin to minimize the seriousness of the problems to calm and appease others, to "get problems behind them," and to have "peace at any price." Become stoic, fatalistic, and resigned, trudging through life as if nothing can be done to change anything. A great deal of anger is simmering under the surface and sometimes explodes in bursts of temper. Have poor judgment. Wishful thinkers, they look for a solution that will solve their problems but that does not require effort or response on their own part.

Unhealthy. Unhealthy Nines are sitting on top of enormous unexpressed rage, and the effort to keep it out of consciousness exhausts them. They can become highly depressed, while the repression of their energy leads to inadequate personal development: they become increasingly helpless and ineffectual, and others must step in to save them from themselves. Terrified that their underlying anger and grief will emerge into awareness, they become obstinate, stubbornly denying that problems and conflicts exist, or that anything is wrong. Tend to blame the messenger, and to become angry with anyone who tries to help them address or even to acknowledge their real problems. Seriously neglectful and irresponsible, dangerous to anyone who needs them. If problems persist, Nines want to block out of awareness anything that could affect them. To defend themselves, they dissociate to a degree that eventually renders them unable to function. They become severely disoriented, depersonalized, catatonic, and immobilized. Emotional breakdown and personality fragmentation are possible.

Triad Issues. As the primary type of the Instinctive Triad, Nine is most out of touch with its own instinctual drives. These are replaced by ruminative thinking and emotional attachments to specific individuals and comforting situations. Instinctive energy is used to maintain boundaries against others and against disturbing elements within themselves. In short, Nines do not want to be "messed with." They martial powerful resistance to being affected or changed by others or by powerful feelings and passions within themselves. To replace the lack of stimulation their instinctive energy would provide, Nines tend to live vicariously through others, identifying with a perceived "stronger," or more passionate, person. They also have problems with *aggression* and *repression:* assertive impulses are repressed, as are the sense of self and other manifestations of their vitality and independence.

Direction of Disintegration. Average Nines are easygoing and agreeable, maintaining a positive outlook and, as much as possible, remaining unruffled by life's ups and downs. But Nines, like anyone else, are not immune to problems or to getting upset by disturbing events. Their powerful defenses usually will help them to remain relatively calm and even-keeled in crises, but when problems get too overwhelming, the resultant stress may cause them to take on some of the behaviors and attitudes of average Sixes. At such times, Nines become visibly more anxious and reactive. Previously, they may have resisted looking closely at problems, but now the full impact registers, and Nines become more nervous and pessimistic. If the source of their problems is interpersonal, they may suddenly become reactive and defiant, like Sixes — in effect, telling people off and discharging their repressed frustrations. While this brings short-term relief from repressed stress, it usually does not resolve the real conflicts and problems that Nines face.

Unhealthy Nines can become extremely stubborn and highly resistant to experiencing their inner pain and anxiety. They martial the powerful defenses of denial and dissociation, but these defenses leave them so out of touch with reality that they can no longer function. When Nines go to unhealthy Six, they become overwhelmed by intense anxiety and paranoia that erupt into consciousness. They react hysterically and become fearful and irrational, lashing out at others while also becoming dependent on others more than ever to take care of them and solve their problems. Deteriorated Nines may masochistically bring about their own downfall so that others will save them from themselves and once again establish a relationship with them.

Direction of Integration. When healthy Nines go to Three, they become interested in developing themselves and their potential. They take control of their lives and value themselves and their contributions. They learn to invest their time and energy in activities that will hone their talents and help them grow as people. As their sense of self develops, Nines become more assertive, independent, and self-assured; their self-esteem also increases. They are more conscious, practical, and live in the real world rather than in their idealizations. Moreover, Nines find that they can enjoy being and expressing themselves fully without losing connection with the people who really love them.

Security Point. Nines can also "act out" the average behaviors of type Three, but most often with trusted friends and intimates. Nines want to be accepted by others and to sustain their relationships, and to this end, they may begin to adapt themselves to others' expectations like average Threes. Nines can become more preoccupied with matters of image and appearance, or behave in ways that will charm others. Having safe and familiar conditions can also bring out more goal-oriented workaholic tendencies in them. With intimates, Nines may also risk behaving more narcissistically, wanting to be the center of attention and enjoying the interest of others.

Childhood Pattern. Connected with both parents or with other parent figures (*PT,* 343–45). Nines have open, receptive psyches, and as young children, they tend to take on much of the emotional tone of their family environment as well as conscious and unconscious expectations from their parents. But while the other two connected types, Six and Three, are able to focus on or react to the expectations of one of their parents (the nurturer for Threes, the protector for Sixes), the Nine is overwhelmed by the connection to both parents. The psyche feels crowded by the covert demands of other family members, so the Nine retreats to the safety of imagination where she or he experiences more freedom, peace, and autonomy than she or he generally finds at home. Some Nines learn to retreat literally, taking refuge in nature or with other children; others withdraw emotionally but remain physically present. In any case, they learn that their home is already full of assertive, demanding energies as well as various problems and conflicts. They attempt to keep a low profile, not to ask for much, not to assert themselves, and to be invisible, in the hopes that their presence will not add any more conflict or confusion to the situation.

Basic Fear. Of loss and separation, of fragmentation.

Basic Desire. To have peace of mind and wholeness.

Secondary Motivations. Nines want to have inner stability, to create and maintain peace and harmony in their world, to mediate conflicts and bring people together, to avoid conflicts, to preserve things as they are, to allow nothing to upset them, to minimize problems and conflicts, to defend the illusion that everything is okay in their world.

In Search of: Harmony and stability. Nines desire oneness, wholeness, and communion for themselves and others. They perceive an ideal order, a way things could be, as do the other two types of the Instinctive Triad, the Eight and the One. Nines attempt to bring a sense of ease, spaciousness, and simplicity to their external affairs by cultivating an inner ease, spaciousness, and simplicity. In effect, Nines want to find a genuine inner peace that will have positive effects on their outer environment.

Healthy Sense of Self. "I am a peaceful, easygoing person."

Hidden Complaint. "I am content with the way things are, although everyone else is always pressuring me to change."

Key Defense Mechanisms. Repression, dissociation, denial.

Characteristic Temptation. To avoid conflicts and self-assertion. For average Nines, directness, making their desires known, or taking a strong position feels like an aggressive act. Nines believe that if they assert themselves, they risk disrupting or even destroying the harmony that exists in their relationships. Thus they begin to think that by being conciliatory and subordinating themselves to others, they can maintain their relationships and their own emotional peace. Nines say yes when they mean no, which avoids conflicts in the short run, but which leaves them angry when others choose a course of action that Nines are not comfortable with. Repressed anger is the first step in creating the resistance, depression, and dissociation that create problems for Nines.

Saving Grace. Despite their growing resistance, unresponsiveness, and fatalism, average Nines may still value their relationships with others so much that they make the effort to break through their resistance and learn to respond to people as they really are rather than deteriorate into serious denial and negligence. Nines' healthy capacity to be receptive to people may allow them to truly put the needs of others first, even at the expense of sacrificing their own peace of mind in the short run.

Suggestions for Personal Growth. See Chapter 10.

Structural Patterns. The keynote is *self-effacement*. There are two aspects to their psyches: first, the inner life of subjective feelings and fantasies, and second, the interpersonal relationships that give rise to their subjective states. Of these aspects, the dominant aspect is their inner world: only truly high-functioning Nines are able to consistently keep their attention on reality rather than on their idealizations of it. As Nines deteriorate, their attention becomes focused not on identifications with people or relationships but on their idealizations of them. For average to unhealthy Nines, the outward pattern becomes one of accommodation and self-effacement to others, but only to maintain their peace and ignore the outside world. Their inner life is dominated by fantasy, while they remain completely defended against reality, impregnable and immovable.

Cognitive Error. To seek peace of mind by diffusing their attention and by disengaging from their instinctual energy. They become "unselfconscious," mistakenly thinking that their presence, engagement, and input do not matter.

Inevitable Consequences. If Nines continue to preserve a false peace of mind through resisting reality, repressing anger, and outwardly accommodating others, they will undermine their Basic Desire (inner stability and peace of mind) while increasingly bringing about their Basic Fear (separation and loss of those they love; *PT,* 375). Their very passivity and complacency, their negligence and obstinacy, and their unwillingness to deal with reality inevitably cause conflicts.

Indeed, Nines' unconscious anger toward anyone who tries to make them respond against their will separates them further from others. The irony is that the type that feels so much at peace with the world is often the cause of frustration and conflicts for everyone else. By not taking responsibility for themselves, they compound problems and then must flee the problems they have caused. Further, the very defenses they employ to protect their inner comfort have the effect of distancing them from others. Others cannot break through to the Nine, and the Nine is gradually isolated, albeit in a numbing world of pleasant daydreams.

Nines must remember that real wholeness and real peace of mind are only possible by embracing the dynamic, changing nature of reality. Nothing stays the same in life, and to try to remain unaffected by the powerful changes around us is to remain in a kind of living death. In a sense, the Nine is like someone standing on the edge of a pool, sticking a toe in the water to see if he or she can take the plunge. Of course, the pool is life, and Nines are actually trying to find the courage to commit themselves to being here fully. When they do, they find the serenity and inner peace they have been seeking.

PERSONALITY TYPE ONE: *THE REFORMER*

The Principled, Purposeful, Self-Controlled, Perfectionistic Person

Healthy. Healthy Ones are conscientious with strong personal convictions: they have an intense sense of right and wrong, as well as a personal code of moral values. They wish to be rational, reasonable, self-disciplined, and moderate in all things. Highly ethical: truth and justice are primary values. Integrity and rectitude make them outstanding moral teachers, personal examples, and witnesses to the truth and other values. Feel they have a mission in life that gives them a sense of purpose. Use their time, energy, and passion to fulfill what they believe is their calling. Articulate communicators, also keep composure under pressure. Extremely principled, always desiring to be impartial, fair, and objective and willing to make sacrifices or delay gratification for the greater good. Embody the Apollonian ideal of cultivating virtue, achieving excellence and balance. *At their best:* Become extraordinarily wise and humane, with superb discernment. By accepting what is, Ones become transcendentally realistic, knowing the best action to take in each moment. Have long-range priorities in view, giving them a transcendental perspective. Profound acceptance of human foibles in themselves and others gives Ones the ability to be inspiring and uplifting to others: the truth will be heard. They give wise counsel, and have nobility of vision and purpose. Life-affirming, hopeful, and kind. Ones balance personal impeccability with a great generosity of spirit.

Average. Average Ones become dissatisfied with reality, and begin to feel a noblesse oblige, that it is up to them, personally, to improve everything: becoming crusaders, advocates, critics, educators, and high-minded idealists. Promote causes. Concerned with working toward an ideal to make things the way they "should" be. Ones feel the need to explain, remedy, debate, point out errors, while striving to maintain standards. Increasingly feel that they have certainty: convinced that their views are correct. The more Ones express their views and standards, the more they become afraid of making a mistake: everything must be consistent with their ideals. Become orderly, methodical, well organized, neat, logical, and detailed, although also more impersonal, no-nonsense, and emotionally constricted: Ones rigidly hold their feelings and impulses in check, resulting in a tense, repressed quality. Bouts of depression begin to enter the picture. Often workaholics — need to feel that they are not "slacking off." Can be puritanical, anal (compulsive), fastidious, meticulous, punctual, and pedantic. Thinking is hierarchical and deductive, separating everything into dichotomies of black or white, good or bad, right or wrong. Highly opinionated about everything — correcting people and badgering them to do the right thing as they see it. Highly critical of self and others: judgmental, nitpicking, and fault-finding. Ones become perfectionistic and impatient, never satisfied unless something is done according to their prescriptions. Feel resentful that others do not share their standards. Others are messing up their good work. Moralizing, scolding, and indignantly angry toward anyone (or anything) they judge is wrong, in error, messy, or out of place.

Unhealthy. Unhealthy Ones can be extremely dogmatic, closed-minded, self-righteous, intolerant, and inflexible. Everyone else is lazy or corrupt. They alone know "the truth" and relentlessly make pronouncements from narrow, forbidding absolutes. Very severe in their judgments; for them to be proved right, others must be proved wrong. Ones use sophistry and rationalizations to maintain their "logical" position. Behind the scenes, however, they are bitter and depressed. Compulsive acting out of "forbidden pleasures" alternates with masochistic periods of guilt and repentance. Become obsessed about the wrongdoing of others, although, ironically, they may do the same thing or worse themselves. Ones' own instinctual drives rebel against their punitive superegos, causing them to do the opposite of what they preach while rationalizing their own contradictory actions or attitudes. Become condemnatory toward others, punitive and cruel to rid themselves of "wrongdoers." May also believe that some part of themselves is responsible for their suffering, resulting in self-punishment or self-mutilation. Severe depressions, nervous breakdowns, and suicide attempts are likely.

Triad Issues. In the Instinctive Center, although Ones' instinctual impulses tend to be repressed or constricted, resulting in a reliance on having strong positions and convictions to compensate. Ability to act spontaneously without guilt or censure from the Inner Critic is undeveloped. Underlying Ones' actions is an attempt to sublimate their instinctive urges in ways more acceptable to society and to their superegos. Issues with *aggression* (anger, resentment, and rage) over the intractability of the self and others, as well as *repression* (of their instincts, sensual gratifications, and other urges) are important elements.

Direction of Disintegration. Average Ones are nothing if not self-controlled and task-driven. Like Threes, they value efficiency and try to get their work done before addressing their own emotional issues. However, stress can build to the point where Ones are no longer able to keep their feelings in abeyance, and at such times they take on some of the attitudes and behaviors of average Fours. Ones at Four start to feel alienated and misunderstood — they are working very hard and no one seems to care about their efforts or their ideals. Self-pity may lead them to indulge themselves like average Fours, often in ways that are in slight contradiction to their expressed values. The typically logical, no-nonsense Ones may also become moody and temperamental, withdrawing from others to sulk or in hopes that someone will see their distress and help them out. Unfortunately, they are unlikely to ask for help directly.

Unhealthy Ones are so driven by their harsh superego that they can seldom escape its withering criticism. Nothing they do seems good enough. They simply cannot seem to measure up. Inevitably, the stress leads them to unhealthy Four behaviors. Ones are filled with self-hatred and hatred of the world for putting them in this situation. They become less functional and feel that they may need extra compensations for their suffering — usually resulting in acting out in ways that bring more harm to them. Eventually, unhealthy Ones may do something so contradictory that their superego pounces on them, with relentless self-criticism and profound feelings of guilt and shame. When Ones deteriorate to unhealthy Four, they regress to a state of severe depression, self-reproach, and self-destructiveness, with suicidal thoughts and feelings. At the least, a nervous breakdown or a severe depression is likely.

Direction of Integration. When healthy Ones go to Seven, they accept reality with its necessary imperfections and become more relaxed and productive. They no longer feel compelled to strive constantly to make everything perfect, nor do they feel that they must save the world single-handedly. Life becomes less stressful and grim; they can allow things to unfold in their own way. They become more joyous, spontaneous, and optimistic. The move to Seven also enables Ones to communicate with others more effectively — their lighter touch helps people to take in the often serious nature of their concerns. They become more curious and more interested in views that are different from their own. Most important, however, integrating Ones increasingly are able to recognize the perfection that is already here. They can stop, breathe, and savor the miracle of their life.

Security Point. Ones can also act out the average behaviors of type Seven, but most often with trusted friends and intimates. In familiar surroundings, Ones like to let their hair down and can display a rowdier, more vivacious side of themselves. In the brief periods of relaxation between missions, they can also get scattered like Sevens, not knowing how best to spend their leisure time or what to order on the menu, trying to cram many experiences into a limited time. Ones can be extremely funny, and actually like to shock people (and to defy their own image) when they feel that it is safe to do so.

Childhood Pattern. Disconnected with the protective figure, who is usually the father or a father figure (*PT,* 382–84). Ones felt that the qualities of guidance, structure, and support in their early childhood were inadequate in some way: either too strict, or too arbitrary, or too vague, or simply lacking. Whatever the specifics, young Ones felt profoundly frustrated with the quality of guidance and discipline they received. Thus they felt that they had to come up with their own set of guidelines and rules, and these are usually stricter than the ones given them by their families. In effect, young Ones were saying, "I'm going to be so good that no one will ever find me at fault. I will never be in trouble because my standards are higher than anyone else's. I will punish myself before anyone else punishes me." Of course, this structure is the One's own superego, and adult Ones continue to depend on it to determine what and what not to do.

Basic Fear. Of being bad, imbalanced, defective, or corrupt.

Basic Desire. To be good, to have integrity.

Secondary Motivations. Ones want to treat others fairly, to act in accordance with their consciences, to strive for their ideals, to improve the world, to prevent mistakes, to be beyond criticism, to justify their position, to be absolutely guiltless, to reproach others for not living up to their ideals.

In Search of: Integrity and improvement. Ones want to make a contribution to the general welfare, to make the world a better place — thereby earning their place in it. Sublimate their own desires and drives. Work hard, having a vision of excellence and what it takes to make "a better world." They are practical idealists. To the degree that Ones have been emotionally wounded by childhood experiences, however, their superegos will be relentless, making it difficult for Ones to take pleasure in whatever good or improvements they actually achieve.

Healthy Sense of Self. "I am a reasonable, objective person."

Hidden Complaint. "I am right most of the time, and it would be a better world if people listened to what I tell them."

Key Defense Mechanisms. Repression, reaction formation, displacement.

Characteristic Temptation. An extreme sense of personal moral obligation. Average Ones begin to think that everything falls on them personally to improve. Average Ones feel that if they do not improve something, no one else will. Or, even if others are willing, they will not do as good and thorough a job as the One will. Ones therefore become increasingly fixated on organizing the environment, correcting and perfecting everything, and on criticizing anyone or anything that does not conform to the ideal as they define it.

Saving Grace. Despite how judgmental and perfectionistic average Ones can be, they may still be objective and sensible enough to prevent themselves from deteriorating into closed-minded intolerance or self-righteous obsessions. Their healthy capacity for reason and moderation can be the means by which they return to a healthier state.

Structural Patterns. The keynote is *objectivity*. Ones attempt to be objective, rational, and fair-minded and to be unmoved and uninfluenced by any personal desire or private passion that would interfere with their obligation to meet their own standards. Hence, there is a division in their psyches between the objective and the subjective, between conscience and desire, between what they would sometimes like to do and what they feel they must do. In the outside world, Ones strive for a higher, more perfect state, attempting to improve everything, including the self (though education, discipline, hard work, high-mindedness). The overall pattern, therefore, is one of constant tension between the objective values they seek to bring to the world and their personal impulses (sexual, aggressive, and personal desires) that tend to erupt if they are not kept under the check of repression and constant self-control.

Cognitive Error. To identify with their Inner Critic (superego) as the judge and determinant of what it means to be good and in balance. This orientation automatically leads to being judgmental and hence to a sense of separation, dualism, reproach, and blame — and, ironically, to a loss of integrity and personal balance.

Inevitable Consequences. Because Ones are rational and logical, of all the personality types, they are most concerned about the consequences of their actions, and it would seem that a rational assessment of their situation would prevent them from falling into fixation. But of course, the ego is never entirely objective, and the very rules and standards by which Ones orient themselves can be the source of their trouble. If Ones continue to believe in their superego's dictates as the sole arbiter of truth and right action, they will gradually become caught in the grip of their Basic Fear (of being bad, defective, or corrupt) while undermining their Basic Desire (to have integrity; *PT*, 408–09). Integrity is a function of wholeness. To have integrity is to be without inner division or conflict. The superego's judgments, on the other hand, always create division and conflict within the self. Some part of us is judging some other part of us with the result that we are divided against our selves. As long as Ones depend on the superego's evaluation of themselves and of reality, they will not find the integrity and wisdom they seek, and will remain blind to the perfection of each moment. When they learn to recognize the action of their own superego and its limitations, the inherent wisdom within them is freed to act in the world.

Placing some of the features we have seen in this chapter on the Enneagram reveals their patterns more clearly.

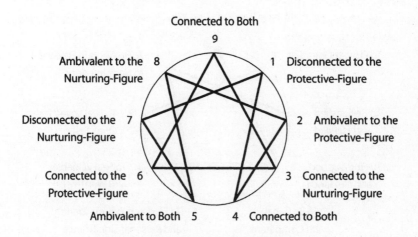

Enneagram of Childhood Pattern

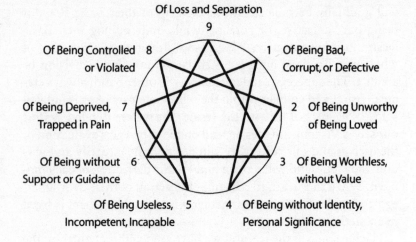

Enneagram of Basic Fears

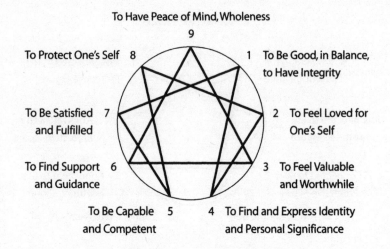

Enneagram of Basic Desires

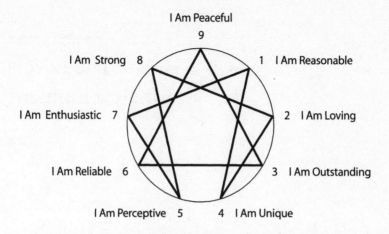

Enneagram of Sense of Self

To become ...

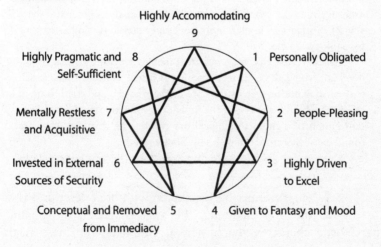

Enneagram of Characteristic Temptations

CHAPTER 4

The Levels
of Development

〜

A total description of any person's character structure would involve an enormous amount of information. Included in it would have to be descriptions of the id, the ego, the superego, anxieties, defenses, conscious and unconscious forces, interpersonal relations, significant features of the life history, interests, attitudes, habits, characteristic patterns of handling the world, symptoms (if any), ideals, goals, and many other features. To avoid such extensive labor, analysts for many years sought shortcuts in briefer, more concise evaluations, similar to trait psychology.

Thus they isolated certain recurrent themes in the life histories of individuals, drew these themes into a consistent constellation (which may or may not be seen as the core of the person), and tried to tie in these themes with the rest of the individual's functioning. Some of the more important characterological descriptions on this basis that are found in the literature can be briefly enumerated.

— Reuben Fine, *A History of Psychoanalysis*

Fine continues his discussion with brief descriptions of the oral character, the anal character, the phallic-narcissistic character, the hysterical character, the masochistic character, the authoritarian personality, the as-if personality, and others — all of which can be accommodated by the Enneagram, as we will see in Chapter 7, "The Centers."

How the Enneagram helps clarify psychiatric categories was briefly covered in Chapter 14 in *Personality Types*. However, a book devoted entirely to theory will be necessary to do complete justice to the complexities of this system and to reveal the many different aspects of the theory. In the meantime, we will limit ourselves to one of the most *practical* aspects of the theory — the Levels of Development.

While the core of the Enneagram — the delineation of the nine personality types — has always rung true, it seemed to us that many further developments and refinements of the system could be made to make it more useful in people's lives. For example, the early descriptions of the types in the Naranjo-Jesuit stream of transmission were short (typically not even a full page) and impressionistic — just enough to convey a sense of each type but not enough for an adequate, satisfying description, much less for any deep understanding. The descriptions needed to be further elaborated upon to account for all the traits of each type.

Moreover, it was enormously difficult to ascertain the precise traits belonging to each type because a "master list" of traits had not been worked out and the inner structure of each type had not yet been discovered. The Enneagram was, and still is, a young and growing field. Those who learned it through the Jesuits were more excited by the basic insights it conveyed and by its psychological and spiritual implications than they were about clarifying what was obscure or even contradictory about it.

This chapter is devoted to revealing more about the Levels of Development, the nine stages within each type, that constitute a Continuum of interrelated traits running from healthy to average to unhealthy states. The Levels of Development are a representation of the inner structure of each type, the conceptual skeleton that is fleshed out with the traits, defenses, interpersonal behaviors, attitudes, and many other complex features. Don Riso recalls how he discovered the Levels.

Like many discoveries, my work on the Levels grew out of a practical need. When I first began to attempt writing descriptions of the personality types, I used a thematic approach, describing each type's behavior in private and at work, its interpersonal relationships, conscious and unconscious attitudes, fears and desires, and so forth. However, I quickly learned that a thematic exposition would involve a great deal of repetition, and my descriptions became long and cumbersome because they lacked an overall structure. There could be no sense of flow and movement from healthy to average to unhealthy states because I had not yet discovered how to organize the material that way. For better or worse, the descriptions seemed to be going around in circles and really going nowhere.

Of course, the thematic approach inadvertently imitates some of the indefiniteness we find in everyday life, although it also suffers from the lack of clarity under which we labor there as well. Ideally, descriptions should not fall into the same traps as human beings but should rise above them. They should clarify human nature, not be as complicated as people themselves can sometimes be. Finding a way to describe the personality types economically depends on cutting through the confusions of everyday life to discover larger patterns. The Levels of Development are the key to doing this.

After two years of struggling with the problem of organizing my thousands of observations into coherent descriptions, a solution finally occurred to me in the form of the Levels. My understanding of them has grown over the years since I discovered them in 1977, but Russ and I are still far from drawing out all their implications.

My working method was to write each trait or observation about the different types onto index cards. Rather than impose an order on them, I decided to see what patterns would emerge if I sorted the cards and allowed what categories there might be to reveal themselves. I started, as I usually do, in the Feeling Triad with personality type Two. After reading through the cards and sorting them into piles of traits that seemed to be related, I finally had eight piles. Sorting the cards for type Three came next, and nine piles emerged; more important, I could also see that they were forming a gradation of some kind. I initially thought that the traits were falling into two groups — healthy and unhealthy (with four healthy piles, one in the middle as a crossover point, and four unhealthy piles).

As I went through the cards of the other types, it gradually became clear that there was also an "average" mid-range of traits. The traits of the types were consistently falling into nine piles, and before long it occurred to me that they could be divided into three groups of three — three piles of healthy, three of average, and three of unhealthy traits. While the preparation for this insight took two years, it took another five years of thought and observation before I was able to work out more details of the Levels of Development, as I began to call them. (And to go further with an important related matter, I was eventually able to work out completely abstract models for each Level that are like blueprints of the psychic activities that happen at each stage. These "Psychic Structures" have not been published yet, but they are the ultimate conceptual bedrock on which the Levels themselves rest; they provide the rationale for the existence and placement of each trait within each type. The Psychic Structures are the abstract "equations" that can be translated into language — language that can then be expanded into full descriptions.)

As helpful as the discovery of the Levels was, it did not automatically clarify either the types or everything about the Levels themselves. We are still learning more about both, a process that will go on for many more years. The information in this chapter is therefore simpler than a complete exposition of the Levels might be. But since the purpose of this chapter is to be practical and to provide an appreciation of the Levels and how they can be used, it is unnecessary to be either encyclopedic or technical. (Those seeking further related information about the theory of the Levels can find it in the Appendix to *PT*, 465–93.) Understanding the Levels within each type (as well as the symmetries between types) is not only intellectually rewarding but also has immense practical implications, as you will see throughout the remainder of this book.

THE PSYCHOLOGY OF THE LEVELS OF DEVELOPMENT

Each Level can be characterized by a specific psychological and interpersonal process that arises at that point along the Continuum. We have described these processes in *Personality Types* (421–26) but will expand on them here.

You will recall that the Continuum for each personality type looks like this:

—
Level 1	
Level 2	Healthy
Level 3	

—
Level 4	
Level 5	Average
Level 6	

—
Level 7	
Level 8	Unhealthy
Level 9	
—

The Continuum

The Levels are numbered in *Personality Types,* and each Level is also accompanied by a two- or three-word title that serves as a descriptive signpost for what happens at that stage along the Continuum. We have also included a master list of the Levels and a more specific description of their inner pattern called the Core Dynamics in the Appendix to *PT.*

The Levels are useful in a number of ways. Theoretically, each Level can be described both as an integral part of the entire type and as a discrete personality subtype, unique to itself. (Indeed, this is more or less what we find in the psychiatric literature, as we will see in Chapter 8.) The vast majority of people, however, are not static examples of one Level; they move up and down within the Continuum, sometimes spiraling downward through the Continuum into neurosis or moving upward toward health and integration. As people shift along the Continuum, different traits and defense mechanisms emerge and combine with existing traits and defenses to form the complex patterns that we see in individuals.

Further, it is almost impossible to make generalizations about the types without taking the Levels into consideration: as each type deteriorates down the Levels, many of its characteristics become their opposite. Everything one can say about the types is Level-sensitive. For instance, healthy Eights are the most big hearted and constructive of the types. They do things to provide the circumstances in which others can flourish and be strong. But the opposite is true of unhealthy Eights: full of rage and feeling that the world is against them, they are extremely destructive and hard-hearted. If one Eight is healthy, and another is unhealthy, they will seem so different that they may be mistyped, or at least misunderstood. Because people range within the Levels of their type, *no single trait will always be true of a type*. Each type is comprised of a continuum of hundreds of interrelated traits and motivations — and as many of them as possible need to be taken into consideration before a self-identification or a diagnosis of someone else can be made. The interlocking fears, desires, and clusters of traits at each Level form an internal spiral of interrelated psychological structures and defenses that, as a whole, make up the type. In other words, each personality type is the sum of the nine Levels. It is therefore unwise to type anyone on the basis of a handful of traits since all of the behaviors associated with each type change at different Levels of Development.

The brief treatment of the eighty-one Levels of Development (nine Levels multiplied by nine types) presented in the following pages allows you to see these patterns more clearly as well as to see how each type fits together as a coherent whole. The descriptive titles represent our effort to compromise between technical language and ordinary language to best describe what is happening at each stage. For descriptive purposes, the charts list the Levels downward from the healthy Levels through the average Levels to the unhealthy Levels, as if the movement were always a progressive deterioration of the person through those stages. However, movement up the Levels is movement toward increasing psychological health and balance (Chapter 10 includes recommendations for personal growth). Movement along the Levels is possible in both directions, and, as we have noted, each of us characteristically oscillates up and down the Levels. For the sake of economy of description, however, we will see the Levels "from the top down" — as if they always moved in one direction — toward increasing unhealth.

Each type has a complex internal structure, as can be seen from the parallel relationships between the Levels. The internal coherence of each type demonstrates that each is a unity — a whole whose parts fit together with precision and elegance. The internal coherence also makes clear why the traits of each type are not arbitrary: each trait must fit within the larger whole that is the type itself.

For example, in type Two, the psychological processes we find at Levels 1, 4, and 7 are parallel. The Disinterested Altruist (at Level 1) deteriorates to the Effusive Friend (at Level 4) and then to the Self-Deceptive Manipulator (at Level 7) — unconditional love deteriorates to people pleasing and then to manipulation. Levels 2, 5, and 8 are also parallel. The Caring Person (at Level 2) deteriorates to the Possessive Intimate (at Level 5), and finally to the Coercive Dominator (at Level 8) — empathy deteriorates to intrusiveness to coercion. Levels 3, 6, and 9 also are parallel. The Nurturing Helper (at Level 3) becomes the Self-Important Saint at Level 6 and at Level 9 the Psychosomatic Victim: generosity deteriorates to uninvited self-sacrifice to feeling victimized and taken advantage of by others. The three sets of symmetries do not exhaust the internal correspondences within each type; other symmetries exist that we will not explore here.

Furthermore, symmetries exist between all of the types. For example, you could compare all the types horizontally at the same Level to see their differences and similarities. While the Levels are a way of helping us understand and organize the types, we must keep in mind that they are a map of the territory — not the territory itself: real people of course are not so highly structured or predictable. Nevertheless, since they can be so accurately represented, the personality types of the Enneagram prove again their remarkable richness in both specificity and sophistication.

The following charts contain lists of the Levels of Development along the Continuum as well as a Summary Overview that make the types' internal coherence more explicit.

Personality Type Two: *The Helper*

HEALTHY:

Level 1: The Disinterested Altruist	Unconditional Love
Level 2: The Caring Person	Empathy
Level 3: The Nurturing Helper	Generosity

AVERAGE:

Level 4: The Effusive Friend	People Pleasing
Level 5: The Possessive Intimate	Intrusiveness
Level 6: The Self-Important Saint	Self-Sacrifice

UNHEALTHY:

Level 7: The Self-Deceptive Manipulator	Manipulation
Level 8: The Coercive Dominator	Coercion
Level 9: The Psychosomatic Victim	Feeling Victimized

Summary Overview. The movement of the Two's Continuum can be seen in the following extremely abbreviated way: Twos progressively deteriorate from healthy disinterested altruism, compassionate concern for others, and generosity, to average effusive friendliness, overenveloping possessiveness, and self-sacrificial self-importance, to unhealthy self-deceptive manipulation, coercive dominance of others, and finally vindicating themselves through psychosomatic suffering (brought on by their suppressed aggressions).

~

Internal symmetries include those between the healthy Two's unconditional love (at Level 1) and the average Two's people pleasing (at Level 4), and the unhealthy Two's manipulation (at Level 7). Other symmetries include empathy (at Level 2), intrusiveness (at Level 5), and coercion (at Level 8). Generosity (at Level 3) parallels self-sacrifice (at Level 6) and the feeling of victimization (at Level 9).

Personality Type Three: *The Achiever*

HEALTHY:

Level 1: The Authentic Person	Inner-Directedness
Level 2: The Self-Assured Person	Adaptability
Level 3: The Outstanding Paragon	Ambition

AVERAGE:

Level 4: The Competitive Status Seeker	Performance
Level 5: The Image-Conscious Pragmatist	Image Consciousness
Level 6: The Self-Promoting Narcissist	Competitiveness

UNHEALTHY:

Level 7: The Dishonest Opportunist	Deceptiveness
Level 8: The Malicious Deceiver	Opportunism
Level 9: The Vindictive Psychopath	Vindictiveness

Summary Overview. The movement of the Three's Continuum can be seen in the following extremely abbreviated way: Threes progressively deteriorate from healthy self-accepting authenticity, adaptable self-assurance, and admirable forms of self-development to expedient concern for their image and self-aggrandizing narcissism to unhealthy unprincipled deceptiveness, unbridled dishonesty and opportunism, and finally malicious psychopathic behavior.

~

Internal symmetries include those between inner-directedness (at Level 1), performance (at Level 4), and deceptiveness (at Level 7). Other symmetries include adaptability (at Level 2), image consciousness (at Level 5), and opportunism (at Level 8). A healthy ambition (at Level 3) deteriorates into competitiveness toward others (at Level 6) and psychopathic vindictiveness (at Level 9).

Personality Type Four: *The Individualist*

HEALTHY:

Level 1: The Inspired Creator	Life-Embracing
Level 2: The Self-Aware Intuitive	Sensitive
Level 3: The Self-Revealing Individual	Creative

AVERAGE:

Level 4: The Imaginative Aesthete	Fantasizing
Level 5: The Self-Absorbed Romantic	Temperamental
Level 6: The Self-Indulgent "Exception"	Self-Indulgent

UNHEALTHY:

Level 7: The Alienated Depressive	Alienated
Level 8: The Emotionally Tormented Person	Hateful
Level 9: The Self-Destructive Person	Self-Destructive

Summary Overview. The movement of the Four's Continuum can be seen in the following extremely abbreviated way: Fours progressively deteriorate from healthy life-embracing self-renewal, self-aware sensitivity, and self-revealing creativity to average fantasizing and aestheticism, temperamental withdrawal, feelings of exemption and self-indulgence to unhealthy resentful alienation, hateful self-torment, and, finally, self-destructive despair.

Internal symmetries include those between healthy life-embracing (at Level 1), fantasizing (at Level 4), and alienation (at Level 7). Other symmetries include those between being sensitive (at Level 2), temperamental (at Level 5), and hateful (at Level 8). Healthy creativity (at Level 3) deteriorates into self-indulgence (at Level 6) and finally into self-destructiveness (at Level 9).

Personality Type Five: *The Investigator*

HEALTHY:

Level 1: The Pioneering Visionary	Understanding
Level 2: The Perceptive Observer	Curiosity
Level 3: The Focused Innovator	Innovation

AVERAGE:

Level 4: The Studious Expert	Conceptualizing
Level 5: The Intense Conceptualizer	Preoccupation
Level 6: The Provocative Cynic	Provocative

UNHEALTHY:

Level 7: The Isolated Nihilist	Nihilism
Level 8: The Terrified Alien	Delirium
Level 9: The Imploded Schizoid	Annihilating

Summary Overview. The movement of the Five's Continuum can be seen in the following extremely abbreviated way: Fives progressively deteriorate from healthy comprehensive understanding, insightful observation, and original innovation to average knowledgeable expertise, detached speculation, and provocative extremism to unhealthy nihilistic rejection of reality, delirious hallucinations, and explosive self-annihilation.

↶

Internal symmetries include those between the healthy Five's profound understanding (at Level 1), conceptualization (at Level 4), and nihilism or loss of meaning (at Level 7). Other symmetries include observant curiosity (at Level 2), preoccupation with ideas (at Level 5), and delirious, distorted perceptions (at Level 8). Healthy innovation (at Level 3) becomes the desire to provoke (at Level 6) and finally may deteriorate into aggressions turned against the self (at Level 9).

Personality Type Six: *The Loyalist*

HEALTHY:

Level 1: The Valiant Hero	Self-Reliance
Level 2: The Engaging Person	Engagement
Level 3: The Committed Worker	Cooperation

AVERAGE:

Level 4: The Dutiful Loyalist	Self-Doubt
Level 5: The Ambivalent Pessimist	Defensiveness
Level 6: The Authoritarian Rebel	Blame

UNHEALTHY:

Level 7: The Overreacting Dependent	Inferiority
Level 8: The Paranoid Hysteric	Paranoia
Level 9: The Self-Defeating Masochist	Masochism

Summary Overview. The movement of the Six's Continuum may be seen in the following extremely abbreviated way: Sixes progressively deteriorate from healthy self-affirming equality with others, engaging reliability, and committed cooperation, to an average self-doubt and investment in structures, passive-aggressive defensiveness, and authoritarian desire to blame others, to unhealthy panicky inferiority, paranoid hysteria, and finally self-defeating masochism.

~

Internal symmetries include those between self-reliance (at Level 1), self-doubt (at Level 4), and inferiority (at Level 7). Other symmetries include their engagement with others (at Level 2), defensiveness (at Level 5), and paranoia (at Level 8). The cooperation found in the healthy Six (at Level 3) parallels their desire to blame (at Level 6) and their masochistic self-defeat (at Level 9).

Personality Type Seven: *The Enthusiast*

HEALTHY:

Level 1: The Ecstatic Appreciator	Gratitude
Level 2: The Free-Spirited Enthusiast	Enthusiasm
Level 3: The Accomplished Generalist	Productiveness

AVERAGE:

Level 4: The Experienced Sophisticate	Acquisitiveness
Level 5: The Hyperactive Extrovert	Impulsiveness
Level 6: The Excessive Hedonist	Excessiveness

UNHEALTHY:

Level 7: The Impulsive Escapist	Dissipation
Level 8: The Manic Compulsive	Compulsiveness
Level 9: The Panic-Stricken Hysteric	Hysteria

Summary Overview. The movement of the Seven's Continuum may be seen in the following extremely abbreviated way: Sevens progressively deteriorate from healthy appreciative gratitude, responsive enthusiasm, and practical productivity, to an average acquisitive seeking of experience, impulsive distractibility, and hedonistic excessiveness, to an unhealthy dissipated escapism, erratic compulsiveness, and finally hysterical collapse.

⤳

Internal symmetries include those between healthy Sevens' gratitude (at Level 1), their average acquisitiveness for more experience (at Level 4), and their unhealthy dissipation (at Level 7). Other symmetries include those between enthusiasm (at Level 2), impulsiveness (at Level 5), and manic compulsiveness (at Level 8). The healthy productivity (at Level 3) deteriorates into excessive hedonism (at Level 6) and panic-stricken hysteria (at Level 9).

Personality Type Eight: *The Challenger*

HEALTHY:

Level 1: The Magnanimous Heart	Compassion
Level 2: The Self-Confident Person	Strength
Level 3: The Constructive Leader	Protective

AVERAGE:

Level 4: The Enterprising Adventurer	Pragmatism
Level 5: The Dominating Power-Broker	Forcefulness
Level 6: The Confrontational Adversary	Belligerent

UNHEALTHY:

Level 7: The Ruthless Outlaw	Ruthlessness
Level 8: The Omnipotent Megalomaniac	Rage
Level 9: The Violent Destroyer	Destructive

Summary Overview. The movement of the Eight's Continuum can be seen in the following abbreviated way: Eights progressively deteriorate from healthy heroic magnanimity, self-reliant strength, and courageous leadership to an average adventurous pragmatism, dominating expansiveness, and confrontational intimidation to an unhealthy ruthless aggression, reckless megalomania, and finally a vengeful destructiveness.

$\backsim$

Internal symmetries include those between their healthy compassion (at Level 1), average pragmatism (at Level 4), and unhealthy ruthlessness (at Level 7). Other symmetries are between real strength (at Level 2), forcefulness (at Level 5), and rage (at Level 8). The constructive and protective traits (at Level 3) foreshadow the belligerent and intimidating traits (at Level 6) and finally may lead to the destructive trait (at Level 9).

Personality Type Nine: *The Peacemaker*

HEALTHY:

Level 1: The Self-Possessed Guide	Autonomy
Level 2: The Receptive Person	Unselfconsciousness
Level 3: The Supportive Peacemaker	Acceptance

AVERAGE:

Level 4: The Accommodating Role-Player	Self-Effacement
Level 5: The Disengaged Person	Passivity
Level 6: The Resigned Fatalist	Fatalism

UNHEALTHY:

Level 7: The Denying Doormat	Neglect
Level 8: The Dissociating Automaton	Dissociation
Level 9: The Self-Abandoning Ghost	Self-Abandonment

Summary Overview. The movement of the Nine's Continuum may be seen in the following abbreviated way: Nines progressively deteriorate from a healthy self-possessed autonomy, receptive unselfconsciousness, and support of others to an average self-effacing accommodation, stubborn passivity, and minimizing resignation to an unhealthy repressed negligence, dissociated disorientation, and finally a self-abandoning fragmentation of consciousness.

〜

Internal symmetries include those between the healthy Nine's self-possessed autonomy (at Level 1), self-effacement (at Level 4), and negligence (at Level 7). Other symmetries are between Nines' unselfconsciousness (at Level 2), stubborn passivity (at Level 5), and dissociation and denial (at Level 8). The acceptance of healthy Nines (at Level 3) foreshadows a potential for resigned fatalism (at Level 6) and a self-abandoning disregard for reality (at Level 9).

Personality Type One: *The Reformer*

HEALTHY:

Level 1: The Wise Realist	Wisdom
Level 2: The Reasonable Person	Conscientiousness
Level 3: The Principled Teacher	Responsibility

AVERAGE:

Level 4: The Idealistic Reformer	Idealism
Level 5: The Orderly Person	Rigidity
Level 6: The Judgmental Perfectionist	Perfectionism

UNHEALTHY:

Level 7: The Intolerant Misanthrope	Intolerance
Level 8: The Obsessive Hypocrite	Obsessiveness
Level 9: The Punitive Avenger	Punitiveness

Summary Overview. The movement of the One's Continuum can be seen in the following abbreviated way: Ones progressively deteriorate from healthy humane wisdom, conscientious rationality, and principled responsibility to an average obligated idealism, self-controlled orderliness, and judgmental perfectionism to an unhealthy self-righteous intolerance, obsessive compulsiveness, and merciless punitiveness (toward self and others).

~

Internal symmetries include the healthy One's wise acceptance of reality (at Level 1), average high-minded idealism (at Level 4), and unhealthy self-righteous intolerance (at Level 7). Other symmetries are between Ones' conscientiousness (at Level 2), rigidity (at Level 5), and consuming (irrational) obsessions (at Level 8). Their responsibility and balance (at Level 3) may deteriorate into a narrow perfectionism (at Level 6) and finally into an inhumane punitiveness (at Level 9).

THE MEANING OF THE LEVELS OF DEVELOPMENT

To provide a fuller explanation of what happens at each Level, the short explanations given in *Personality Types* (465–68) have been expanded here. The descriptions and profiles (given in this book and in *Personality Types*) fit the following patterns.

In the *Healthy* Levels

At Level 1: The Level of Liberation. By confronting and surmounting the Basic Fear (which arose in childhood as a result of the loss of contact with the ground of our being), the person becomes liberated and moves into a state of ego transcendence where he or she begins to actualize the true self. Paradoxically, the person also attains his or her Basic Desire, and therefore begins to fulfill his or her real needs. Moreover, particular spiritual capacities and virtues emerge, different for each type. The ego self has become highly transparent and flexible, providing more balance and freedom. The person is on the brink of shifting from "personality" to "essence," and has opened to many of the positive qualities from the Direction of Integration. Level 1 marks the end of the journey *to* essence, but is also the beginning of the journey *as* essence. In other words, from Level 1, we experience ourselves as essential, spiritual presence. (See Chapter 11, "Personality, Essence, and Spirituality," for more.)

At Level 2: The Level of Psychological Capacity. If the person succumbs to his or her Basic Fear, a Basic Desire arises at this Level to compensate. The person is still very healthy, but the ego and its defenses begin to develop in response to anxieties created by succumbing to the Basic Fear. The person's Sense of Self (see Chapter 3) and "cognitive style" (which can be correlated to Jung's attitudes and functions) manifest themselves at this stage. The Basic Desire is a universal psychological human need, but it can also be considered as "the ego ideal." ("When I become or achieve this, then everything will be great.") The Basic Desire can only be resolved through contact with our true nature. Ironically, the ego's efforts to achieve the Basic Desire actually prevent us from contacting our true nature. When our fear-based ego activity relaxes, we reconnect with our source, and our Basic Desire is fulfilled.

At Level 3: The Level of Social Value. In response to succumbing to secondary (derivative) fears and desires, the person's ego becomes more active, producing a characteristic persona, with its social and interpersonal qualities. The person is still healthy although less so because both the ego and the persona are protected by defense mechanisms (see Chapter 3). At this Level, we see the healthy social characteristics that the type brings to others. While the personality, ego, and defenses are operative, the person is highly functional and is capable of attaining (or regaining) the qualities at Level 1 by overcoming the Basic Fear and by acting properly on the Basic Desire — that is, by relaxing the ego activity.

In the *Average* Levels

At Level 4: The Level of Imbalance. As a result of the person's succumbing to a significant Characteristic Temptation (see Chapter 3) that violates his or her own best interests and development, the ego is reinforced, defenses increased, and imbalances introduced. Imbalances are maintained by drawing on the type's source of psychic energy. Actually, from a day-to-day perspective, an individual at Level 4 would be seen as relatively high functioning and probably likable. But the person's capacity for self-awareness, for presence, becomes markedly diminished. At Level 4, we become more powerfully identified with our egos. This Level also marks a clear shift into the fixations and passions of the type (see Chapter 2). While not yet a problem, this degree of ego fixation ultimately becomes a psychological dead end, which, if not resisted, will create increasing intrapsychic and interpersonal conflicts.

At Level 5: The Level of Interpersonal Control. The ego inflates significantly as the person tries to control the environment (especially other people) in characteristic ways. Specifically, each type tries to manipulate the environment and other people to provide the person with his or her Basic Desire. Defense mechanisms are more active and cause interpersonal and intrapsychic conflicts as well as increasing anxiety if they fail. The traits emerging at this Level are noticeably more problematic than any seen prior to this stage. This Level is a turning point in the deterioration of the type since from here downward, the traits become more egocentric, defensive, and conflicted.

At Level 6: The Level of Overcompensation. The person begins to overcompensate for conflicts and anxieties brought about by the increasing inflation of the ego, as well as by the failure of the behavior seen at Level 5 to provide the person with what he or she has wanted. A characteristic form of self-centeredness emerges (different for each type), as well as overcompensated, extreme forms of behavior, usually found by others to be objectionable (neurosis). All nine types are prone to acting out anxieties and to aggressive tendencies at this Level. Conflicts with others arise as the person acts on self-centeredness to maintain ego inflation and to defend against underlying painful feelings of rage, shame, or fear.

In the *Unhealthy* Levels

At Level 7: The Level of Violation. If a person suffers a major life crisis, or if he or she has grown up in an environment of abuse of one kind or another, the person's defenses can begin to break down, and serious reactions occur. Each type employs a different survival tactic, an unhealthy "self-protective" response, in a desperate attempt to bolster the ego (now assailed by seriously increased anxiety) and defend the self from more intolerable feelings. The problem is that this response is usually compulsive, and violates the integrity of the self or that of others (or both), creating serious interpersonal conflicts. This state is severely imbalanced and unhealthy although not fully pathological yet.

At Level 8: The Level of Delusional Thinking and Compulsive Behavior. As anxiety increases, very serious intrapsychic conflicts occur, and the person attempts to remake or escape from reality rather than succumb to anxiety. Thinking and perceiving, feeling and behavior all become severely distorted and unfree; hence, this is a fully pathological state. (We find the fully developed personality disorders of the DSM at this Level — see Chapter 8.) The person begins to lose touch with reality (becoming delusional in some way); the resulting behavior can be characterized as highly compulsive. Note that the psychological capacity that emerged at Level 2 and became inflated at Level 5 has become delusional by this Level.

At Level 9: The Level of Pathological Destructiveness. This Level includes states of extreme pathology (psychosis) in which openly destructive behavior is often expressed. Having become delusionally out of touch with reality, the person becomes willing to destroy others, the self, or both to spare the self from the massive pain and anxiety produced by whatever crises or violations have been visited on the person. Different forms of immediate or remote, conscious or unconscious destructiveness (including latent self-destructiveness) manifest themselves, resulting in serious psychotic breakdown, violence, or death.

↩

These brief descriptions of the meaning of the Levels do not do them justice. Nevertheless, with even such a brief explanation, it should be possible to understand the overall rationale of the Levels and therefore to understand the patterns presented by each type. Note that the ego emerges at Level 2, becoming increasing inflated and destructive by 9. Note also that a reverse process happens with personal freedom: the person is most free at Level 1 and becomes increasingly unfree ("compulsive") as he or she deteriorates into pathology at Level 9. Pathology is fundamentally unfree, while health is marked by an increasing personal freedom.

Note also that while Levels 2 through 9 comprise the gradations of ego consciousness as they become denser and denser, the Level of Liberation (Level 1) is the doorway to Essential states. At this Level, we rediscover our connection with the Divine. It is no longer an abstract idea or a matter of belief or something that someone has told us about, but a real, felt experience. We no longer need "faith" — we have Being, Knowledge, Gnosis. We come fully in contact with reality because we are not perceiving it through the distorting lens of ego. We feel intimately and compassionately connected with ourselves, others, and the environment, experiencing life with an exhilarating immediacy. We are relaxed, strong, subtle, and clear, seeing everything exactly as it is without alteration or judgment.

As we have seen, Level 1 is the beginning of the vast realm of possibility that lies beyond the ego. Level 1 is not our final destination, however. While Levels 2 through 9 could be thought of as the "octave of personality," Level 1 marks the first note of the higher "octave of Essential Being." It is the beginning of another whole movement and an entirely new set of possibilities in the world of Essence. Level 1 represents the moment when we show up completely, here and now, and fully express our Being — the Divine Spark that we essentially are. When we experience such moments, all of our defenses, boundaries, stories, and strategies fall away, and who and what we really are can shine forth.

The characteristics of the Levels can be depicted as follows:

Ego Inflation	Level of Development	Characterized By	Most Freedom
	1	Liberation	
	2	Psychological Capacity	
	3	Social Value	
	—		
	4	Imbalance	
	5	Interpersonal Control	
	6	Overcompensation	
	—		
	7	Violation	
	8	Delusion and Compulsion	
	9	Pathological Destructiveness	Least Freedom

THE CHARACTERISTICS OF THE LEVELS

A review of *Personality Types* shows that each Level has certain core characteristics. While here they are simplified and presented schematically, it is possible to see how these traits form the major theme for each Level; it is also possible to use the following key traits as the basis for comparing each trait "horizontally" from type to type at the same Level of Development.

The following core characteristics will be displayed in two ways — as a list of traits and then arranged around an Enneagram.

Level 1	Characterized by Liberation (Self-Transcendence)
Type One:	Acceptance: Wisdom
Type Two:	Self-Nurturance: Unconditional love
Type Three:	Self-Acceptance: Authenticity
Type Four:	Self-Renewal: Inspiration
Type Five:	Clarity: Gnosis
Type Six:	Inner Guidance: Courage
Type Seven:	Assimilation: Gratitude
Type Eight:	Self-Surrender: Magnanimity
Type Nine:	Self-Remembering: Indomitable

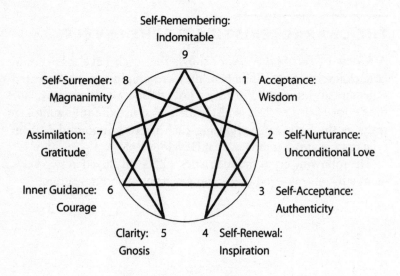

Enneagram of Liberation

Level 2	Characterized by Psychological Capacity and Sense of Self
Type One:	Conscientiousness: "I am reasonable."
Type Two:	Empathy: "I am caring."
Type Three:	Adaptability: "I am outstanding."
Type Four:	Self-Awareness: "I am sensitive."
Type Five:	Observation: "I am perceptive."
Type Six:	Engagement: "I am reliable."
Type Seven:	Responsiveness: "I am enthusiastic."
Type Eight:	Self-Assertiveness: "I am strong."
Type Nine:	Receptivity: "I am peaceful."

Enneagram of Psychological Capacity

Level 3	Characterized by Social Value (Contribution to Others)
Type One:	Principles: Responsibility
Type Two:	Generosity: Service
Type Three:	Ambition: Self-Development
Type Four:	Self-Revelation: Creativity
Type Five:	Focus: Innovation
Type Six:	Commitment: Cooperation
Type Seven:	Realism: Productivity
Type Eight:	Self-Confidence: Leadership
Type Nine:	Stability: Support

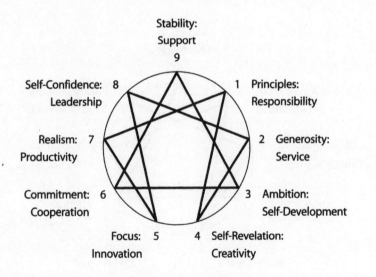

Enneagram of Social Value

Level 4	Characterized by Imbalance
Type One:	Constantly feeling personal obligation
Type Two:	People-pleasing, winning over others
Type Three:	Driving oneself to excel, comparisons
Type Four:	Constantly living in the imagination/heightened feelings
Type Five:	Retreating into the mind
Type Six:	Investing oneself in external sources of security
Type Seven:	Restless, seeking sources of stimulation
Type Eight:	Constantly asserting oneself, pushing oneself
Type Nine:	Avoiding conflicts through accommodation

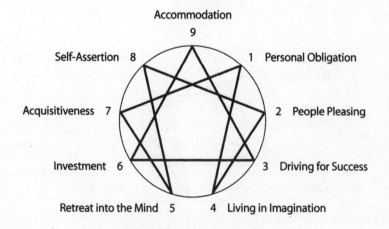

Enneagram of Imbalance

Level 5	Characterized by Interpersonal Control (Cause and Result)
Type One:	Self-Control: Rigid orderliness
Type Two:	Possessiveness: Intrusiveness
Type Three:	Image-Consciousness: Expediency
Type Four:	Self-Absorption: Temperamental
Type Five:	Preoccupation: Detachment
Type Six:	Ambivalence: Defensiveness
Type Seven:	Distraction: Hyperactivity
Type Eight:	Self-Glorification: Domination
Type Nine:	Disengagement: Complacency

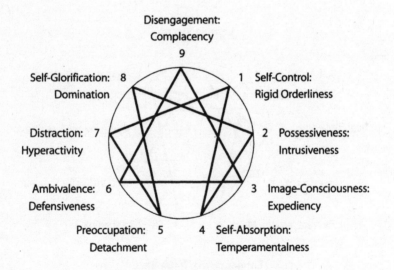

Enneagram of Interpersonal Control

Level 6	Characterized by Overcompensation (and Defensive Behavior)
Type One:	Judgmentalism: Criticizing others
Type Two:	Self-Importance: Patronization
Type Three:	Grandiosity: Self-Promotion
Type Four:	Exemption: Contempt
Type Five:	Extremism: Provocation
Type Six:	Authoritarianism: Assigning blame
Type Seven:	Self-Centeredness: Excessiveness
Type Eight:	Confrontational: Intimidation
Type Nine:	Resignation: Appeasement

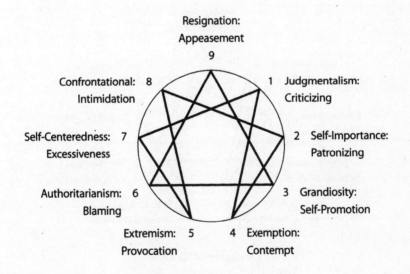

Enneagram of Overcompensation

Level 7	Characterized by Violation (of Self and Others)
Type One:	Self-Accusation: Intolerance of others
Type Two:	Self-Deception: Manipulation of others
Type Three:	Self-Rejection: Deception of others
Type Four:	Self-Sabotage: Hatred of others
Type Five:	Self-Negation: Rejection from others
Type Six:	Self-Betrayal: Defiance of others
Type Seven:	Self-Dissipation: Callousness with others
Type Eight:	Self-Hardening: Ruthlessness with others
Type Nine:	Self-Repression: Neglect of others

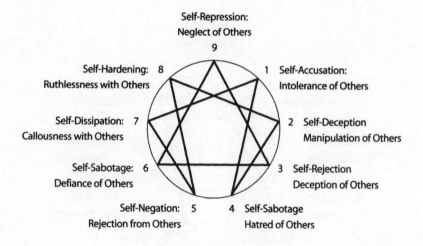

Enneagram of Violation

Level 8	**Characterized by Delusions and Compulsions (Thinking and Behavior)**
Type One:	Obsession: Compulsive behavior
Type Two:	Entitlement: Coerciveness
Type Three:	Duplicity: Exploitation
Type Four:	Self-Hatred: Clinical depression
Type Five:	Schizoid withdrawal: Retreating behavior
Type Six:	Paranoia: Volatile behavior
Type Seven:	Manic mood swings: Reckless behavior
Type Eight:	Megalomania: Terrorizing behavior
Type Nine:	Dissociation: Disorientation

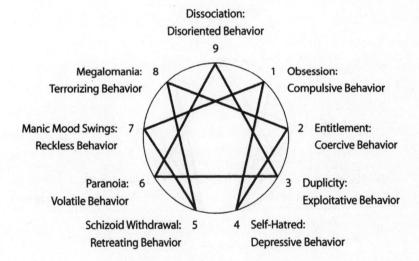

Enneagram of Delusions and Compulsions

Level 9	Characterized by Pathological Destructiveness (Pathology and Result)
Type One:	Condemnation: Retributive behavior
Type Two:	Conversion reactions: Psychosomatic problems
Type Three:	Psychopathy: Monomaniacal behavior
Type Four:	Clinical depression: Suicidal behavior
Type Five:	Psychotic states: Annihilating behavior
Type Six:	Self-Abasement: Self-destructive behavior
Type Seven:	Hysteria: Panicked behavior
Type Eight:	Sociopathy: Antisocial behavior
Type Nine:	Self-Abandonment: Depersonalized behavior

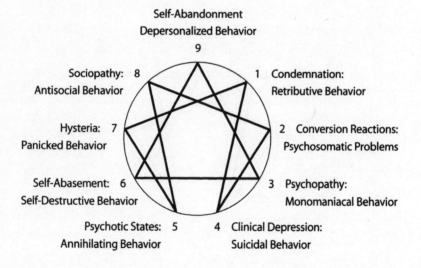

Enneagram of Pathological Destructiveness

Assessment

CHAPTER 5

Identifying Your Type:
A Questionnaire

$\backsim$

Since the initial publication of *Understanding the Enneagram*, we have produced several questionnaires to help people find their basic type. Among the best known of these is the RHETI (Riso-Hudson Type Indicator), available in the book *Discovering Your Personality Type*. The test presented here, however, is an update of our first test instrument. By taking the test, many people have been assisted in finding their type. We have revised some of the statements for the types, but we have kept the basic structure of the test intact to preserve its ease of use. We hope that this instrument, as well as the others that we have created, will be helpful to those who are still uncertain about their type and to those who want a questionnaire to help confirm their diagnosis. A questionnaire can never be foolproof, but it can certainly provide a valuable piece of evidence for determining one's type, or at least to narrow the choices.

Even after devising these questionnaires, however, we would like to remind readers of the limitations of questionnaires in general. To be accurate, questionnaires should be more sophisticated than those usually found in self-help books, especially if they are to be administered by readers themselves. The questionnaire might have to include several hundred items so that a broad range of traits can be tested; sophisticated statistical techniques should be employed to analyze the responses. Taking the test and grading it are time-consuming and can introduce errors; and even in the case of a sophisticated questionnaire administered by trained psychologists, the results can be ambiguous or downright misleading.

Rather than provide a questionnaire in *Personality Types,* we offered an incremental method (33–43). The nine types were introduced first, one word at a time, then by four words, then by a paragraph describing the major traits and dynamics of each within its Triad. Next were the Profiles that began each descriptive chapter with keywords and motivations, then the Overview, and then, finally, the full descriptions themselves. With this method, the descriptions started simply and got increasingly complex — literally going from one word to approximately ten thousand words for each type.

The drawback with this method was that readers were required to choose which description fit them best and to judge whether the descriptions continued to do so as they were expanded. Thus, some degree of prior self-knowledge was necessary for readers to be able to recognize themselves. If someone had absolutely no self-awareness, then he or she would be at a loss about where to begin — and even the most accurate diagnosis (by this or any other method) would remain relatively meaningless to her or him.

Since self-knowledge is precisely what is missing in many people, some were unable to use this incremental method effectively. The desire to obtain self-knowledge is the reason many people are interested in the Enneagram in the first place; while it might be unrealistic to expect a high degree of self-knowledge from beginners, some degree of it is a prerequisite if there is to be any progress at all. Thus, paradoxically, we need some self-knowledge before we can acquire more of it. Those who have no idea of who they are (or who are completely uninterested in understanding themselves) will have extreme difficulty trying to make progress on their own.

One way out of the problem of ignorance of ourselves is to enlist the aid of friends who can tell us which type they think we are. The old observation that others can see us better than we can see ourselves is often true. Even those who feel confident of knowing their type can be helped by discussing it with someone who knows them well and who will discuss the description of their type with them frankly.

Those who have some self-understanding but who still remain confused about which type they are should reflect on those two or three types that are the most likely candidates. (You can also consult Chapter 6, "Misidentifications," for comparisons and contrasts between types that you think you might be.)

The Type Profiles in this book (and the Profiles in *Personality Types*) are also a kind of "second questionnaire": the two sets of Profiles can be read as if they were questionnaires. To use this approach, go to the Profiles and read them carefully, pausing over each word or phrase and turning it into a question.

Each Profile is, in effect, a long questionnaire with the questions and qualifying statements omitted. Each Profile is a checklist that can be turned into either a question or a descriptive statement that should be potentially true of you all the time. A typical question might be, for instance, "When I am healthy or average or unhealthy, am I _____?" Someone reading the Profile of the Two (*PT*, 59–60) could ask, "When I am healthy am I unselfish? Am I also disinterested? Am I also altruistic? Do I also give unconditional love to others? Am I also empathetic? Am I also compassionate? Am I also caring? Am I also warm? Am I also concerned?" The *combination of all of these healthy traits* will apply uniquely to healthy Twos because, of course, any type can occasionally be caring or warm or loving. The essential difference is that healthy Twos are not only caring, warm, and charitable, they are *also* unselfish, disinterested, compassionate, concerned, unconditionally loving, and so forth — virtually at the same time. In varying degrees, healthy Twos possess *all* the healthy traits listed in the Profile and act consistently on them. These traits are typical of healthy Twos because they are what make up this particular personality type.

No matter which method you use — the questionnaires, talking with friends, the Profiles, or the descriptions — it is important to allow time for the full descriptions to have an impact on you. Much of the material is complex and subtle, and, even more important, it is difficult to overcome our natural resistance to seeing ourselves clearly. There are elements in each of us that are painful to look at; it takes courage and time to acknowledge and deal with them.

You might also keep a few other general observations in mind as you use this or any questionnaire. People often choose the type they would like to be rather than the one they actually are. This is by no means universally true, and perhaps most people identify their personality type correctly right away. (Without controlled research, it is difficult to say.) In any event, understanding our type — and seeing ourselves more objectively — often causes emotional turmoil (at least in the beginning) and presents us with a new set of challenges. Gaining self-knowledge is not always comforting, particularly if we have been protecting ourselves from painful past experiences or feelings of shame — although the more honest we are, the more liberating self-knowledge becomes. After all, if we purposely choose a type that flatters us rather than the one we suspect we really are, whom are we shortchanging? By choosing the wrong type, not only are we not transforming ourselves, we may be deceiving others. And instead of availing ourselves of the insights it has to offer, we will be rendering the Enneagram worthless.

Even so, a related legitimate problem remains: how to know with certainty whether we have correctly chosen our true type. Is the type we have chosen *really* our type? Several "rules of thumb" can be applied.

If the type you have chosen not only stirs up deep feelings but also helps you understand aspects of yourself you have never seen before, then it probably is your type. If your choice leads you to make new connections and see new patterns in yourself and your relationships, then you have probably accurately typed yourself. If the type in which you have seen yourself not only upsets you but, more important, encourages and excites you, then you have probably made the correct choice. And if your friends and family concur in your choice, then you are almost certainly on the right path.

However, there is no way to know with total assurance whether the type we have chosen really is our type. We will never find a book in which our personality type has been inscribed or see a tattoo of our Enneagram number on our body. We can be assured of gathering objective evidence only if we see ourselves as we really are. With time and experience, confidence in our self-assessment will increase, although it will always depend on making a judgment based on the best available evidence. Perhaps most individuals can determine their type immediately; others take longer. You may be in either group.

The greatest mistake many people make is that they select a personality type by *taking a few traits out of context* rather than by trying to understand each type as a whole. For example, some Nines think they are Fives because they like to think (ruminate) and they convince themselves that they therefore must be Fives — "the thinking type." Likewise, some Sixes are creative and have artistic talents and therefore think that they must be Fours, and so forth.

Individual isolated traits such as thinking and artistic talent should not be taken as the basis of a diagnosis. As general a trait as "thinking," for instance, must be distinguished from type to type because, of course, every type thinks — and the thinking of Fives and Nines can be clearly contrasted. Taking a trait out of context and making a diagnosis based on that alone often leads to mistyping. (We will see many more examples of this kind of misdiagnosis in Chapter 6, "Misidentifications.") The important thing is to discern the whole pattern and the underlying motivations for each type, not to take the individual traits out of context. In time, and with attention, the true patterns will emerge.

The caricatures in *Personality Types* and the new ones in this book should also give you additional impressions of each type. The caricatures embody many traits and, for those who are visually oriented, convey valuable information.

INSTRUCTIONS FOR THE QUESTIONNAIRE

The questionnaire is *organized according to type* instead of as a list of random statements. All statements for each type are true.

↩

There are twenty statements for each personality type. They reflect a range of attitudes and behaviors between the *healthy* and *average* traits of the type. In our experience, people tend not to admit to unhealthy traits and to see themselves in all of the healthiest traits. Therefore, most of these questions are from the upper-average, normal range and as such *do not indicate anything about a person's mental or emotional health* — only their basic personality type.

To determine your type with this questionnaire, you should "agree" or "strongly agree" with fifteen or more of the twenty questions listed. In other words, *most* of the statements should describe you either as you were in the past or as you are in the present or as you could be in the future. Some of the statements may touch only on your potential behavior, although even in these you should be able to see your own *tendencies* clearly.

The most important thing to remember as you take this and all questionnaires is to answer spontaneously, without thinking of extreme circumstances under which the statement might possibly be true of you. The statement should obviously be true or untrue, applicable or not, reflect a true tendency or not. Don't strain to answer the question.

A scoring sheet has been provided on which you can mark the number of "agree" answers for each set of statements, especially if you would like to take the questionnaire for all nine types. Doing so should give you a full profile and indicate which wing you have, depending on the type on either side of your basic type that you scored higher on.

You might have relatively high scores on more than one set of statements because several other questions express attitudes held by that part of you that can be attributed not only to your wing but to the types lying in your Directions of Integration or Disinte-gration. For instance, a person taking the test might produce the following pattern of answers: agreement with about eighteen of the statements in the person's basic type, with about twelve to fourteen in their wing, and with two to six of the questions in the remaining seven types, with more agreement (five to ten) for those two types in the Directions of Integration and Disintegration from the basic type. In any event, one type should stand out most clearly, and that type is the person's basic type.

However, if someone agrees with virtually all the questions in all the types or, at the other extreme, with none of the questions in any of the types, the problem might be caused either by a faulty understanding of the questions and the need to discriminate be-tween them or by the person's inability or unwillingness to under-stand and discriminate between them.

Another explanation is also possible: many average Nines tend to have a high score for all the types, often seeing themselves ev-erywhere because their sense of self is characteristically undefined. (For more about distinguishing between Nines and other types, see Chapter 6, "Misidentifications.") Other types may well pro-duce other "typical" overall patterns if resistance is operative. Time and research will tell.

THE QUESTIONNAIRE

Personality Type Two

1. At my best, I love others unconditionally and do not concern myself with how people repay what I do for them.
2. People would say that I really care about the welfare of others.
3. Some people may think of me as a saint, but I know my imper-fections and don't think of myself that way.

4. I can be generous without calling attention to myself or whatever I have done for other people.

5. I am happy when good things happen to people, and I go out of my way to help others in whatever ways I can.

6. I am a caring person, and my personal feelings for others make me deeply concerned for them.

7. Love is the greatest value in life; without love, what would life be?

8. Part of being a good friend is letting others know how much you love them.

9. It's good to be close to people, and I don't feel at all embarrassed to express how I feel, especially by hugging and kissing my friends.

10. I think a lot about my friends and friendships, and I could count five or ten people who are my very close friends.

11. I enjoy having my family and friends around me, and I like it when they come to me for guidance and advice.

12. I am not really possessive of people, although I suppose I do find it difficult to let go of those who are important to me.

13. I suppose it's true that I need to be needed — but doesn't everyone?

14. Maybe I am too good for my own good and should think of myself more instead of caring so much about everyone else.

15. To be perfectly candid, I'm an extremely generous and thoughtful person, and others are lucky to have me in their lives.

16. It's really important to me that the main people in my life are aware of how much I care about them and how much I want to do for them.

17. I don't think I really manipulate others, but even if I occasionally have to, it's to get them to do what is best for them.

18. One of these days my family and friends will have to take care of me the way I have taken care of them.

19. I've often worried that people take me for granted and don't care about my needs very much.

20. It seems that I have had more than my share of illness in my

life — I guess I don't take care of myself as well as I take care of others.

Personality Type Three

1. I accept myself as I am and am honest about my limitations and talents.
2. It is easy to affirm myself as a person because I feel worthwhile and valuable.
3. I come across to others as self-assured and poised, as someone who has a lot of self-esteem.
4. I like myself; I feel valuable and desirable, and I enjoy being who I am.
5. I believe in developing myself and think that other people should also spend time and effort improving themselves in whatever ways they can.
6. I have worked hard to distinguish myself, and other people see me as an outstanding person.
7. Other people usually don't say it, but I can tell they are often jealous of me for one reason or another.
8. I want to be the best at what I do. If you can't be outstanding, why bother?
9. I'm efficient, I know how to get things done, and I don't let someone else's agenda get in my way, especially in my career.
10. Accomplishing things in life often requires making a good impression on others. I am diplomatic and have a knack for charming people.
11. It is important to know how to project the right kind of image if you want to be successful.
12. People create their own reality, and if they hold themselves back or fail, then that's their choice and they will have to deal with it.
13. When something isn't working, the thing to do is to change your tactics and do what it takes to accomplish your goal.
14. What others think about me is important to me. I don't have much patience with inappropriate behavior.

15. Being effective and achieving my goals have been my top priority for much of my life.
16. I like to think that I have my act together. I work to make the most of my talents and to have a successful life; in many ways, I have it all.
17. I have bent the rules now and then to get ahead, but everybody does, so what difference does it make?
18. I have usually been able to attract people, but I have tended to get nervous if they got too close.
19. A lot of people look up to me and think I'm pretty wonderful — but I worry tht they wouldn't like the "real" me.
20. I may *look* confident, but I'm terrified of failure — I can't imagine anything worse.

Personality Type Four

1. One of my strengths is that I am a sensitive human being, and I make the most of my experiences, even if it hurts.
2. At my best, I am able to create something that seems to come out of nowhere — to be an inspiration of some kind.
3. For better or worse, I have tended to follow my intuitions.
4. I am deeply convinced that I must be true to myself and, as much as humanly possible, I always try to act authentically.
5. The power of my creativity comes from expressing my deepest feelings in some form, whether personally or artistically.
6. I am aware of what I feel, and I try to be honest with myself about what my feelings are telling me.
7. For better or worse, I have a vivid imagination and am able to create a world of fantasies that is very real to me.
8. I spend a lot of time in long conversations with people and reveries about them in my imagination.
9. I have a poetic sensibility; however, it often leaves me feeling melancholy and emotionally vulnerable.
10. I question myself about everything — my motives and behavior, what I have said to someone, whether or not I will be up to a certain task — to the point where I can sometimes do little else.

11. I have tended to become infatuated with new romantic interests, only to later feel disappointed and disenchanted with them. I'm sure this confuses people — it confuses me!
12. When someone says something I find upsetting, I can't do anything except turn it over in my mind until I have resolved it.
13. I often feel uncomfortable around people, even my friends, and I am not always sure why; maybe I'm just a loner.
14. When I am feeling vulnerable, I tend to withdraw into my shell to protect myself for being hurt any more.
15. It's very painful to me, but I can become so angry at people that I can't bring myself even to be in the same room with them, much less to talk with them about what's bothering me.
16. Everyone else seems to be happier than I am; I seem to be emotionally damaged and unable to function very well.
17. I don't seem to be able to "pull myself together." I don't know where to begin, or, if I do make some progress, it seems it can all be lost in a second.
18. Thank God nobody talks to me the way I reproach myself; a voice inside me says the most cruel, contemptuous things to me.
19. I have thought about suicide: it's a way out I might be forced to take someday.
20. Life is full of pain and loss and sadness — at least my life has been.

Personality Type Five

1. I have the capacity to have deep insights into the world around me, and I almost always perceive things that others miss or ignore.
2. Foresight is one of my great capacities: I seem to be able to predict the way things will turn out before they take place.
3. I have always had the ability to concentrate very deeply on my work or whatever I turn my attention to.
4. I have had more than my share of original thoughts and innovative ideas.
5. People come to me to get answers to complex or difficult ques-

tions because they realize that I know what I am talking about.

6. The life of the mind is the most exciting kind of life.

7. I treasure the pursuit of knowledge: leave me alone with a book and I am perfectly happy.

8. I am not always aware of time passing when I become involved with fine-tuning my work.

9. I am a rather intense person: I can totally lose myself in my interests because I get so completely immersed in them.

10. I have been made fun of by people who think that I am a bit strange; they have called me an "egghead" or "nerd" — and I suppose it's been true enough.

11. My ideas are so complex that it is sometimes difficult for me to express them and difficult for others to understand what I am trying to say.

12. My relationships are frequently rocky because I can overwhelm others with my curiosity, intensity, passion, and desire to understand them in depth.

13. Genius is usually misunderstood, and my ideas are sometimes so far ahead of their time that I don't even try to discuss them with anyone.

14. Once or twice, I have discovered an extraordinary new insight, a long-sought key that explains a great many other things.

15. I seem to be able to live with far fewer physical comforts than most people.

16. The fact is that most people are too stupid to understand what is really going on; in fact, most people are really just too stupid to notice anything.

17. Most religions pander to the infantile, superstitious needs that other people cannot live without.

18. It is safer and easier to live alone; I do not want others to become close to me or to know what I am doing or thinking.

19. Sometimes my thoughts seem to have a life of their own — they come so fast that I find it difficult to slow down my mind, to relax, or to go to sleep.

20. My most secret thoughts may be strange and frightening, but they express the world as I see it.

Personality Type Six

1. At my best, I realize that I have tremendous courage, faith, and endurance: people know they can count on me.
2. I am more vigilant and aware of potential problems than most people.
3. I have an ability to find common ground with others, and I like the feeling of being liked.
4. It is important to me to feel secure in my job and relationships.
5. I am very committed to those who are committed to me — my family and friends know that I meet my responsibilities.
6. I am a reliable, hard worker and have invested a lot of myself to build a secure life for myself and my family.
7. Although I've had many successes in my life, I still doubt myself.
8. I can get really nervous when I have to make an important decision, but I can't stand having other people make decisions for me.
9. I spend a lot of time trying to understand who and what I can trust.
10. I am not always sure about what other people think about me — sometimes I feel they like me, sometimes I feel they don't.
11. My sense of humor throws people off because I often say the opposite of what I really mean, so they don't know whether I'm serious or not.
12. I can be extremely prudent and cautious about a problem, but then do something impulsive just to get it over with.
13. Although I usually do what's expected of me, there are times when I rebel.
14. I don't always follow the rules or procedures, but I really want to know what they are so I know when I'm breaking them.
15. I become furious when I see others breaking the law and getting away with it.

16. I can drive myself nuts with all my worrying and indecision, but I'm usually certain about how I *feel* about things.
17. I can be really tough and stubborn when I have to be, although I don't always feel all that tough inside.
18. I can really get down on myself for not being as aggressive and independent as I would like to be, especially if I have let down someone who was counting on me.
19. I tend to be suspicious of some people and feel that they don't like me and are out to get me — or they would if they could.
20. I tend to get tense and overreact when I am really upset or when I am under pressure and things are not going well for me.

Personality Type Seven

1. Life is really wonderful, and when I stop and think about it, I have so much to be grateful for.
2. When I am at my happiest, I am exhilarated, spontaneous, and full of life — in fact, I am one of the happiest people I know.
3. I get a kick out of things and am enthusiastic about everything because everything seems to give me pleasure.
4. I have a lot of different talents and am one of the most accomplished people I know — really good at a lot of different things.
5. I am also very practical and productive: I have my feet on the ground and know how to get things done.
6. I enjoy going to restaurants, entertaining, traveling, and enjoying myself with my friends.
7. I keep myself amused by having lots of different things to do; after all, you only live once, but, as they say, if you do it right, once is enough.
8. I love the good things in life; if I want something, I don't see why I should deny myself.
9. I hate being bored and I enjoy staying on the go as much as possible: my calendar is filled with things to do, and that's the way I like it.

10. It's fun to talk, gossip, joke around, and "let it all hang out," even if I sometimes am outrageous or overdo things.
11. I am one of the most uninhibited and outspoken people I know: I say what others wish they had the nerve to say.
12. I don't care if people think I'm too much — I like to stay on the go and jump into life fully.
13. I tend to go to extremes — with me it's feast or famine, although, of course, I feast as much as possible.
14. I agree with the statements that "nothing succeeds like excess" and "you can never get enough of a good thing."
15. Inconveniences and other frustrations can make me so mad that sometimes I just feel like screaming until I get what I want — and I usually do!
16. I have a tendency to become "addicted" to different things; once I get used to something, I want to have more of it.
17. It's better to be an escapist than to be depressed and gloomy; I'd rather be on the go and not look back.
18. Some people may say I'm pushy about getting what I want, but who cares what they think — I go after what I want in life.
19. There have been periods in my life when I was either out of control or nearly out of control.
20. Sometimes I feel panicky and anxious, but I throw myself into something new and the anxious feeling goes away.

Personality Type Eight

1. I am self-assertive and I have a lot of self-confidence.
2. I can see opportunities; I see how I want things to be and I can rally others around me to achieve it.
3. I have a lot of guts — I'm courageous and have frequently taken on difficult challenges and succeeded in them.
4. People look to me for leadership because I am strong and decisive and can make tough decisions.
5. I like the thrill of danger and adventure; I have often placed myself in tight spots and succeeded despite the odds.
6. I command respect: others look up to me.

7. I am a passionate, direct person: people always know where they stand with me.

8. When I see something I feel is unfair, I can't help but get involved to straighten it out.

9. I make it my business to be as independent as possible: I don't want anyone to have any power over me.

10. I am a tough negotiator: I know how to push and how to say no, and I don't back down.

11. I know how to get what I want. I'm pretty persuasive with people.

12. When you get right down to it, it's a matter of survival — them or me — and I am going to be the one who comes out on top.

13. There is no question that I'm tougher than most, but only those who know me well seem to know how much I care.

14. I don't mind knocking heads when I have to; when you get right down to it, the only thing people really respect is strength.

15. People are always telling me to restrain myself. They don't realize that I *am* restraining myself.

16. You definitely don't want to get me angry: I can make people wish they hadn't tangled with me.

17. At times in the past, my philosophy has been "might makes right" — and I can be pretty ruthless when I have to be.

18. Sometimes I feel like no one will ever accept me, so why even try to be nice?

19. People being wimpy or indecisive drives me nuts. If you can't take the heat, stay out of the kitchen.

20. If someone hurts me or someone I love, they're going to have to pay for it.

Personality Type Nine

1. At my best, I can assert myself; yet I am still close to people, particularly my spouse and children.

2. I enjoy creating a warm, supportive atmosphere in which oth-

ers can flourish and everyone can be happy and loving with each other.

3. People say that I am not judgmental or aggressive, that I'm comfortable and easy to be around.

4. People are basically good, and I trust them and don't question whether they have so-called ulterior motives.

5. I don't think I am a very complicated person: I am optimistic and contented with myself and with my life as it is.

6. There is a contemplative and mystical side to me; I love to commune with nature, and I often feel at one with the universe.

7. I want to be close to my family and friends, so I try to go along with whatever they want me to do for them — it seems to make them happy.

8. Many things in life are just not worth getting worked up about — but in some matters, I really dig in my heels.

9. A lot of other people are too critical — they worry too much, but I don't see any point in worrying about most things.

10. I want everything to be pleasant, and I don't like it when people argue or bring up problems or cause upsets.

11. Most problems aren't really such a big deal, and they usually work out for the best eventually anyway.

12. Some people may think that I am forgetful, but there are things I would rather not pay attention to, so I just don't think about them.

13. People really can't change: you just have to accept them as they are.

14. I take life as it comes because things are going to happen and they are going to happen no matter what you do.

15. I don't want to think about myself very much: nothing is going to come of it anyway, so why get upset?

16. I have found that if you ignore problems long enough, they will go away.

17. The past is done, and it's best to get problems behind you as soon as possible.

18. People are sometimes angry at me and I don't understand why

— I'm a good person, and I haven't done anything to hurt anyone.

19. Now and then anger or other upsetting feelings of mine seem to come out of the blue, although once I've had my say, that's the end of it.

20. If something terrible happens to me, it is as if everything is suddenly unreal, like a dream, and it really isn't happening to me.

Personality Type One

1. I have very good judgment and am extremely prudent: in fact, good judgment is one of my deepest strengths.

2. I have a strong conscience and a clear sense of right and wrong.

3. I tolerate others, their beliefs and actions, even though I don't necessarily agree with them or think that they are right.

4. My conscience leads me to do what I think is best, whether or not it is convenient for me or in my immediate self-interest.

5. I always try to be as fair as possible, especially by not allowing my personal feelings to sway my objectivity.

6. Integrity is very important to me, and I couldn't go to sleep at night if I felt that I had seriously wronged someone.

7. I feel that I should improve whatever I can whenever I see that something is wrong so that the world will be a better place.

8. Unfortunate but true: always striving to attain my ideals can be exhausting.

9. I can sometimes seem to others to be a little unemotional or too "cut-and-dried," but they don't know the real me.

10. Being organized is necessary if anything is going to get done and if things are going to be under control.

11. I often feel that if I don't do something, no one else will — and sure enough, I'm usually right.

12. Very few people do things as well or as thoroughly as I do: most people are too lazy and they let themselves off the hook too easily.

13. I don't think I'm that much of a workaholic, but there is so

much that needs my attention that it's difficult to find time to relax.

14. I have opinions about most things, and I think I am right about them — if I didn't, I wouldn't hold the opinions that I have.

15. The fact is, other people would be better off if they would do what I tell them to do more often.

16. Right is right, and wrong is wrong, and I don't see any reason to make exceptions.

17. I don't have to tolerate nonsense, and when people are wrong, I think I have an obligation to set them straight.

18. I am so effective in my life that few people would guess how sad and lonely I sometimes feel.

19. True, I can get obsessive and rather picky about certain things, but they simply must be done the way they should be — the right way.

20. It seems like no matter how hard I try, I never quite live up to my standards, and that can sometimes get me down.

Questionnaire scoring sheet

Personality Type

Question	Feeling Triad			Thinking Triad			Instinctive Triad		
	TWO	THREE	FOUR	FIVE	SIX	SEVEN	EIGHT	NINE	ONE
20									
19									
18									
17									
16									
15									
14									
13									
12									
11									
10									
9									
8									
7									
6									
5									
4									
3									
2									
1									

CHAPTER 6

Misidentifications

∽

Whenever we teach people about the Enneagram, we inevitably encounter those who have misidentified their type — Twos who are convinced they are Fours, Nines who think they are Fives, Threes who are persuaded they are Ones, and so on. This chapter has grown out of the need to clarify similarities and differences between the types.

It is necessary to be more precise about the similarities and differences so that people may understand them more clearly. After all, a deepening self-understanding is the primary aim of the Enneagram. If a person misidentifies himself or herself, the Enneagram will do him or her little good. It will be no more than a fascinating curiosity or, worse, a way of obtaining insight into others while avoiding insight into oneself.

It is admittedly easy to misidentify people, and there are good reasons why aspects of virtually all the types can be confused. First, the Enneagram is complex — and human nature is even more complex. People are extraordinarily varied and ever-changing. Unless we see individuals in different situations over a period of time, it may be difficult to feel confidence in the accuracy of our diagnosis.

Second, it is inherently difficult to identify others because we must infer their type based on less than complete information about them. In fact, the ability to determine personality types accurately is something of an art in itself, yet it is a skill that anyone can become proficient in, given time and practice. Moreover, the fact that some people misidentify themselves or others is to be expected, at least at the present time, considering the state of the art of the Enneagram. There are different interpretations in circulation, some containing significant contradictions, as well as misattributions of traits from type to type. This is why it is essential to think critically and independently.

Third, since the Enneagram can accommodate more than 486 variations of the types (*PT*, 425), it is inevitable that some of them will be similar. For example, Sixes (at Level 6, the Authoritarian Rebel) can resemble Eights (at Level 6, the Confrontational Adversary) in that both are belligerent and authoritarian, although in noticeably different ways — if you are aware of them.

Fourth, types are easily confused when they are thought of as narrow entities — as if Nines, for example, were always peaceful and serene. If this is our idea of Nines, then when we encounter someone who is occasionally irritable or aggressive, we may automatically conclude that the person cannot be a Nine. While peacefulness and serenity are two of the principal traits of *healthy* Nines, there are also times when Nines can be angry, aggressive, and anxious. However, they virtually always think of themselves as peaceful and return to various forms of peacefulness (for instance, passivity and complacency) as their home base. And as important, when Nines are aggressive, angry, or anxious, they manifest these traits in distinctive ways: they express their anger as a coolness toward the person they are angry with and deny that they are angry. Severe outbursts of aggression can erupt suddenly and subside quickly. To understand subtle distinctions, we must discern the overall style and motivations for each type rather than look at individual traits in isolation.

Fifth, other variations can color our impression of a person's type. The wing, for instance, can significantly affect the person's behavior. Similarly, the Instinctual Variant can powerfully affect the way the person expresses his or her type (*PT*, 426–30). If the person has been under stress for a period of time, he or she may strongly behave, and even feel like, the type in his Direction of Disintegration. Also, people who are high-functioning can be more difficult to identify because they are less identified with the patterns of their type and can freely express a wider range of coping styles. Clearly, the Enneagram types are not static or simple: many factors can influence a person at any given moment, and it takes time and dedication to really understand all the subtleties and variations of the nine basic types.

Sixth, we may confuse some types because our exposure to the full range of the personality types is limited. It may be that because of our individual experience, we simply do not know many Fives, or Eights, or Twos, etc. Until you have correctly identified (and thought about) a wide variety of examples from all the types, it is likely that some of them will remain vague.

Furthermore, even if you do know examples from every type, it is important to keep in mind that *no one manifests all the traits of his or her type*. It is probably exceedingly rare for an individual to have traversed the entire Continuum, and even more unusual (if, indeed, it is possible) to manifest the full range of the traits at one time. Each of us moves along the Levels of Development around a certain center of gravity, varying by no more than a few Levels. Or, to put this differently, there is a certain "bandwidth" of Levels within which our own center can be found. (For example, someone might be fundamentally healthy, and the range of his or her behavior might be characterized as being within Levels 2 and Level 5, inclusive. Thus, the person would not manifest Level 1 traits, or, at the opposite end of the Continuum, traits from Levels 6 downward into the extremes of unhealth.) We simply don't act out the entire range of the potential traits of our type: if we were to do so, we would be simultaneously healthy and unhealthy, balanced and neurotic, integrating and disintegrating — an impossibility.

Because no person manifests the full range of traits at any one time, it is worthwhile to discuss the types (and their many variations) with others. It's interesting to discuss the traits that others observe in the person you're trying to identify and see if your perceptions agree. When they don't agree, it's even more helpful to debate as you search for the best available evidence to determine the person's type. Remember, however, that the most we can do is discern a person's type based on the traits he or she manifests in his or her long-term behavior. Observation over a period of time (and under a variety of circumstances) is the best way to arrive at a sound conclusion.

Seventh, it is helpful to personally know the individuals you want to identify, although this is not absolutely necessary. We can identify people at a distance, without direct contact, because they manifest their personalities so clearly or because a great deal of information is available about them, or both.

For example, former president Ronald Reagan seems to be a personality type Nine. He is genial, unassuming, optimistic, and easygoing; he has also sometimes been detached, passive, inattentive, and forgetful. These and many other traits evidenced in Mr. Reagan's behavior belong to the healthy and average Nine, and so it is reasonable to assume, since Mr. Reagan has manifested them so clearly and consistently during his lifetime, that he is a Nine. And, of course, while it remains possible that he is not a Nine (and that another type might better explain his personality), given the evidence, the probability is high that Mr. Reagan is a Nine. We can therefore have confidence in our diagnosis of him.

The diagnoses of other famous people given in *Personality Types* have been made on the same foundation, as educated guesses based on reading, intuition, and observation over a period of years (*PT,* 52–53). While no claims for infallibility have been made, we felt that all of the diagnoses were helpful to give an impression of the range of each type because people of the same type (particularly those with the same wing) are noticeably similar to each other. We *can* at least say that the *public personas* of these individuals serve as excellent examples of the type in question.

Eighth, one of the most important ways to distinguish similar traits of different types is to try to discern the different *motivations* behind their behavior. Different types can act in virtually identical ways although their motives are quite different.

For instance, every type gets angry, but the anger of Ones is differently expressed from that of every other type and also has different causes. It is essential to be aware of underlying motives rather than deal solely with the more superficial behavior.

Ninth, the longer you are familiar with the Enneagram and the more you practice using it, the more perceptive you can become. In the last analysis, however, learning how to identify people depends on knowing how to match the traits of individuals with those of the personality types. Thus, two areas must be learned: first, which traits go with which types, and second, how to recognize those traits in individuals. Even though there are hundreds of traits for each type (and scores of subtle distinctions to be made), the first area is easier to learn than the second. It is admittedly very difficult to perceive the true behavior, attitudes, and motivations of others, especially since they often do not recognize those things in themselves, much less want them recognized by anyone else.

↬

After taking into consideration the difficulties that stem from misinformation or misunderstanding — as well as from the inherent difficulty of the undertaking itself — there lies the fact that legitimate similarities exist among the personality types. It is precisely these similarities that contribute to mistypings and confusion.

The following comparisons and contrasts are based on similarities between types and between Levels from one type to another. Thus, some familiarity with the Levels of Development is necessary (*PT*, 45–47, 421–26, 465–93 and Chapter 4 in this book). Unless stated otherwise, the comparisons and contrasts made in this chapter are between *average* people of each type.

↬

The order of the discussions begins with type One and ascends numerically.

MISIDENTIFYING ONES AND OTHER TYPES

Ones and Twos

This is not a common mistype, but it does occur when a wing is mistaken for the dominant type. In other words, 1w2's can sometimes be confused with 2w1's, but the confusion is far less likely with 1w9's (owing to their reserved and relatively unemotional demeanor) and 2w3's (owing to their outgoing, effusive demeanor). Gender can influence this mistyping as well. Women who are 1w2's tend to see themselves as 2w1's, and men who are 2w1's may see themselves as 1w2's.

Both types are serious and conscience-driven, both like to feel that they are of service, and both can be very altruistic; however, their styles and motivations differ significantly. Ones try to transcend the personal in their dealings, appealing to principles and the evident "rightness" of their positions or suggestions. Twos are highly personal and see their service in personal terms. Ones defend their autonomy — they do not want people to interfere with them. Twos seek close connection and even merging. Ones are restrained in the expression of their positive feelings, although they let people know when they are dissatisfied or irritated. Twos may have difficulty with hostile or angry feelings, but they are fairly unrestrained in expressing their positive feelings. Compare Sandra Day O'Connor (a One) with Sally Jesse Raphael (a Two).

Ones and Threes

Average Ones and average Threes are sometimes mistaken because both types are efficient and highly organized. If an isolated behavior is the only thing being considered (chairing a business meeting or planning a vacation, for instance), their organizational abilities are similar — hence the confusion between them. Both are highly task-oriented and tend to put their feelings on the back burner to get things done. Both share a desire to improve themselves and to meet high standards, although the basis of their standards and their key motivations are quite different in nature.

Average Ones are idealists, striving for perfection and order in every area of their lives. They are trying to control both themselves and their environment so that disorder and errors of all sorts will not be introduced. Inner-motivated by strong consciences, they are organized and efficient so as not to waste time or allow themselves to be in a position for their consciences to rebuke them for being imperfect, for not trying hard enough, or for being guilty of some form of selfishness.

Average Threes, by contrast, are efficient pragmatists, not idealists. Threes are driven more by their goals than by standards — they care more about getting the job done than about the particulars of *how* it gets done. Ones tend to be attached to particular methods or procedures ("This is the best way to do this."). Threes are more adaptable, and will change tactics quickly if they feel they are not getting the desired result. Average Threes are primarily interested in success and prestige, and they are efficient in attaining their goals.

While both types tend to put their feelings aside for the sake of efficiency, average Threes are more able to mask whatever is bothering them. On the surface, they rarely appear emotionally disturbed by anything for long (although they may become momentarily discouraged or even depressed by setbacks), nor are they often distracted by their feelings. They invest most of their energy in remaining focused on and achieving their goals. Ones are far less able to conceal their irritations and disappointments. Others are almost immediately aware of their agitation.

Both types can be cool and impersonal, although they are usually polite and well mannered. With average Ones, we get the impression of deeper feelings being held in check or sublimated elsewhere, for example, organizing and maintaining their office space or volunteering at a local ecological organization. Even though Ones do not ordinarily express their passions, their emotions are potentially available if they lift their typical self-control. (Their most prevalent negative emotions are righteous anger, indignation, irritation, and guilt.) In average Threes, however, the impression of aloofness and of emotional coolness is due more to a detachment from their feelings rather than a suppression of them. At the same time, average Threes tend to present whatever emotion seems appropriate at the time. If seriousness is called for, they tend to project seriousness. If levity is required, they will cooperate, smiling and being chatty, even if they are feeling frightened, overwhelmed, or sad. For better or worse, Threes are more skilled at projecting charm and personality than Ones. However, we can discern the underlying detachment from deeper feelings when Threes are "performing" by the abruptness and ease with which they can adjust their affect from situation to situation and from person to person. (In contrast to Ones, their most prevalent negative emotions are hostility, arrogance, and underlying feelings of shame and humiliation.)

Ones are trying to be perfect to fend off their own superegos, while Threes are trying to excel to overcome feelings of family shame. In effect, Ones say, "Listen to me — I know the right way to do things," whereas Threes say, "Be like me — I have it together." Ones offer themselves as examples of those who are striving for perfection, particularly moral perfection: they see themselves as those who can meet the highest standards. Threes offer themselves as exemplars of individual perfection, particularly personal desirability, and as those who can accomplish and be the best.

These two types are similar because both are thinking types — the One corresponds to Jung's extroverted thinking type (*PT*, 381), who attempts to be objective and impersonal, while the Three's thinking is goal-oriented and pragmatic, similar in orientation to the extroverted thinking of the average One (although technically there is no direct Jungian correlation). Both types have in mind some sort of goal that they want to achieve. The difference is that Ones attempt to discover which objective means will best lead to the desired ideal, whereas Threes are pragmatists who work backward to find the most efficient means to achieve their goal. The differences between these types can be seen by compar-

ing Al Gore (a One) with Bill Clinton (a Three) or betv
Thompson (a One) and Jane Pauley (a Three).

Ones and Fours

Since Ones and Fours are so different, it might seem strange that
they can be confused. The confusion seems to arise when a One
(who may be going to Four under stress) begins to think that he
or she is a Four. Invariably, Ones who misidentify themselves as
Fours focus almost exclusively on the traits of the unhealthy Four
and not on the type as a whole. Because Ones feel melancholy, depressed, and alienated from others, they may convince themselves
that they are Fours. If Ones experience difficulties, they may shunt
to Four more continuously to avoid falling into more unhealthy
Levels of type One — a far more serious problem. At such times,
Ones are typically guilt-ridden, feel worthless, and are subject to
excruciating self-contempt and self-hatred. (They may even feel
suicidal.) Their confusion would be alleviated if they were to look
at themselves historically and see both themselves and the Four as
a whole.

In the average Levels, Ones usually attend to their responsibilities first and deal with their feelings later. Their lack of focus on
their feelings is actually one of the main causes of their not infre-
quent depressions. (It is also worth mentioning that Ones are one
of the types more vulnerable to depression.) Fours, on the other
hand, want to sort out their feelings first, dealing with their duties
only after they have worked through their emotions. As a result,
they may have difficulty mobilizing themselves to meet responsibilities. Most Ones would not give themselves permission to indulge their feelings in this way for long.

Despite these differences, there are similarities. Both tend to be
perfectionistic and dissatisfied with things as they are. Both are often frustrated with themselves and their environment, and can be
perceived by others as fussy, or picky. Both can be very particular
about their environment and the rules that they want others to observe in their personal space. ("No one comes in here without
removing their shoes.") Both types can be angry: average Ones

are frequently critical and irritable, but usually over others' inefficiency or failure to follow agreed-upon procedures. Average Fours are often critical and picky over others' lack of awareness of their sensitivities. They may feel irritable about others' apparent coarseness. Similarly, Fours can also become resentful when they feel that others do not appreciate their depth and creativity. If upset in this way, Fours attempt to punish offenders by coldly withdrawing emotionally or even physically. They refuse to engage in further communication. Average Ones do not withdraw from people. On the contrary, they press themselves and their opinions on others with increasing urgency as they become more angry at what they see as the irresponsibility of others.

It is also possible for an occasional healthy Four to be mistaken for a One; such a misidentification would, however, be a compliment to the Four since it indicates that he or she has integrated to One and is living with purpose beyond the self. Fortunately for them, some Fours actually do integrate and begin to manifest the reason, moderation, and attraction to objective values of healthy Ones. Further, some Fours may well be teachers and in a teaching situation be called on to move beyond their feelings and interior states. But a Four who has genuinely integrated some of the healthy qualities of type One is still a Four — and besides having either a Three-wing or a Five-wing, other important characteristics will continue to be present in the Four's overall personality. Contrast a Four such as Anne Rice and a One such as Martha Stewart or a Four such as Tennessee Williams and a One such as Arthur Miller for more insight into these types.

Ones and Fives

Ones and Fives both correspond to Jungian thinking types — the One to the extroverted thinking type (*PT,* 381–82) and the Five to the introverted thinking type, or to what might be better termed the "subjective" thinking type (*PT,* 177–78). They are in two different Triads: Ones are an instinctive type and Fives are a thinking type. While Ones certainly think, they are primarily people of action, and are only interested in ideas that lead to some practical result. Fives, however, are truly a mental type: they can ponder any proposition or idea and do not particularly care about its practical ramifications.

Contrary to popular notions, opinions and beliefs have their basis in the instincts, in the gut. When we assert a position ("This is absolutely the way it is!"), the certainty of our view comes from our gut. If we are present enough to notice, we can feel this when we express a strong opinion. And indeed, Ones are people of strong convictions and opinions as befitting a type in the Instinctive (or Gut) Triad. Average to unhealthy Ones are entirely convinced of the rightness of their views, and respect people who hold similar strength in their convictions. They think as a way of buttressing their already established beliefs. Average to unhealthy Fives tend to get lost in a maze of *uncertainty.* They may develop elaborate theories or positions only to overturn them soon after. While less healthy Fives may assert provocative views, they are more interested in disturbing the certainty of others than in convincing others that they have the correct view. Unhealthy Fives may want to feel *smarter* than the other person, and even argue points that they do not personally agree with just to prove to themselves that they can mentally "run circles" around others. As they become less healthy, Ones become more rigid and fixed in their views about things: Fives become more uncertain, nihilistic, and afraid that they cannot arrive at any kind of meaning or truth.

Similarly, they differ most markedly in the One's emphasis on certainty and judgment and the Five's relative lack of certainty and difficulty with discernment. (While healthy Ones have excellent judgment, average Ones are merely judgmental — still, making judgments about the world around them is one of the principal ways in which their extroverted thinking manifests itself.) Judgment is not as centrally important to Fives. They want to understand how the world works on a theoretical level or create inner worlds of imagination that are interesting and amusing to them. Thus, Fives tend to be detached from the practical world and intensely involved with complex mental constructs. And while healthy Fives observe and interact with the real world around them, average Fives, as they become more deeply enthralled by their own cerebral landscapes, lose their capacity to make accurate assessments about the truth, significance, or accuracy of their ideas. They gradually care less about an idea's objective rightness than about how their ideas relate to other thoughts that arise in their minds. By contrast, Ones employ thinking so that they can relate more perfectly to their ideals: their focus is on making rules and procedures for the progress and improvement of themselves and their world. Average Ones are not as detached from the world, or as withdrawn as average Fives are: although they may be cool and impersonal, and somewhat overly reserved, Ones are keenly interested in applying their principles to daily life.

Thus, Ones and Fives are opposites in the way they judge and evaluate reality. Ones judge situations from idealistic standards based on what they think should be the case. Fives are constantly investigating and questioning assumptions, not to mention standards and principles. Ones are deductive, operating from principles to specific applications; Fives are inductive, operating from given data to form more sweeping theories. Both are philosophical, and love knowledge: Ones as a means of perfecting the world, Fives as a way of discovering more about the world. Ones tend to be teachers and moralists, not inventors and iconoclasts like Fives. The difference between these types can be seen by comparing George Bernard Shaw (a One) and James Joyce (a Five), Margaret Thatcher (a One) and Susan Sontag (a Five).

Ones and Sixes

Both are among the compliant types of the Enneagram. As noted in *Personality Types* (434–36), Ones are compliant to the demands of their superegos and their ideals, while Sixes are compliant to the demands of their superegos and other people, especially perceived allies or authority figures. We say that Ones have an "Inner Critic" in their heads, while Sixes have an "Inner Committee." What these two types have in common is the tendency to feel guilty when they do something contrary either to their ideals (Ones) or to the commitments to allies, beliefs, and authorities they have made (Sixes). Guilt feelings owing to strong consciences and the need to organize their environments are the main points of similarity between them. While Sixes may rarely mistake themselves for Ones or Ones misidentify themselves as Sixes, other people may be confused by some superficial similarities between them. (And, in fact, a Six with a Five-wing will more likely be confused with a One than a Six with a Seven-wing because of the seriousness and intensity that the Five-wing brings to the Six's overall personality.)

These two types are easy to distinguish, however, by noting the overall emotional tone of each type. Average Sixes are anxious, indecisive, ambivalent, and, above all, reactive. They find it difficult to relate to others with self-confidence as equals, tending either to become too dutiful and dependent or to go to the opposite extreme and become rebellious and defiant. Sometimes they get stuck in the middle and become ambivalent, indecisive, and vacillating.

These traits are almost completely absent in average Ones. Their overall emotional tone is one of self-controlled, impersonal efficiency, orderliness, and propriety. Ones are emphatically *not* indecisive: they know their own minds and have opinions about everything, which they are more than willing to express to others. Ones are certain, and try to convince others that they know the optimal way to do things. Sixes are uncertain, and rely on reassurance, back-up, familiar procedure, or the sanction of previously tested ideas and philosophies to help them come to decisions.

Average Ones are often so tightly self-controlled that they are able to keep their feelings at bay. They are frequently unaware of the degree of their tensions. Average Sixes struggle with more volatile feelings and have difficulty putting them aside — although they seldom express their feelings to others. Sixes carry considerable anxious tension and are more aware of it. Righteous anger, irritation, and moral indignation are the principal negative emotions in Ones, whereas fearfulness, suspicion, and anxiety are the principal negative feelings in Sixes. Moreover, while lower functioning Ones can be sarcastic and verbally abusive, they almost never let themselves get out of control and are seldom physically violent, whereas low functioning Sixes can more easily lose their tempers, sometimes erupting into hysterical reactions or even physical violence.

When it does arise, confusion about distinguishing Ones and Sixes seems to stem from both types' overactive superegos. Both are "should" and "must" people: both feel obligated to take care of all duties before relaxing or attending to their own needs. Further down the Levels, both types exhibit a legalistic streak: Sixes at Level 6 are The Authoritarian Rebel and Ones at the same Level are The Judgmental Perfectionist. When their superegos are even more severe, both types are quite capable of telling others what to do, although in different ways and for different reasons. Ones moralize and scold, lecturing others in the name of an ideal about whatever issues are of concern to them. ("Do you have any idea how wasteful it is to use an air conditioner?") Ones do not hesitate to order others around, telling them what they should be doing to improve themselves or to be more effective.

Sixes can also give orders, not because of rigid inner standards, but because they are afraid of what they see as the erratic, irresponsible conduct of others potentially disrupting the security and stability they are trying to maintain. They are angered and threatened by others' "breaking the rules" and becoming more unpredictable. Sixes identify with certain beliefs or authority figures and internalize the values that they have learned from these sources of guidance. Once they have identified with what they have taken to be trustworthy sources of information about the world, Sixes can be aggressive toward anyone who does not accept the same values as they do. This is especially true when Sixes are more insecure — the more anxious they are, the more they want to cling to whatever positions or allegiances they still believe in. The indifference of others to their beliefs may infuriate Sixes as much as outright rejection of them does. Compare the personalities of George Bush (a Six) and Al Gore (a One), Meryl Streep (a One) and Meg Ryan (a Six) for examples of the similarities and differences of these two types.

Ones and Sevens

Ones are unlikely to mistype themselves as Sevens, but Sevens occasionally mistype themselves as Ones. Sevens who have been under stress for prolonged periods of time may notice many average One behaviors, such as perfectionism and a need for order, and conclude that they must be Ones. While these traits may surface in certain extreme circumstances, a quick review of the Seven's life will usually reveal that rigid self-control, harsh inner criticism, and repression of impulses are not their dominant issues.

Another source of confusion is the shared idealism and sense of "mission" of the two types. Both types hold high ideals about the world and about human beings, but express these in markedly different ways. Sevens are usually very optimistic about the future and about things working out positively. Ones are far less so — they hold high standards and *expect* to be disappointed by people and by the world. Ones are fairly certain that they know their "mission" while for Sevens, it is more of a feeling. In Sevens, uncertainty about the nature of their mission creates a great deal of underlying anxiety. ("What if I miss my chance?")

Sevens may also think they are Ones because they see themselves as "perfectionists," but their style of perfectionism is very different. Ones' perfectionism drives them to berate themselves for days because they misplaced a comma in an otherwise excellent one-hundred-page report. Sevens' "perfectionism" may lead them to become frustrated because the seafood salad the Sevens ordered in a restaurant was not exactly the way they wanted it. Sevens mistake their frustration or impatience with the quality of their experience for perfectionism.

The two types are quite different in a number of other ways. Sevens are spontaneous and adventurous — they like to be free to change plans and to follow their inspiration. Ones get frustrated when plans are changed, and usually do not like to deviate from the careful preparations they have made. Sevens are usually unselfconscious socially, Ones are usually very self-conscious socially. Ones are methodical and sticklers for time management and for following efficient procedures. Sevens have a more fluid sense of time, and balk at being "bogged down" by procedures. Sevens are curious and open-minded, but tend to get distracted and scattered. Ones are more focused and directed, but can be opinionated and closed-minded. Sevens are driven by anxiety, Ones by simmering anger, and so forth. Compare George F. Will and Julie Andrews (Ones) with Larry King and Cameron Diaz (Sevens).

Ones and Eights

Both Ones and Eights are in the Instinctive Triad, both have powerful wills, both are action-oriented, and both have strong notions about how to do things. However, Ones try to persuade others to do the right thing (as they see it) from the standpoint of a moral imperative — because it is the right thing to do. They try to logically persuade others of the soundness of their views, but become irritated and less logical when others resist their reasoning. Eights, on the other hand, rely on their own self-confidence, and attempt to sway others by their gutsy convictions and sheer personal charisma. ("I don't know if it's the right way, but it's *my* way.") Ones try to *convert* those who resist them: Eights try to *power through* them.

The greatest misunderstanding between these two types involves their concern with justice, although the nature of their sense of justice can be quite different. Ones hold justice as an extremely important value — many judges, attorneys, advocates, and criminal prosecutors actually are Ones. Ones think a great deal about issues of providing suitable standards for human beings and about the specifics of how to administer a fair and equitable system. Ones at all Levels of Development refer to justice and think that they seek justice (no matter how skewed their interpretation of it may become). In any case, justice is a matter of *principles* — part of their idealism. They strive after justice and want to rectify injustices wherever they find them because, among other reasons, to do otherwise would be to fail to live up to their high moral standards and would make them feel guilty.

In Eights, justice is more of a visceral response, a reaction to witnessing injustices occurring. Eights, generally speaking, do not walk around thinking about these matters, but if they saw a helpless person being harmed or bullied by others, without thinking about it, Eights would rush in to "level the playing field." For Eights, justice has little to do with abstract principles. Eights see themselves as protectors of others, and when they are healthy, they actually are. Eights are more likely to seek justice for "their people" — their family, friends, coworkers, ethnic group, and so forth. It is usually expressed in a concern that those in their care (or under their power and authority) be treated fairly. The cowboy marshal protecting the town against criminals and the union chief negotiating a just wage for the rank and file are examples of this more restricted concern for justice. With Eights, the sense of justice usually involves addressing an imbalance of power. This is quite different from the One who seeks to make sure that people are appropriately rewarded for good actions and punished for bad ones.

Of course, in their unhealthy manifestations, both types can be extremely *unjust*. Even if they are being cruel, unhealthy Ones still believe they are being fair — the punishments they are meting out are for the good of the person being punished, or at the very least, for the good of society. Ones feel they need to rationalize their punitive activities. Eights do not. For unhealthy Eights, administering justice is simply meting out vengeance. ("You hurt me or my people, and I'll *destroy* you." "He ripped me off. Now he has to pay.") Needless to say, others may question the "justice" in either of these types' unhealthy behavior.

The confusion between Eights and Ones probably also stems from the fact that some Ones may misidentify themselves as Eights since they would like to have the authority and influence of Eights. They may also recognize that they have aggressive impulses and misidentify themselves as an "aggressive type," although they are really compliant to their ideals; the Eight is the true aggressive type *par excellence*. On the other hand, Eights almost never misidentify themselves as Ones, viewing Ones as lily-livered and bloodless —

moral only because they are too weak to be strong. Although Eights themselves are unlikely to think they are Ones, other people sometimes misidentify Eights as Ones because they see them as reformers. But clearly, many natural leaders, including Eights, lead reforms when they are needed. Contrasting Ones such as Pope John Paul II, Ralph Nader, and Hillary Rodham Clinton with Eights such as Lee Iacocca, Franklin Delano Roosevelt, and Barbara Walters gives a vivid sense of their differences.

Ones and Nines

Usually this mistype is caused by confusion about the wing and dominant type: is the person a Nine with a One-wing or a One with a Nine-wing? In some cases, with a strong wing, this can be a difficult call. Both can be idealistic, philosophical, and somewhat withdrawn. Neither feels comfortable with his or her anger. Usually, the Nine's reluctance to get into conflicts is the easiest way to discern these adjacent types. Average Nines want to maintain peace in their lives, and while they may hold strong personal convictions, they generally do not want to argue about them with people — especially people with whom they have an emotional attachment. For Ones, however, the principle is foremost, and Ones will drive home their point to convert others to their view, even if it risks creating upsets and arguments. ("The truth is the truth.")

While Nines can be hard workers, it does not take much to convince them that a break would be useful. They enjoy downtime, and tend to have difficulty shifting gears from relaxation to activity or vice versa. Ones are extremely driven and have difficulty tearing themselves away from their various projects to take a rest or relax. They feel anxious when they are not being productive (like Threes), and want to get back to work to avoid attacks from their superego.

Another distinction can be found in how the two types handle stress. Nines initially become more emotionally disengaged and resistant, but eventually they become more anxious and reactive as they go to Six. Ones initially become more fervent in their efforts to convince the other that they are right, but then collapse into moodiness and a tight-lipped testiness as they go to Four. Compare Ones Ted Koppel and Meryl Streep with Nines Walter Cronkite and Andie MacDowell.

MISIDENTIFYING TWOS AND OTHER TYPES

Twos and Ones

See Ones and Twos.

Twos and Threes

Here again, confusion about wing versus dominant type is likely to be the problem. A Two with a One-wing is unlikely to be mistyped as a Three, and a Three with a Four-wing is unlikely to be mistaken for a Two. With the 2w3 and the 3w2, however, personal charm and the desire to be liked and to please others can make these types more difficult to distinguish. Confusion sometimes arises, for instance, because the word "seductive" has often been applied to type Two. But clearly, all types can be seductive in their own way, and Threes can be very seductive indeed. Therefore, it is important to distinguish how these two types "seduce" attention from others. Basically, Twos attempt to get others to like them by doing good things for them — by focusing on the other person. ("How are you feeling this afternoon? You look sad.") Twos give the other person lots of appreciative attention in the hopes of being valued as a friend or intimate by the other. Twos are primarily motivated by the desire to please the other as a way of creating closeness or intimacy — to enhance a relationship.

Threes get others to like them by developing the excellence of their own "package." Threes seldom lavish attention on the other; rather, they are trying to be so outstanding and irresistible that the other will want to focus attention on them. And while Threes enjoy the attention, and want relationships, they actually fear intimacy, becoming more uneasy as the relationship becomes closer.

Twos and Threes are different in several other key areas. While

Twos can be ambitious, they feel uncomfortable going after their goals directly, feeling that to do so would be too selfish. Threes are extremely goal-driven, and feel they are not living up to their potential if they are not the best at what they do. Twos are openly sentimental and emote easily. Threes tend to be more composed, and to have difficulty accessing their feelings. Twos keep trying to do nice things for others until they lose their patience and blow up when they go to Eight. Threes keep driving themselves to excel until they burn themselves out and become more detached and passive when they go to Nine. Compare Twos Stevie Wonder and Jerry Lewis with Threes Sting and Dick Clark.

Twos and Fours

Twos and Fours can be confused primarily because they are both Feeling types, and because they both put great emphasis on the ups and downs of their personal relationships. Even with these similarities, however, these two types are seldom mistaken for each other. When they are, it is usually because they are being defined too narrowly. For instance, some Twos might mistype themselves as Fours if they have been through a depression or have recently experienced the end of an important relationship. They may learn that Fours are a depressive type and deduce that since they have been depressed that they are probably Fours. In fact, all nine types can be depressed: feeling sad or alienated in itself is not an indication of being any particular type. Twos may also hear that Fours are romantic, and seeing themselves as romantic, mistype themselves. Female Fours who have been reared in traditional or strongly religious environments may identify themselves as Twos, but this is a danger for women of all types. Some Fours who have been under stress for some time may also recognize many Two-ish behaviors.

Their differences are not difficult to recognize, however. Twos tend to move toward others and engage them, sometimes excessively. Fours tend to withdraw from others, while hoping that others will seek them out. Twos look for people to rescue, Fours look for someone to rescue *them*. Twos are very aware of others' feelings, but tend to be unaware of their own motivations and needs. Fours are highly attuned to their own emotional states, but can fail to recognize their impact on others, and so forth. Compare Bill Cosby and Sally Struthers (Twos) with James Dean and Judy Garland (Fours).

Twos and Fives

This is an extremely unlikely mistype. Few people of either type would be likely to mistype themselves as the other type, but others might occasionally be fooled. Surprisingly, it is more likely for some Fives to be mistaken for Twos, but only in very narrow circumstances. Because Fives do not form emotional bonds easily, they can be highly dependent on the few they *do* form, and can become needy with their significant others. At such times, they do not want their loved ones far from them, apparently like Twos.

Otherwise, these types are almost opposites. Twos are emotionally expressive and highly people-oriented. Fives are emotionally detached and can be the true loners of the Enneagram. Both feel rejected easily, but Twos cope by winning people over and Fives cope by detaching from the hurt and isolating themselves further. Twos go by their feelings and can get flustered or irritated by overly intellectual approaches or complex ideas and procedures. Fives grow flustered or irritated by sentimentality and gushiness; Fives, however, are in their element with intellectual concepts and complexity. Twos tend to move toward others: Fives tend to withdraw from others, and so forth. Compare Barry Manilow and T. Berry Brazelton (Twos) with Philip Glass and Oliver Sacks (Fives).

Twos and Sixes

This is a fairly common mistype because these two types share a number of key traits. Both are warm and engaging and want to be liked — although, more precisely, Sixes want to have the approval and support of others, whereas Twos want to be loved and to be important to others. Both ingratiate themselves with people, although Sixes do so by being playful and silly, by bantering and teasing those they want to elicit an emotional (protective) response from. Average Twos also ingratiate themselves, but more from an implied position of superiority — they are warm and friendly, although the implication is that they are offering their love and friendship, their approval and advice, rather than that they are seeking it from the other, at least at first.

In short, the feeling-tone of both types is completely different: Sixes warily invite selected others into their lives, whereas Twos throw out the net of their feelings with more abandon and see whom they can sweep into the fold. Sixes want to create partnerships with others that will support them in their bid to be more independent, but start to feel anxious if the relationship becomes too merged or "mushy." Twos want to be close with others, and the more intimacy and merging they have with their loved ones, the better.

Both types are emotional, corresponding to the Jungian feeling types — the Two is the extroverted feeling type (*PT,* 62–63), and the Six, the introverted feeling type (*PT,* 222–23). Twos "wear their hearts on their sleeves" and are openly warm and demonstrative about how they feel toward others. Sixes, by contrast, are often ambivalent about their feelings, frequently sending ambiguous, mixed signals to other people. As they deteriorate, average to unhealthy Twos become increasingly covert in their dealings with people, ultimately becoming manipulative while concealing their true motives even from themselves. By contrast, average to unhealthy Sixes become wildly reactive (overreacting) and consciously confused about their feelings, ultimately becoming paranoid.

Indeed, Sixes are consciously assailed by anxiety, indecision, and doubts — and they look to trusted others (especially some kind of authority figure) to reassure them and help them build their confidence and independence. Twos are also sometimes anxious, of course, as all human beings are; however, they are not as indecisive or assailed with doubts, nor do Twos consult an authority figure for answers. On the contrary, as they grow in self-importance, average Twos usually make themselves into authority figures, dispensing advice on all life issues to the people within their spheres of influence. In short, average to unhealthy Twos believe they will only get love by having others depend on them, whereas average to unhealthy Sixes increasingly fear becoming dependent on others, while actually becoming more dependent. At the end of the Continuum, the differences can be seen most starkly between the unhealthy Two's psychosomatic suffering and romantic obsession and the unhealthy Six's paranoia and volatile lashing out. Contrast Twos such as Merv Griffin and Sammy Davis, Jr., with Sixes such as Johnny Carson and Mel Gibson.

Twos and Sevens

These types are frequently mistaken because both can be emotional and histrionic, although the emotions of Sevens are more labile (changing quickly) than the feelings of Twos. Average Twos are friendly and effusive, even gushy and dramatic, although they take pains to express their warm, personal appreciation of other people. They are deeply feeling (one of the types in the Feeling Triad), and their feelings are intimately connected with their sense of self, their behavior, and their interactions with others.

Average Sevens are also histrionic in that they dramatize their emotions flamboyantly, although their emotions are usually shorter lived and wide-ranging — from elation to delight to giddiness to flightiness to highly negative displays of anger, frustration, vituperation, and rage at others. Twos, while needing to express their feelings, tend to be more low-keyed. (Unless they are very unhealthy, Twos do not express their anger at others as openly, nor do they ever display the range of emotions — or such a dazzling variety of them — as Sevens.)

Although both types are gregarious and enjoy being with people, their interpersonal styles are noticeably different. Twos are more interpersonal, genuinely friendly and warm, and interested in others — they would like to be the heart and soul of a family or community, the best friend or confidant everyone comes to for attention, advice, and approval. Twos want to be significant to others and on intimate terms with them, although sometimes they go too far, meddling too much and being too solicitous to make sure they are needed.

By contrast, Sevens do not get as involved in other people's lives. Sevens do not see themselves as the center of a community or family, but as members of a free-floating band of fellow adventurers whose own enjoyment is enhanced by being with others. Sevens do not like to eat or drink alone, or go to the theater alone, or go on vacation alone, but this does not always mean that they are great lovers of people. But it is certainly true that their activities are more enjoyable when others are around to contribute to the excitement and stimulation they seek. To provide themselves with the company of others, Sevens may pay for the pleasure, buying tickets for poorer friends, inviting them to dinner or the country house, and so forth. Sevens may thus exhibit a certain generosity, although their motives may well have less to do with helping needier friends than with making sure that they themselves have a good time by having others around.

While average Twos want others to need them, average Sevens do not want to be needed by anyone: just the reverse, they have little patience for anyone who is too dependent on them since dependents become a drain on their resources and limit their freedom. Average Twos can be possessive of their friends because they feel they have invested a lot of time and emotional energy in them and do not want to see them drift away. Average Sevens tend to be less attached to people. ("Fine. If you don't want to be with me, there are always more fish in the sea.") Sevens can be devoted to loved ones like anyone else, but they refuse to cling. Once they decide that a relationship is not working, they can end it fairly quickly. They may feel sad for a time, but seldom have regrets about their decisions. Twos can leave relationships behind as well, but have a lot more difficulty letting go.

Last, although Sevens are action-oriented and expressive, they are primarily thinking types. They are quick-witted and like to fill their minds with interesting possibilities and concepts. Although Twos can certainly be bright and knowledgeable, they really are feeling types and the juice for them is in the sharing of feelings and intimacies. It is probable that more Sevens misidentify themselves as Twos than vice versa. The differences between Leo Buscaglia and Ann Landers (Twos), and Timothy Leary and Joan Rivers (Sevens) may clarify these two types.

Twos and Eights

It is not difficult to see how Twos and Eights can be confused, although there is a world of difference between them. Some average Twos may realize that they are forceful and dominating, two of the significant traits of Eights. A particularly aggressive Two may find himself or herself in a work-related role that requires leadership and discipline. For these and other reasons, it is possible for some Twos to misidentify themselves as Eights. This is especially true for male Twos, who, for cultural reasons, may prefer to emphasize these traits.

It is worth noting that both types struggle with underlying feelings of *rejection,* although they cope with these feelings in different ways. These feelings probably predispose both types to have stormy relationships and, should conflicts occur, to express their intense passions in interpersonal conflicts (Eights) or in covert neediness and manipulation (Twos).

The probable source of the confusion is that both types have strong wills and egos and a tendency to dominate others. Eights are openly aggressive, forceful, and egocentric, but they are very direct in their communication. When Eights are not happy about something, they have no difficulty letting the other person know that they are angry or disappointed. Twos can also be aggressive, forceful, self-satisfied, egocentric, and so forth, although covertly and indirectly, under an increasingly thin veneer of love. Twos have great difficulty communicating their anger openly, even though they may be very upset with someone. Thus, they use indirect approaches, trying to hint at, or failing that, to manipulate others into meeting their needs. By contrast, less healthy Eights intimidate people openly and when they are frustrated, they push harder to get what they want, possibly using direct threats. They make it clear that they are in a power struggle with the other.

When Twos are frustrated, they try to make others feel guilty, especially by dramatizing the suffering they feel. Twos do not dominate others for self-protection or to extend their power as Eights do; rather, they attempt to control in order to prevent others from leaving. Of course, as Twos become more overwhelmed by stress, they increasingly resemble Eights since Eight is the Two's Direction of Disintegration. Contrasting Twos such as Mother Teresa and Barbara Bush with Eights such as Indira Gandhi and former governor of Texas, Ann Richards, will yield more insight into these two types.

Twos and Nines

There are a number of similarities between these types. Both are interpersonal, both tend to put others' needs before their own, both believe in service, both like to keep things positive, and so forth. Nonetheless, the differences between them are significant.

It is usually average Nines who mistakenly think that they are Twos; it is rare for average Twos to make the reverse misidentification. Some average Nines (particularly women) would like to be Twos because they believe that Two is the loving type, and since these Nines also see themselves as loving, they feel that they must therefore be Twos. But of course, the capacity to love is not restricted to Twos, and other types (including Nines) are equally capable of loving others. As with other general traits that are common to all the types (such as aggression and anxiety), love is expressed differently from type to type and must be distinguished.

In fact, the way Twos and Nines love others is quite different. Nines are unselfconscious, seldom focusing on themselves. They are self-effacing and accommodating, quite content to support others emotionally without looking for a great deal of attention or appreciation in return. Of course, while Nines want to feel that their love is returned, they are patient about it and can be satisfied with fewer responses than Twos. (Some of this is because Nines secretly do not want others to bother them or to affect them too strongly — they attempt to stay in connection with others while withdrawing within themselves to feel safe and independent.) Av-

erage Nines tend to idealize others and fall in love with a romantic, idealized version of the person rather than the person as he or
she actually is. Average Twos, on the other hand, have an acute
sense of other people and their hurts, needs, and frailties. Twos
may focus on these qualities as a way of getting closer to others
and as a way to be needed.

Unlike average Nines, average Twos have a very sharp sense of
their own identities. Although highly empathetic, they are not particularly self-effacing or accommodating. Rather than being unselfconscious, they are highly aware of their feelings and virtues
and are more likely to talk about them.

At their best, healthy Twos can be as unselfish and humble as
healthy Nines, but by the average Levels, there is quite a marked
difference: Twos need to be needed, they want to be important in
the lives of others, and they want people to come to them for approval, guidance, and advice. Average Twos almost "go after"
people, and are always in danger of subtly encouraging people to
become dependent on them. They tend to do things for people so
that others will reinforce their sense of themselves as selfless, all
good, and loving. By contrast to average Nines (who become silent, uncommunicative, and show few reactions when they get
into conflicts with others), average Twos have no hesitation about
telling people how selfish they are or informing them in no uncertain terms how much others are indebted to them. In short, as they
become more unhealthy, the egos of Twos inflate and become
more self-important and aggressive, whereas the egos of Nines become more self-effacing, withdrawn, and diffused.

Healthy Nines offer safe space to others. They are easygoing
and accepting, so that others feel safe with them. There is almost
no tendency in healthy Nines to manipulate others or to make
them feel guilty for not responding as they would like. (Healthy
Nines are more patient and humble — traits Twos could learn
from them.) They are less willing than Twos, however, to go out of
their way for others. By contrast, healthy Twos are willing to get
down to the nitty-gritty and help out in difficult situations. They
have an energy and staying power that average Nines tend to lack.

Moreover, the help that healthy Twos give has a direct, personal focus: it is a response to *you* and your needs. In general, Twos will walk that extra mile with others, whereas while Nines sincerely wish others well, they generally offer more comfort and reassurance than practical help. (The particularity of the love of healthy Twos is something that Nines could learn.) The similarities and differences between these two types may be seen by contrasting Eleanor Roosevelt and Lillian Carter (Twos) with Lady Bird Johnson and Betty Ford (Nines).

MISIDENTIFYING THREES AND OTHER TYPES

Threes and Ones

See Ones and Threes.

Threes and Twos

See Ones and Threes.

Threes and Fours

Here also misidentifications are probably the result of a confusion over wing versus dominant type: 3w4 and 4w3. The primary difference between these types can be seen in their relationship with their emotional life. Threes tend to focus on task, on efficiency, on performance. Of course, Threes have feelings, but as much as possible, they put them on the back burner whenever there are things to get done — and with many Threes, that is most of the time. As Threes become less healthy, they increasingly see their own feelings as "speed bumps" — annoyances that must be dealt with but that interfere with their effectiveness. Threes want to get their goals accomplished, and then, time permitting, process their feelings.

Fours are almost the exact opposite. Naturally, Fours want to accomplish things too, but when difficult feelings arise, Fours want to stop what they are doing and process them before returning to their tasks. The less healthy the Four, the more he or she will need lots of time to sort through troubling feelings and reactions. Threes can see the Four's preoccupation with feelings as unprofessional and immature. Fours can see the Three's obsession with performance as inauthentic and shallow.

It is far more common for Threes to mistype as Fours than vice versa. This is especially true for Threes who grew up in families in which artistic self-expression was particularly valued. They may mistakenly believe that only Fours are creative, while failing to recognize that there have been many noted artists who are Threes. Compare Threes Barbra Streisand and Richard Gere with Fours Sarah McLachlan and Jeremy Irons.

Threes and Fives

The principal reason these two very different types are confused is that some average Threes (especially if they are intelligent) would like to see themselves as "thinkers." Since Fives are most stereotypically seen as the "intelligent, thinking type," average Threes may choose type Five rather than the type they actually are. This misidentification is made almost exclusively by Threes since Fives are not likely to think that they are Threes. Average Threes are set up to fulfill the hidden expectations of their parents; so in a family that values intelligence, originality, and intellectual brilliance, it is quite natural for Threes to grow up thinking that they must be those things in order to be worthwhile. Thus, narrow conceptions of the types, or unflattering and unfair presentations of type Three in some Enneagram literature, may cause some average Threes to want to be Fives.

Some Threes may well be thinkers and have original ideas; they may excel academically and be brilliant students. But these traits alone are not sufficient to be a Five. Once again, the root of the misidentification lies in focusing on one or two traits rather than considering the type as a whole, including its central motivations.

There are many significant dissimilarities between these two types. The kind of thinking they engage in is very different: Fives are very process-oriented: they do not care about final goals and can be extraordinarily involved in abstract ideas for the sake of acquiring knowledge, virtually as an end in itself. The pursuit and possession of knowledge enthralls Fives, and not only do their interests not need to have any practical results for them to be satisfying, average Fives are just as likely never to seek fame or fortune for their discoveries or creations. Fives follow their ideas wherever they take them, with no particular end in view. Their ideas need not even be related to making discoveries. Creating their own private inner realities can be reward enough. In any case, average Fives will stay with a project for years until they exhaust their subject or themselves, or both.

Threes, by contrast, are not usually involved in subjects for their own sake: they may change their interests and careers rapidly if the success and recognition they seek elude them. Moreover, average Threes pursue their intellectual work with personal goals in mind (either consciously or unconsciously): to impress others, to be famous, to be known as best in their field, to be acclaimed as a genius, to beat a rival at a discovery, to win a prestigious prize or grant, and so forth. The essential consideration is that their intellectual work is frequently undertaken to achieve long-range goals and garner recognition rather than for the love of knowledge and the excitement of intellectual discovery. Average Threes want to feel successful and so tend to talk about their brilliant achievements, whereas average Fives tend to be secretive and reticent about their work and discoveries. Furthermore, the pragmatic thinking of average Threes calculates how to achieve goals in the most efficient manner, something completely alien to impractical, curiosity-driven Fives.

In addition, Threes are highly sociable and well groomed: they know how to present themselves favorably. Fives are usually loners and often put little to no effort into their personal appearance: their appearance means less to them than pursuing their interests until the problems are solved and the work is done. Average Threes are highly aware of what others think about them, whereas average Fives care little about anyone else's good opinion. Average Threes want to be considered as sexually and socially desirable and will conform to and set social standards. Fives are often strange, eccentric, and isolated from others — not at all concerned about conforming to social standards. Contrast the personalities of Threes such as Michael Tilson Thomas and Carl Sagan with those of Fives such as Glenn Gould and Stanley Kubrick.

Threes and Sixes

These types are not often mistyped, but they do have some similarities. Both can be very focused on work and performance but can play very different roles in the workplace. Threes see themselves as soloists: they cooperate with others, but want to excel, to be the best at what they do. They need recognition and acknowledgment for their accomplishments, and as long as those are forthcoming, can be tireless workers. Sixes are hard workers, too, but unless they are moving to Three in stress, tend to feel awkward about taking the spotlight. ("Everyone takes pot shots at the guy out front.") Sixes work hard to ingratiate themselves with their superiors, to build up security: they want to convince others of their dependability. Threes tend to be more smooth and composed; Sixes tend to be more nervous and awkward, although sometimes endearingly so.

Another common source of mistyping here comes from the sexual instinctual variant of type Six (*PT*, 426–30). In short, some Sixes focus on cultivating personal magnetism and attractiveness like Threes, but their insecurities about their desirability is far more visible. Further, Threes tend to project a cool, emotional reserve, while Sixes project more volatile and intense feelings. Compare Threes Tom Cruise and Whitney Houston with Sixes Tom Hanks and Bonnie Raitt.

Threes and Sevens

Both Threes and Sevens are aggressive types (*PT*, 433–36) and both are interested in enjoying different aspects of success. Both types may pursue the acquisition of wealth and status symbols, but with significant differences: Sevens because their sense of self is maintained by acquiring things, Threes because status symbols reinforce their feeling of self-worth and hence their sense of self.

Sevens love the material world and want to acquire a variety of exciting experiences because having a steady stream of sensations makes them feel alive. They are sensation seekers, whose sense of self is maintained and reinforced by heightening their experience of the world, regardless of anyone else's knowledge of their acquisitions. For them what is important is the stimulation that the pursuit and acquisition of experiences and things give them, whether or not anyone else is part of the picture. For example, taking a first-class cruise on an ocean liner is a source of pleasure for Sevens, whether or not anyone else knows that they are doing so. By contrast, for Threes, such a trip would be a symbol of their success — that they have "arrived." Of course, it would be more important to have other key people know about their vacation.

As another example, money might allow Threes to hire a governess for their children so they can pursue their careers and so that they can let everyone know that they are successful enough to afford a governess. By contrast, Sevens may engage a governess so that they can travel and not be tied down by having to raise their children themselves.

One of the fundamental reasons why Sevens and Threes are confused in the traditional Enneagram teaching is that *unhealthy* Sevens in a manic phase have grandiose delusions similar to the grandiose feelings of self-esteem we find in narcissistic Threes. The difference is that Sevens are grandiose about their plans while Threes are grandiose about their ability to achieve things: Sevens have great expectations about their future activities. When they become manic, everything seems possible for them. By contrast, unhealthy Threes are grandiose about their self-worth: narcissistic, exhibitionistic, and prone to exaggerating their accomplishments.

It is likely that these two very different types have been confused because both seem to be narcissistic — that is, inflated with self-love or self-regard. However, average Sevens are not really narcissistic in the classic sense; they may be selfish, self-centered, greedy, insensitive, and so forth, but they are not looking for constant mirroring of their excellence, nor are they particularly vulnerable to narcissistic hurt. Threes are classic narcissists and are far more concerned with avoiding potential shame and humiliation. Furthermore, when Sevens become grandiose, they are trying to escape from pain and anxiety, whereas grandiose Threes are overcompensating for their fear of failure.

Last, one of the simplest ways to distinguish these two types is by marking the difference in their overall emotional tone and style. Average Threes are cool, in control, projecting the impression that they are perfectly together, with no emotional or personal problems. By contrast, Sevens have many more rough edges, rarely seeming as perfect or as coolly self-contained as Threes. For better or worse, Sevens do not censor themselves and can be funny, outspoken, vulgar, ill mannered, and outrageous — allowing far less polished behavior and attitudes to be displayed for public view. Contrast Sevens such as Bette Midler and Howard Stern with Threes such as Shania Twain and Bryant Gumbel.

Threes and Eights

Threes and Eights are both aggressive (*PT,* 433–36), although the confusion between them centers on the competition found in average Threes and a similar competitiveness in average Eights.

In general terms, both Eights and Threes are ambitious and competitive: both types want to rise above others. The difference is that average Eights are self-assertive and want others to give them their way immediately so they do not have to waste time and energy fighting with people — not that they are afraid to do so. Eights compete for material, political, or sexual dominance, less over purely social or status issues. For instance, Eights usually do not spend a lot of time comparing themselves with others, and certainly never to the degree that Threes do. For the same reason that Threes confuse themselves with Sevens and Fives (because they are looking for a flattering identity), it is far more likely that Threes identify themselves as Eights rather than vice versa.

Despite some superficial similarities, the differences are profound: Eights are leaders, deal makers, and power brokers who want to make the world conform to their personal vision. They want to have a large impact, to build and accomplish great things, possibly something that will live as a testament to the greatness of their audacity and will. Strong and implacable, they can be ruthless when something or someone gets in their way. They have large egos, and achieving some form of glory is important to them. Achieving personal power is the dominating drive in Eights, and there is nothing ambiguous, much less furtive or duplicitous, about them.

By contrast, power is not the key motive of Threes; achieving enough success and prestige to feel valuable and worthy is. Further, it is important for Threes to have significant people in their lives recognize and acknowledge their success. (By contrast, Eights do not care about popularity; they do not particularly care about the approval of others, so long as they get their way.) If Eights are natural leaders, Threes are natural managers and technicians. Further, Threes fear failure deeply because they see it as a personal humiliation, a potential occasion for being rejected as worthless, their deepest fear. By contrast, Eights see failure as an opportunity to learn something and come back stronger. If Eights are too busy achieving their purposes to worry about public opinion, Threes live and die on the opinions of others and desperately want to be in demand socially. If average Eights are combative and intimidating and can "take the heat," despite a certain bravado, average Threes will turn to diplomacy, "get even" more covertly, or back down: they cannot take pressure or open confrontation for long. Compare Eights such as Telly Savalas and Bette Davis with Threes such as Sylvester Stallone and Sharon Stone.

Threes and Nines

Threes and Nines can be mistaken for each other in that both are highly adaptable and both can be interested in gaining acceptance from others. Although it is not always obvious in the case of Threes, both can also have trouble recognizing who they are or what they really want. Threes can also resemble Nines when they move to Nine in their Direction of Disintegration, becoming more disengaged and unmotivated by their usual goals.

The differences between these types can be quite pronounced. Threes are highly motivated self-starters who launch into projects with a sense that they can and will succeed. They are determined to meet goals and have trouble slowing down and relaxing. Nines can be highly accomplished in life and hugely successful, but many such Nines have friends or spouses who keep them motivated and on track with their goals. Generally speaking, Nines have trouble doing good things for themselves, but they have a much easier time relaxing than Threes do. Threes try to garner attention from people who they believe are important to them. Nines are reluctant to ask for attention, and discount themselves easily. Threes get excited about their projects, Nines about their free time and comforts. Compare Nines Ronald Reagan and George Lucas with Threes Bill Clinton and Tony Robbins.

MISIDENTIFYING FOURS AND OTHER TYPES

Fours and Ones
See Ones and Fours.

Fours and Twos
See Twos and Fours.

Fours and Threes
See Threes and Fours.

Fours and Fives
Fours and Fives can resemble each other in that both are withdrawn types (*PT,* 433–36), both can be individualistic and eccentric by mainstream cultural standards, and both can be highly creative. Of course, there is a greater risk of mistyping with 4w5's and 5w4's.

Fives are more likely to mistype as Fours than vice versa, primarily because of simplistic definitions of the types. Some Fives have learned that Fours are more feeling-oriented. Fives are more intellectual, and, seeing that they have deep feelings, presume that they must be Fours. (This is especially true with female Fives.) Also, Fives are often portrayed as scientists or engineers while Fours are creative artists. In fact, it is true that Fours are less likely to be scientists than some other types, but there are as many Fives who are artists as Fours, although their styles are somewhat different.

Fours are self-absorbed and emotionally volatile — they express their feelings one way or another, and need people to respond to them in an emotional way. Their artistic work tends to be autobiographical, based on their families, on relationships, past or unrequited, and on the content of their subjective experience. Fives may have intense feelings but share them with few people. Their feelings tend to fuel their thoughts and their imagination, leading them to more abstract or fantastic forms of creative expression. Their work is less autobiographical, and more often portrays their vision of reality. ("I paint what I see!") Fives tend to be more experimental and outlandish in their artwork. Although both types can explore personal darkness more thoroughly than most, Fours tend to focus on their disappointments in love and with their childhoods and their attendant pain. Fives tend to focus on inner emptiness and feelings of meaninglessness. Fives are more driven to penetrate the surface of things in order to understand, Fours to get in touch with feelings and cathartically express them. Compare Fours Ingmar Bergman and Anne Rice with Fives David Lynch and Clive Barker.

Fours and Sixes

While there are real similarities between these two types, there are even more differences. The principal difference is that Sixes relate well to people; they have the ability to unconsciously engage the emotions of others so that others will like them and form secure relationships with them. Fours, in contrast, do not relate primarily to people but to their own inner emotional states. Fours tend to feel that they are alone in life (even when they are not), and find it difficult to form bonds with others — something that comes more easily to Sixes. The psychic structures of the two types are also very different: Fours are true introverts, while Sixes are a blend of introversion and extroversion — true ambiverts who possess qualities of both orientations.

Confusion arises between these types principally on the part of Sixes who think that they are Fours for two main reasons. First, some Sixes identify with the negative side of the Four (depression, inferiority, self-doubt, and hopelessness, for example) and think they must be Fours because they recognize similar traits in themselves. The difference lies in the motivations for these traits. For example, while all the types can become depressed, Fours do so because they are disappointed with themselves for having lost some opportunity to actualize themselves. They become depressed when they realize that in their search for self, they have gone down a blind alley and now must pay the price. Unhealthy, depressed Fours are essentially angry at themselves for bringing this on themselves or for allowing it to happen.

By contrast, Sixes become depressed when they fear that they have done something to make their allies or authority figures angry with them. Their depression is a response to their self-disparagement; it comes from the fear that the authority is angry at them and will punish them. Thus, the depression of Sixes is based on repressed *anxiety*. This is not the case with Fours, whose depression is based on repressed feelings of *hatred* toward the self and others.

Second, we have characterized the Four as the Individualist, and some Sixes who are artistic think that they therefore must be Fours. However, as noted above in the discussion of Fours and Nines, artistic talent is not the sole domain of Fours, so it is entirely possible for Sixes to be artists of one kind or another. Even so, there are important differences in the creative work produced by these two types.

In general, Sixes tend to be performing artists, while Fours tend to be solo creators. Sixes are more likely to be actors or musicians than poets and playwrights, and can be more comfortable performing the words or music of someone else than creating it themselves. Even those Sixes who are creative tend either to be traditionalists, creating within firmly established rules and styles, or they go to an extreme and become rebellious, reacting against traditionalism — such as rock stars and experimental novelists who purposely defy traditional forms. In either case, both tradition and reactions against it are an important aspect of their art. The themes typically found in the art of Sixes have to do with belonging, security, family, politics, country, and common values.

Creative Fours, by contrast, are individualists who go their own way to explore their feelings and other subjective personal states. The artistic products of Fours are much less involved either with following a tradition or with reacting against it. Fours are less apt to use political or communal experiences as the subject matter for their work, choosing instead the movements of their own emotions, their personal histories, the darkness and light they discover in themselves as they become immersed in the creative process. By listening to their inner voices, even average Fours may speak to the universal person or fail to communicate at all, at least to their contemporaries. They may be ahead of their time not because they are trying to be rebellious or avant-garde, but because they develop their own forms to express their personal point of view. What is important to Fours is not the tradition but personal truth. Tradition is no more than a backdrop against which Fours play out their own personal dramas. Compare and contrast the personalities of Rudolf Nureyev and Peter Ilich Tchaikovsky (Fours) with those of Mikhail Baryshnikov and Johannes Brahms (Sixes) for further similarities and differences.

Fours and Sevens

Fours and Sixes are vastly different, and except for a superficial similarity at Level 6 of both types, it would be difficult to see how anyone familiar with both could misidentify them for long.

It seems, however, that the basis for mistaking them is that both types tend to be excessive — Sevens go to extremes in the external, material world with the lavishness and number of possessions and experiences they acquire. At Level 6, Sevens tend to become jaded and hardened, insensitive and demanding, selfish and uncaring about others. We have characterized them as the Excessive Materialist.

Fours at the same Level (The Self-Indulgent Aesthete) are also excessive and go to extremes, although emotional extremes. Emotionally self-indulgent, average Fours go for the big emotional charge in their fantasy lives, allowing themselves to feel and imagine anything, no matter how ultimately unrealistic or emotionally debilitating it might be. They wallow in their feelings and fantasies, squeezing the last breath of life from them to reinforce their sense of self. Thus the Fours' self-indulgences are more internal and private, centered on the emotional world they inhabit. Outwardly, their emotional excess is expressed in an increasing preciosity and impracticality, an effete, overripe decadence and sensuality that is the main point of similarity between the two types. While both types may become decadent and sensual, Sevens do so to stay "happy" and thus flee from anxiety and negative feelings. By contrast, Fours embrace sensuality, luxuriating in sex or drink or drugs to heighten their emotional fantasies and to deaden the pain of their self-consciousness.

Both types share a love of fine, expensive things, although here too there are differences. Fours make do with fewer material things, cherishing beautiful objects for the sake of their beauty and the feelings that beauty awakens in them. A stone picked up on the beach or a twig with a single bud can quicken their aesthetic feelings and satisfy them. By contrast, while average Sevens want to possess beautiful objects, they become increasingly unappreciative and insensitive to the beauty or value of those objects. They become acquisitive not because they enjoy things for themselves but because the acquisition of possessions provides a sense of security. And even more fundamentally, what excites Sevens is the stimulation they feel when they desire something new. The stimulation of their appetites reinforces their sense of self, although once they have actually acquired what they want, they usually lose interest in the acquisition. The pair of shoes that they were "dying" to have joins the racks with dozens of others; the fur coat they were drooling over for weeks suddenly becomes "that old thing" as they turn their attention to acquiring something else. Sevens may also mistype themselves as Fours because they have suffered from depression. Indeed, Sevens can suffer from loss, sadness, and depression as much as anyone. As quickly as possible, however, Sevens will seek out positive activities in order to feel better. They can even become manic in their efforts to avoid painful feelings. Fours, on the other hand, feel much more comfortable with feelings of sadness and pain because these feelings are an important part of Fours' identities. In short, average Sevens tend to be upbeat experience-seekers, while average Fours tend to be languishing aesthetes — very different types. Compare the styles of Bob Dylan (a Four) and of Elton John (a Seven) and those of Ingmar Bergman (a Four) with Steven Spielberg (a Seven) to understand the difference.

Fours and Eights

At first, it would seem extremely unlikely that Fours and Eights would be mistyped for one another, but it does occasionally occur. More often, Eights mistake themselves for Fours because they see themselves as passionate and as having intense feelings, and this is usually true. Similarly Eights may well recall childhood hurts and identify with the Four's sense of alienation or loneliness. But Eights cope with these feelings in radically different ways than Fours do. Eights learn to toughen themselves up and to "get over it" so that they can do what they need to do to maintain their independence and personal authority. Fours find it difficult to let go of their childhood wounds and do not want to "get over it." Fours do not necessarily want to be dependent on anyone, but they are willing to rely on others if it gives them the time and resources to work out their feelings or to develop their creativity.

Eights *do* feel vulnerable inside, but as much as possible, they steel themselves against any feelings of insecurity and weakness in themselves. Eights tend to see such feelings as self-indulgent luxuries for people who have no serious responsibilities. Fours show their vulnerability, but can be much tougher and controlling than they generally realize. In fact, Fours are quite resilient and can endure emotional difficulties and losses that would cause most other types to collapse. In a strange way, Eights are like Fours turned inside out. Contrast Fours like Roy Orbison and Johnny Depp with Eights like Frank Sinatra and Sean Penn.

Fours and Nines

Some average Nines think that they are Fours because they have artistic talents and creative inclinations of one kind or another. As in the case of love not being the sole domain of Twos, artistic capacity is not the sole province of Fours. Other types can be, and often are, artists.

Even so, the artistry of Fours is much more personal and self-revealing than that of Nines. The art of Nines often expresses idealized, mythological, and archetypal worlds — usually the real world fictionalized into something fantastic and wondrous. Nines are often gifted storytellers in which " . . . and they all lived happily ever after" is assured. (There are no unhappy endings in the Nine's world of make-believe.) By contrast, the art of Fours is generally more personal and realistic, the expression of the Four's (and of everyone's) deep longing for love, wholeness, and meaning. Fours often deal in the tragic, finding redemption in understanding loss and sorrow (Tennessee Williams, Joni Mitchell); Nines deal in the commonplace, finding comfort in ordinary lives and simple situations or in reassuring fantasy (Walt Disney, J. R. Tolkien).

The principal reason these types may be confused is that they are both withdrawn types (*PT*, 433–36). Fours withdraw from others so that they can give themselves time to deal with their emotions. Nines, on the other hand, are withdrawn in the sense that they remove their attention from people or situations that threaten them, disengaging themselves emotionally so that they will not be anxious or upset. They cut off their identification with others (or never identify with them in the first place), identifying instead with a private, idealized version of reality. Average to unhealthy Nines tune out any unpleasantness by dissociating from whatever upsets them, whereas Fours do just the opposite, brooding over their hurts in an attempt to come to terms with them. Fours are certainly not detached from their emotions — just the reverse, they are keenly aware of them, perhaps too much so.

Both types can therefore be shy, absent-minded, confused, and detached from the real world. The difference is that Nines are detached both from the external world and from their emotions, whereas Fours withdraw from whatever has caused them pain. (In the end, that may add up to quite a lot.) Nines see the world through rose-colored glasses, and their view of it is comforting, whereas Fours see the world from a garret window as outsiders and are not comforted: everyone else seems to be living a happier, more normal life. Contrast the personalities of Mahler (a Four) and Aaron Copland (a Nine), Saul Steinberg (a Four) and Norman Rockwell (a Nine).

MISIDENTIFYING FIVES AND OTHER TYPES

Fives and Ones

See Ones and Fives.

Fives and Twos

See Twos and Fives.

Fives and Threes

See Threes and Fives.

Fives and Fours

See Fours and Fives.

Fives and Sixes

Fives and Sixes are both thinking types and, when educated, can both be quite intellectual. It is far more common for Sixes to mistype as Fives, but for some easily understood reasons. Of the two types, Sixes tend to be more linear and analytical in their thinking because they are interested in troubleshooting, in prediction, and in establishing methods that can be repeated. Thus, contrary to popular belief, the world of academia and higher education is more the realm of Sixes than of Fives. Academia teaches students to work with advisers and mentors, to cite sources and back up arguments with quotations from authorities, to follow proper procedures in papers and theses, and so forth — all type Six values.

Fives are much more nonlinear in their thinking. They are interested in finding out where established theories break down and in developing iconoclastic ideas that shake up structures and established methods. Fives are, generally speaking, bolder than Sixes in their positions and creativity, but also far less practical. Fives feel that they can trust only their own minds to come to conclusions — they believe that everyone else is likely to be less well informed. Sixes get frantic trying to find something to trust precisely because they do not trust their own minds to come to meaningful conclusions. The difference between them can be seen in the difference between Umberto Eco (a Five) and Tom Clancy (a Six), or Peter Gabriel (a Five) and Bruce Springsteen (a Six).

Fives and Sevens

These types are seldom mistyped for one another, but they do have some similarities. Fives and Sevens are both thinking types: they are both highly curious, exploratory, and willing to try new ways of doing things. Both types also have a propensity to collect things and to be nervous and high-strung. They are quite different emotionally and in their characteristic preoccupations and avoidances.

Fives tend to be more socially isolated and withdrawn, spending long hours alone working on their projects, reading, listening to music, and so forth: Fives prefer cerebral entertainment. Sevens are highly gregarious, and like to stay active. They enjoy a good read too, but get impatient with sitting around for extended periods of time. The gift of the Five is intense focus and concentration. The gift of the Seven is breadth of vision and synthesis. Sevens are also the optimists of the Enneagram, seeing the positive side of most things and wanting to avoid topics that get too dark, painful, or heavy. Fives are almost the opposite, seeing optimism as unrealistic and being drawn to the dark, the macabre, and the nihilistic side of life.

Of course, Fives can resemble Sevens when they are under increased stress and moving in their Direction of Disintegration. At such times, they can become distracted and scattered like average Sevens. But as soon as the stressful situation is relieved, Fives will return to their more focused, withdrawn ways. Compare Fives like Gary Larson and Stanley Kubrik with Sevens like Robin Williams and Leonard Bernstein.

Fives and Eights

These two types are not often mistyped, but they share similar attitudes. Eights and Fives both see themselves as outsiders and easily feel rejected. Both are highly independent and willing to battle with anyone who threatens their independence. Both believe in direct communication, can be aggressive, and tend to protect their vulnerability.

Eights sometimes see themselves as Fives because they go to Five in stress, and therefore recall times when they have withdrawn from others to strategize and think about their future courses of action. Nonetheless, Eights more often deal with problems head on, and can be highly assertive in going after what they want. Fives, by contrast, tend to retreat from others and to cut themselves off from many of their needs in order to avoid risking dependencies.

Eights are highly instinctual and intimately related to their bodies: as a result, they are people of practical action, pragmatism, and sensuality. Fives tend to stay in their heads more and often have an ambivalent relationship with their bodies. Staying grounded and practical can be a problem for Fives — it is almost never one for Eights. Compare James Joyce (a Five) with Ernest Hemingway (an Eight).

Fives and Nines

A detailed comparison and contrast between Fives and Nines is warranted because so many Nines mistakenly think that they are Fives; typically, the misidentification almost never happens the other way around. Particularly if they are well educated and intelligent, average male Nines tend to think that they are Fives. (As noted in the discussion of Twos, average female Nines tend to think they are Twos.)

Of all the personality types, Nines have the most difficulty identifying which type they are because their sense of self is undefined. Average Nines have little sense of who they are apart from those they have identified with; hence, they are usually at a loss to know where to begin to find their type. (As we have seen, either they think they are Fives or Twos or they see a little of themselves in all the types and make no further effort at identifying themselves. If they have no guidance, Nines in this predicament usually shrug their shoulders and give up on the Enneagram and, more important, on acquiring self-knowledge.)

Even relatively healthy Nines still have a somewhat diffused sense of self because it is based on their capacity to be receptive to others — and to be unselfconscious. Moreover, average Nines have problems identifying their type because doing so arouses anxiety, something completely anathema to them. Whatever disturbs their peace of mind is ignored or met with a blind eye. They avoid introspection in favor of entertaining comforting notions about themselves, whatever they may be. Maintaining an undefined understanding of themselves, and thus, maintaining their emotional comfort, is more important to average Nines than acquiring deeper insights.

None of this is true of Fives, and the two types are opposites in many ways. Nines are gentle, easygoing, patient, receptive, accommodating, and drawn to comforting thoughts, whereas Fives are intense, strong-minded, high-strung, argumentative, and drawn to disturbing thoughts. Nines like people and trust them;

perhaps at times they are too trusting. By contrast, average Fives are suspicious of people and are anything but trusting, perhaps at times too cynical and resistant. Both types employ a schizoid defense of the self — they detach from their feelings — and both are among the three withdrawn types of the Enneagram, but (as we have seen with Fours and Nines), while there are genuine similarities between them, they are only superficial ones (PT, 433–36).

Despite their similarities, the main point of confusion for Nines arises around the notion of "thinking." Nines believe they are Fives because they think they have profound ideas: therefore, they must be Fives.

Part of the problem stems from the fact that individuals of both types can be highly intelligent, although as a group Fives are probably the most innovative and mentally focused of the nine personality types. (When Nines are highly intelligent, they can be as brilliant as Fives, although they may be highly self-conscious about their intelligence, even to the point of discounting it.) Although intelligence can be manifested in different ways, to be intelligent or intellectual does not make a Nine a Five. Since all the types think in one way or another, thinking alone, with no further distinction, is not a sufficient basis for a personality diagnosis.

The fundamental difference between the thinking of Nines and that of Fives is that Nines are impressionistic and involved with generalities, synthesis, imaginative ruminations, and fanciful situations. Nines typically do not want to take their ideas deeper or question them once they have reached certain conclusions, nor are they usually good at following up once they have acted. By contrast, the thinking of Fives is highly concentrated, penetrating, laserlike, and almost microscopic in the specificity of its focus. Fives love details, losing themselves in research, scholarship, and complex intellectual pursuits. They think in-depth, concentrating so much that they block out other perceptions (eventually to their detriment). By contrast, even brilliant Nines tend to have problems concentrating; they also tend to lose interest quickly and to allow their attention to drift off when they become bored or anxious.

Nines tend to spin grand, sweeping, idealistic solutions to problems, while Fives tend to speculate on problems, then on the problems that their problems have raised, then on those problems, ad infinitum. Nines may be gifted storytellers, able to communicate simply and effectively to others, even to children. Fives usually communicate to only a few or keep their ideas entirely to themselves. (Moreover, their ideas may be so complicated that they are difficult to communicate to all but other specialists.) Nines usually do not consider the consequences of their actions; Fives are extremely interested in predicting the consequences of every action. Nines idealize the world and create imaginary worlds in which good always triumphs over evil; Fives analyze the real world and create horrifying scenarios in which evil usually triumphs over good or exists in tension with it. Nines simplify; Fives complexify. Nines look to the past; Fives to the future. Nines are fantasists; Fives are theorists. Nines are disengaged; Fives are detached. Nines are utopians; Fives are nihilists. Nines are optimists; Fives are pessimists. Nines are easygoing and nonthreatening; Fives are intense and disturbing. Nines are at peace; Fives are in tension. Nines end in dissociation; Fives in delirium.

The thinking of intelligent, well-educated Nines tends to be in the direction of simplifying reality and cutting through abstruse thickets to get at the kernel of truth beneath. Nines tend to see things the way they want them to be; they reinterpret reality to make it more comforting and less threatening, simpler and less daunting. By contrast, the thinking of Fives is complex. By attempting to arrive at a grand unifying theory that encompasses and explains everything, average Fives end up involved in increasing complications and abstractions. Their thought is focused on specifics, often highly technical and concerned with foresight and the consequences of acting one way rather than another. But at an extreme, Fives risk seeing reality not as it is but as a projection of their preoccupations and fears. They distort their perceptions of reality so that reality seems more negative and threatening than it actually is.

Nines feel at ease in the world, and their style of thinking reflects their unconscious desire to merge with the world. Fives are afraid of being overwhelmed by the world, and their intellectual efforts are an unconscious defense against the world, an attempt to master it intellectually. There is a world of difference between these two types since they see the world so differently. Compare Charles Darwin (a Five) and Walt Disney (a Nine), Albert Einstein (a Five) and Jim Henson (a Nine) to understand the similarities and differences between these two types more clearly.

MISIDENTIFYING SIXES AND OTHER TYPES

Sixes and Ones
See Ones and Sixes.

Sixes and Twos
See Twos and Sixes.

Sixes and Threes
See Threes and Sixes.

Sixes and Fours
See Fours and Sixes.

Sixes and Fives
See Fives and Sixes.

Sixes and Sevens
Sixes and Sevens can be mistyped when there is confusion between main type and wing: that is, between a Six with a Seven-wing and a Seven with a Six-wing. Both are thinking types, and both are driven by anxiety, although they cope with their anxious feelings in strikingly different ways. Sixes tend to react to their anxiety by fretting and becoming more anxious. They may react counter-phobically by reacting against their fears, but react they do. Fur-

ther, anxiety tends to make Sixes more pessimistic and negative about themselves and their prospects. They can be full of self-doubt, while being suspicious of the motives of others.

Sevens, by contrast, are extremely optimistic, and react to anxiety by looking for enjoyable distractions. Sevens suppress their self-doubt as much as possible, and try to keep everything upbeat. Sevens tend to deny the dark corners of their souls, Sixes tend to get stuck in them. Sixes, however, have a heightened sense of responsibility and do not allow themselves to "goof off" until all of their obligations have been met. Sevens, for better or for worse, are far more spontaneous, and resist having too many expectations placed on them. They want to be free to come and go as they please, and they find the Six's persistent sense of commitment potentially limiting and dull. Sixes tend to find the Seven's lifestyle flighty and irresponsible. In short, Sixes seek out structure and guidelines: Sevens resist both. Compare David Letterman and Princess Diana (Sixes) with Jim Carrey and Carol Burnett (Sevens).

Sixes and Eights

Sixes and Eights are aggressive, although only the Eight is an entirely aggressive personality. Sixes react both to their fears and to other people and constantly oscillate from one state to another, from Level to Level. They are ambivalent and passive-aggressive, evasive, and contradictory. In contrast, Eights have solid egos and formidable wills; they keep pushing others until they give them what they want. Eights reveal little softness; they are not often willing to comply with the wishes of others. They have little desire to please others or to ingratiate themselves with people. Rather than look to others for protection, Eights offer protection (patronage) in return for hard work and loyalty.

As different as these two types are, they are nevertheless similar at Level 6 — but only at this Level. At this stage, both Sixes (The Authoritarian Rebel) and Eights (The Confrontational Adversary) show similar aggressive traits — belligerence, defiance, a willingness to intimidate others, a quick and threatening temper, the threat of violence, hatred of others, and so forth. However, Eights arrive at this stage as a result of constantly escalating their pressure on others to get what they want until they have become highly confrontational and combative. Sixes arrive at their state from a very different route — in reaction to their suspiciousness and fear of dependency. Sixes become aggressive because they do not want to be pushed around anymore; Eights become aggressive to push others even more.

The essential difference is that Sixes eventually will yield and their defenses will crumble if enough pressure is applied to them, whereas opposition to Eights only encourages them to remain defiant and to meet their adversary with renewed aggression.

When unhealthy, both types can be dangerous; ironically, Sixes are probably more dangerous at this stage than Eights since they are anxious and may strike out at someone impulsively or irrationally. On the other hand, average Eights are more rational: they take the odds of success into account at every move. If and when they finally do become violent, however, Eights are more dangerous than Sixes because they are more ruthless, and the momentum of their inflated egos makes them feel that they can and must press onward until their enemies are utterly destroyed. Eights eventually become megalomaniacs (and may be destroyed after they have destroyed others). By contrast, unhealthy Sixes eventually become self-defeating (and may be destroyed by their own fear). Compare G. Gordon Liddy and Mike Tyson (Sixes) with Henry Kissinger and Muhammad Ali (Eights) to understand more about the similarities and differences between these types.

Sixes and Nines

These types are actually frequently mistyped. Sixes and Nines are both concerned with security and with maintaining some kind of status quo situation. They are both family-oriented, and both tend to take modest views of themselves. Their affect, however, is the easiest way to distinguish them.

In short, Nines like to remain easygoing and unflappable. Nines work steadily at their tasks, but they show little sign of being upset by the day's ups and downs. Sixes, on the other hand, cannot easily disguise their feelings. They more readily grow agitated and become rattled by mishaps. While Nines can remain silent within their own inner peace, Sixes need to vent with others periodically to discharge their fears and doubts. Sixes are more obviously nervous and defensive when they believe there are problems. Nines remain strangely bland in the face of problems, although beneath the pleasant surface of average Nines, there is stubborn resistance and an unwillingness to be upset or troubled by conflicts or problems. Sixes tend to be suspicious of unknown people and situations — they need to test people before they let them get close. Nines may be protected by the disengagement of their attention, but they tend to be trusting of others — almost to a fault.

Of course, under stress, when moving in their Direction of Disintegration, Nines will begin to act out some of the behaviors of average Sixes, and for this reason, some Nines will mistype themselves as Sixes. But such periods of overt anxiety generally do not last long. As soon as possible, Nines revert to their more easygoing approach to things. Compare Sixes George Bush and Dustin Hoffman with Nines Gerald Ford and Jimmy Stewart.

MISIDENTIFYING SEVENS AND OTHER TYPES

Sevens and Ones
See Ones and Sevens.

Sevens and Twos
See Twos and Sevens.

Sevens and Threes
See Threes and Sevens.

Sevens and Fours
See Fours and Sevens.

Sevens and Fives

See Fives and Sevens.

Sevens and Sixes

See Sixes and Sevens.

Sevens and Eights

Sevens and Eights are both aggressive types (*PT,* 433–36) and can resemble one another in certain respects. Both are powerful personalities who are able to go after what they want in life, but what they want, and how they attempt to get it, are different.

Sevens are primarily interested in variety — they want to sample as many different experiences as possible and become practical inasmuch as their practicality gives them the means to pursue the experiences they want to try. Eights, by contrast, are more interested in intensity — they care less about variety than about having intense experiences that they enjoy. Eights are also interested in power, both as a way to maintain their independence and as a way of asserting their dominance in the environment. Sevens are not particularly interested in having power, seeing the work necessary to maintain it as possibly infringing on their freedom.

Eights are an instinctive type, and as such, they make decisions from their "gut" instincts. They prefer dealing with practical matters, and although emotionally volatile at times, generally remain grounded and down to earth. Sevens are thinking types; they can have brilliant, quick minds. At the same time, Sevens can get ahead of themselves with their plans, schemes, and interests: they can have trouble remaining grounded and focused on their projects. Sevens see themselves as idealistic optimists, while Eights see themselves as hard-nosed realists. Compare Sevens Mike Myers and Goldie Hawn with Eights Danny DeVito and Roseanne Barr.

Sevens and Nines

Sevens and Nines might seem difficult to confuse because average Sevens are the hyperactive extroverts of the Enneagram, while average Nines are more easygoing and complacent, living at a much lower energy level than Sevens.

The main reason they may be confused is that both types can be extremely busy; both are usually rather ebullient and happy. Furthermore, the defense mechanisms of Sevens and Nines are similar: both have repressed the darker parts of their inner worlds — Nines to maintain their idealized identifications with others, Sevens to suppress potentially overwhelming pain and anxiety.

The points of similarity are reflected in their psychic structures — the fact that both are sensation types in the Jungian model, Sevens corresponding to the extroverted and Nines to the introverted sensation type (*PT*, 262–63, 345–46). While it is clear, even when maintaining a superficial acquaintance with Sevens, that they are highly extroverted and orient themselves to the world via sensation, what is unclear is that Nines are introverted. The nature of the sensation that they introvert on is yet more unclear. This is why the inner world of Nines is so obscure and difficult to describe (and why others have not understood this type's proper correlation to the Jungian category).

The Nine orients itself to the world by introverting on the "sensation" of possessing union with another — by introjecting another and then idealizing that introjection. Their sense of self comes from the emotion they feel when they sense their identification with another person, much as a pregnant woman introverts with thoughts of love for her unborn child. By talking to the child in her womb, she gains a sense of herself as a mother. In a similar way, Nines commune with their inner sensations (identifications), maintaining their sense of self by living through an identification with another person. Hence they correspond to the Jungian introverted sensation type.

This introversion accounts for the inner life of Nines, which is largely out of view, protected in the inner sanctum of their psyches so that it cannot be easily disturbed or changed. It is in their dealings with the outside world that Nines can resemble Sevens.

Average Sevens can become hyperactive, busy with too many things to complete many of them. They dabble around to amuse themselves and to stave off boredom and anxiety. Similarly, Nines are highly intolerant of anxiety, and they stay busy to avoid it, using errands and hobbies to occupy their minds in undemanding, nonthreatening ways. They want to avoid conflict or overexcitement; by contrast, Sevens love excitement. Sevens become demanding, excessive, and manic as they deteriorate, while Nines become more passive, indifferent, and unresponsive as they become more unhealthy. Sevens want to be stimulated, whereas Nines want to avoid anything that would overly stimulate, much less upset, them. The essential difference is that average Nines do not want to be emotionally involved in their activities (since these can threaten their identifications), whereas Sevens want to have an increasingly high emotional charge from their activities (since they have few subjective identifications).

Furthermore, Nines do not seek the same kind of happiness (euphoria and elation) that Sevens do. Instead, they wish to maintain a state of placid contentment, of being neither too excited nor in discomfort. Indeed, if they could, they would be completely free of excessive stimulation of any kind. The Nine's desire to avoid becoming deeply involved with anything lest it arouse too high a response is the polar opposite of what we find in the average Seven. As we have seen, like all opposites, these two types can nevertheless be alike in many ways. Consider the differences between John F. Kennedy (a Seven) and Ronald Reagan (a Nine) or between Bette Midler (a Seven) and Ingrid Bergman (a Nine) for further insight into these two types.

MISIDENTIFYING EIGHTS AND OTHER TYPES

Eights and Ones
See Ones and Eights.

Eights and Twos
See Twos and Eights.

Eights and Threes

See Threes and Eights.

Eights and Fours

See Fours and Eights.

Eights and Fives

See Fives and Eights.

Eights and Sixes

See Sixes and Eights.

Eights and Sevens

See Sevens and Eights.

Eights and Nines

Eights with a Nine-wing can sometimes be mistaken for Nines with an Eight-wing, although this is not a common mistype. Eights are openly assertive and don't mind debating to make their point. In fact, Eights often seek conflicts and debates, finding them energizing. Nines dislike contention of any kind and, if possible, they would rather agree with the other to keep the peace. As they deteriorate down the Levels, Eights become more angry, aggressive, and domineering; Nines become more passive, disengaged, and depressive. Compare the Nines Geena Davis and Walt Disney with the Eights Susan Sarandon and John Huston.

MISIDENTIFYING NINES AND OTHER TYPES

Nines and Twos

See Twos and Nines.

Nines and Threes

See Threes and Nines.

Nines and Fours
See Fours and Nines.

Nines and Fives
See Fives and Nines.

Nines and Sixes
See Sixes and Nines.

Nines and Sevens
See Sevens and Nines.

Nines and Eights
See Eights and Nines.

New Connections,
New Directions

CHAPTER 7

The Centers

〜

The Centers relate to the idea that there are three main components to human intelligence. *The intelligence of the body,* or the instincts, is traditionally located in the belly. *The intelligence of the heart* is associated with emotion and feelings. And *the intelligence of the head* encompasses the cognitive functions.

In *Personality Types* we discussed the basic functions of the three Centers (associated with the three Triads) and explained some of the Essential qualities connected with them. Several other systems from sacred tradition also describe "centers" in various ways (the *Chakra* system from India, for example), yet they all contain striking similarities. We have based our understanding of the Centers primarily on the work of Gurdjieff, who called the three Centers the Moving-Instinctive Center, the Emotional Center, and the Intellectual Center, corresponding to the Instinctive, Feeling, and Thinking Centers, respectively.

Experientially, the three Centers (or Triads) manifest differently from the ordinary ways we think about them. Few people think of themselves as "identified with their gut," for instance. In fact, most people have difficulty experiencing themselves "in their gut" at all. For most of us, caught in the world of our personality as we usually are, it is difficult to distinguish these components of ourselves. Nothing in our modern education has taught us how to do so.

Although it is convenient to look at the issues of each Center separately (as we did in *Personality Types*), in reality, all three operate simultaneously. Once any one of them is triggered, the various responses and defenses of the other two Centers work together to keep the ego in place. Any response from a Center will cause the other two to actuate as well.

The ego responds to stress and threats to itself by causing our bodies to become tense and constricted and by withdrawing our attention from a direct engagement with reality (activities of the Instinctive Triad). Tension and disengagement create an imaginary boundary within which we feel safer. However, having tensed the body into numbness and disengaged our attention from contact with reality, we have also lost connection with the ground of our Being, with our true nature.

We must then create a substitute for this authentic personhood, and so begin to absorb emotional patterns from others, as well as our own reactions to these patterns, to construct some kind of identity to replace the lost Self (activities of the Feeling Triad). Over time, we construct self-definitions, stories, likes and dislikes, personal associations, and interpretations of events to reinforce the patterns of feelings. Since this assumed identity is not the True Self, it is always at risk of being exposed as the artificial construct it is. Thus, we are obliged to function in our lives with a false self that must be defended from others, as well as a sense of inner emptiness and insubstantiality that we must continually guard against.

The only possible result of this arrangement can be deep anxiety and fear. To be able to function, therefore, we must develop some strategy for coping with life that will substitute for the more direct inner knowing that comes from our Essence (activities of the Thinking Triad). We are thus placed in the position of doing what we believe we must do without experiencing the support of our own authentic Being. Fears therefore arise both about our own inner deficiencies, and about threats in our environment that could at any time either unmask or destroy our assumed self.

Fear also causes us to erect more rigid boundaries, to further disengage from reality, and to tense the body even more (symbol-

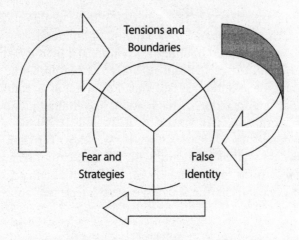

Tensions and
Boundaries

Fear and
Strategies

False
Identity

How the Centers Reinforce One Another

ized by a return in the cycle to the Instinctive Triad). Subsequently, there is even less sense of Being, and we have an even greater need to invest in our false self as well as in strategies to sustain this false self. This, of course, leads to yet more fears, and around and around the cycle goes.

As we can see, the structure of the ego is like a "cat's cradle," a pattern of related reactions and responses maintained by the mutual tension between these reactions. We can work on any one of these three primary issues — resistance and tension in the body, identification with a false self, or with fears and mental strategies to justify and defend our ego structures — and all of them will temporarily come to the foreground and be released. Thus, if we start exploring the artificiality of our identity, we will quickly come into contact with fear and problems with resistance. If we start exploring the tensions of the body, we will soon uncover the artificiality of our identity and our fear of letting go of it. And, if we work on fear directly, we will discover bodily tensions and resistance and the false identity that has been covering our fear.

We can therefore begin working with any one of these areas as a way of unlocking the mechanisms of our personality. When we do, we discover that the three Triads represent three qualities of Essential Being that the personality is attempting to imitate. Instead of tension and imaginary boundaries (symbolized by the Instinctive Triad), we find the reality and substance of our authentic Being: we are real, here, and present. Instead of an identity constructed from emotional reactions, imagination, and limited pictures and ideas about the self (symbolized by the Feeling Triad), we actually experience our True Identity directly. We know our uniqueness and value, as well as our unity with all of creation, and we feel the richness of the many qualities of our Essential nature. Instead of anxiety, mental chatter, and desperate strategies to "solve" life's

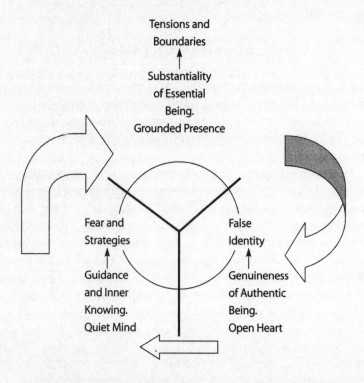

The Relation of Essential Qualities to Personality Qualities

problems (symbolized by the Thinking Triad), we discover a peaceful, spacious, quiet knowing. We function with a confidence and certitude that arise directly from the ground of our Being, rather than being led by reactions to circumstances, or by borrowed strategies.

In this arrangement, groundedness in our physicality supports the opening of the heart, which supports the quieting of the mind, which supports the groundedness in Being. Again, we speak of these things as if they were separate and sequential activities, but whether we are speaking about the Essential qualities, or the different components of the ego, we can see that they are really a unity: no one of them can function without the other two.

THE IMBALANCES OF THE THREE CENTERS

Gurdjieff asserted that the greater potentials inherent in all human beings, the aspects of higher consciousness, were manifestations of two additional Centers which he called the "higher emotional" and "higher intellectual" Centers. However, Gurdjieff said that we did not need to add or develop these two higher Centers. On the contrary, he taught that they were fully operational and ready to manifest through us. He claimed that the reason we seldom experience the action of these higher Centers was due to what he called the scrambling or misuse of the three "regular" or lower Centers. In other words, the lower Centers of thinking, feeling, and instinct are so distorted and off balance that the "signals" from the higher Centers cannot get through to us.

If we reflect on the themes of the Triads, we may sense the truth of Gurdjieff's assertion. For instance, we seldom hear our inner knowing or guidance because our minds are too noisy and cluttered with daydreams, anxieties, sexual fantasies, and imagined conversations. Similarly, we are seldom open to the tremendous power of love and compassion because our feelings are distorted into habitual reactions, desires, irritations, and either depression or narcissistic grandiosity. In these cases, the natural qualities of our souls cannot manifest because our inner space is filled up with something else.

Gurdjieff called this "something else" the formatory apparatus, a side effect of the scrambling of our three lower Centers. The three Centers are not naturally scrambled, but become so because we are educated by people who themselves had their Centers scrambled. According to Gurdjieff, few people in the modern world have their Centers working properly. For instance, we might tend to think with our feelings, to feel with our instincts, and to have little or no communication between our thinking and our instincts. Of course, other scrambled combinations are also possible.

Amazingly, *the formatory apparatus, the scrambling of Centers, is the basis of our personality. We are not identified with the proper functions of the Centers, but with the side effects of their misuse.* If our Centers were to return to their proper function, our personality, as we have known it, would cease to exist. We would still have a personality, but it would be quite different from our habitual experience of ourselves.

Gurdjieff explained our plight by describing the human being as a "house in disorder," like a mansion full of servants but without a master. In this house, the servants, lacking proper supervision, have begun to do what they want rather than the work they are suited for. The cook is driving the limousine, the driver is gardening, the gardener is cooking the meals, and the maid is doing the accounts. As a result, nothing is carried out as expected — no one is performing the tasks that he or she has been trained to perform — and the house is in a state of genteel inefficiency or even outright chaos. The master is unlikely to return home until the servants have put the place in order: for this to happen, the servants must return to their proper tasks, just as we must with the functions of our Centers.

From the perspective of Inner Work, our personality is a temporary patchwork designed to hold our Centers together until they can be brought into a more conscious and natural alignment.

Unfortunately, this state of affairs causes two problems. First, it maintains a distorted relationship between the Centers; and second, as long as it is in place, it is very difficult for the Centers to come together in another way. Essential awareness, which could truly restore the proper function of the Centers, cannot do its work because the personality is already usurping the job. Since the personality is largely an artificial construct that uses the energy of the Centers to sustain itself, it is both an expression of and a compensation for the imbalance of the Centers. And, to the degree that we are identified with the structures of our personality, we will be disconnected from many of the qualities that distinguish a conscious human being.

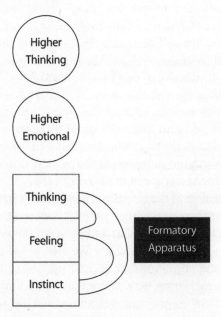

Gurdjieff's Diagram of the Scrambling of the Centers

Indeed, Gurdjieff taught a proposition that is extremely challenging: when we are in our ordinary ego consciousness, *we are not really in any of these Centers.* We are not really feeling, we are

not really thinking, we are not really in our bodies. We are somewhere else, in "formatory apparatus," a mode of consciousness
that is almost completely unrelated to what we are actually experiencing here and now. As we have begun to see, in ordinary awareness, we are caught in the compulsive and repetitive reactions of
our personality instead of being present to what is occurring in
and around us. This has many implications with regard to the
Triads.

Any single Center can be out of balance with one of the other
two Centers, or with itself. Simple permutations reveal that, since
there are three Centers, there are nine possible combinations or
ways of scrambling them. Thus, *the nine personality types of the
Enneagram are based on nine possible permutations of the imbalances of the three Centers of Thinking, Feeling, and Instinct.*

As shorthand, we will designate the function of thinking as "T,"
the function of feeling as "F," and the function of Instinct as "M,"
for "Moving-Instinctive Center." (We could use "I," but it is
harder to distinguish visually from "T.") If you refer to the diagram below, you will see each of the nine types accompanied by
the letters "T F M" and that each set of three letters is accompanied by several underlines, connecting lines, or boxes. These symbols are our shorthand to represent the particular imbalance of the
three Centers for each type in the average range.

In our discussion of the Levels of Development in Chapter 4, we
mentioned that there are "shock points" between the healthy and
average range (at Levels 3 and 4) and between the average and unhealthy ranges (at Levels 6 and 7). We also noted that it usually
requires extreme conditions or special intentions to cross these
thresholds in any lasting way. Obviously something significant is
occurring at these points, and we can understand this more fully
by looking at the imbalances of the Centers.

The "significant occurrence" is that, as we move down the
Levels, at each shock point *another Center becomes imbalanced
by the personality.* Thus, in the healthy range, only one Center is
being drawn on by the personality. However, between the healthy
and average ranges (Levels 3 and 4), a "shock point" is crossed,

and another Center is knocked off balance. In the average range, then, *two* Centers are being scrambled by the personality. The second shock occurs between Levels 6 and 7, marking the descent into the unhealthy range of the type, and here, *all three* Centers have become distorted. Outside intervention is required, in effect allowing the unhealthy person to use the outside agent (the therapist, spiritual teacher, etc.) as a stable Center with which to temporarily identify.

What is especially noteworthy is that in the unhealthy range,

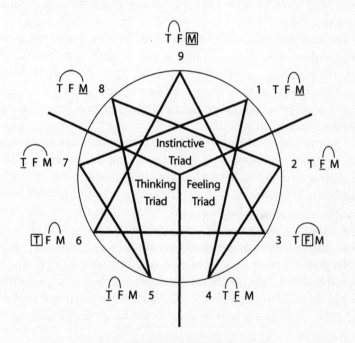

The Imbalances of the Centers

Key to Symbols:

— An underline indicates the Center the type primarily identifies with

☐ A box around a Center indicates that the Center is "segregated" or cut off from the other Centers

⌒ A curved line indicates a linkage or scrambling between two centers

the third Center also becomes a problem, whereas in the average to healthy range it has not been part of the picture. This raises an interesting point: we have found that *for people who are within the average range of their type,* it is very helpful to work first on the third Center, the Center that is not part of the knot of typical identifications.* Because we are mostly identified with the first Center and its interactions with the second if we are in the average range, the third Center is not a part of our ordinary self-image. We could describe it as virgin territory, unused psychic space, because it is a largely undeveloped part of ourselves that we have never really explored.

The primary types (Three, Six, and Nine) are somewhat unlike the other types because they require a different approach to growth than the secondary types (One, Two, Four, Five, Seven, and Eight). The primary types need to work directly on the Center that is most problematic for them, the Center in a "box" (see the illustration on page 255).

The expression of the problematic Center in the primary types is not necessarily suppressed, or even lacking or "broken"; rather, it is segregated, boxed off, or out of communication with the other functions. You could also think of it as being out of sync or out of step with the others. Because of this, over time the primary types may begin to neglect this Center, leading to its lack of development. In a certain way, we might say that the problematic Centers of the primary types need to be educated by experience. When this happens, the primary types start to learn that it is safe for them to use these functions. Specifically, Threes need to learn that they can feel their feelings without being rejected by others, Sixes need to

---

* We are encouraged to see that our colleagues, Hurley and Donson, who have done significant work on the Centers, have arrived at a similar conclusion. They emphasize the importance of developing the third Center, which they call the "Repressed Center." We agree that understanding the Third Center is extremely important for growth and for therapy. As we previously mentioned, our understanding of the Centers developed from our experience in the Gurdjieff work, and differs from theirs in several important ways. Those seeking another perspective on this subject are directed to their book, *What's My Type?*

learn that they can follow their own inner guidance without losing support from others, and Nines need to learn that they can assert themselves without losing their connection with others.

Therapeutic work for the primary types may be more difficult initially: these types are forced to directly confront their problems by working on the Center that is fundamentally imbalanced. Once the disconnected Center (the one in the box) is integrated to some degree, however, progress may be rapid. For this reason, we say that the developmental path of the primary types is revolutionary, while that of the secondary types is evolutionary. The process for the secondary types may begin more easily but then proceeds at a slower pace, in small steps, as the balance of the Centers is gradually restored.*

THE NINE TYPES AND THEIR IMBALANCES

We will now discuss the nine types, beginning with type Two in the Feeling Triad, to explain what our shorthand annotations mean in practice, and to comment briefly on some of the main practical and therapeutic implications of the particular imbalances of the Centers for each type. This information will be of interest not only to those engaged in transformational work but to therapists and counselors of all kinds: knowledge of the "imbalance of Centers" is the key to an awareness of personality structures and therapeutic strategies for unlocking them.

Personality Type Two: The Helper   T F̂ M

In the illustration on page 255, we see that there is an underline under the letter "F." The underlined term indicates that Twos identify mainly with their Feeling Center. However, as we have seen in our discussion of the Triads in Chapter 3, the true qualities of the Feeling Center are blocked when Twos are functioning in ego. Thus, Twos attempt to compensate for this blockage *by dem-*

---

* See *Personality Types* (revised edition, 1996), pp. 416–18.

onstrating their loving feelings through action — by doing things for people. In simple terms, Twos begin to "do their feelings" instead of "feel their feelings." We can see the reason for this in the line between the F and the M: in the average range, the Feeling Center of the Two, "F," is interfering with the function of the Moving-Instinctual Center, "M."

The emotional energy in Twos mixes with that of the instincts, making it difficult for Twos to separate these two functions. We could even say that their emotionality interferes with their instinctual responses. As a result, the instincts of Twos (their sense of strength and self-preservation, their ability to feel their own substantiality), are overwhelmed by their feelings, and by their identifications with and reactions to other people. Twos are trying to develop a sense of Being (which comes from the instinctive function) through their feelings for other people. As Twos become more identified with this pattern, they focus entirely on their feelings for others and stop taking care of themselves. Twos also confuse emotional and instinctual responses to others. They are unable to simply "feel their feelings" without needing to act on those feelings — feeding people as a sign of love, for example. The Instinctive Center also governs our habits, and in combination with the Feeling Center can lead to compulsive talking about their feeling reactions, including gossiping, complaining, and florid reactions. This might lead people to conclude that Twos are more feeling than other types. This is not necessarily true; Twos only *appear* more feeling because they are constantly compelled to demonstrate their feelings through action due to the increasing scrambling of these two Centers. Their feelings are simply more visible to others.

As Twos go down the Levels, this imbalance intensifies, eventually causing their third Center, the Thinking Center, to become caught in the Feeling-Instinctual "knot." In the unhealthy range, Twos' thinking can become highly distorted by the scrambling of emotional needs and instincts, leading to denial, rationalization, and obsessive thoughts. Simultaneously, the Moving-Instinctual Center, their physical apparatus, can become broken down by the constant strain of their imbalanced feelings. They can literally damage their health over emotional issues. As we have seen, unhealthy Twos often abuse food or medications, taking out their emotional imbalances on their bodies.

By contrast, average Twos can reverse this process and begin to loosen up their identifications with their personalities by developing their Thinking Centers. Many Twos report that their emotions affect them so much that they have difficulty finding inner quiet or getting perspective on what to do; they tell us that it is difficult for them to see the big picture or to connect ideas easily. Twos also frequently report that they are often uncomfortable with linear, verbal forms of communication. All of these self-disclosures confirm the idea that Twos are least engaged with their Thinking Center.

It is important to remember, however, that a Two's lack of identification with the Thinking Center has nothing to do with his or her intelligence. Twos could be geniuses in terms of their mental capacities but they tend not to rely on their intellectual gifts as much because they are so identified with their Feeling and Instinctive Centers. It is necessary to have a correct understanding of what the Thinking Center is: the real, Essential quality of the Thinking Center is concerned with developing the inner guidance of quiet mind — not with reading more books, attending graduate school, or becoming a scholar.

Ultimately, Twos develop their healthiest qualities by learning to discriminate their emotional reactions from their basic instinctual responses and needs. To disentangle their emotions from their doing, they must become more conscious of their genuine feelings and motivations — particularly when these feelings are not positive. As Twos are able to sit with their emotions without instantly acting on them, their Feeling Center begins to come into balance as repressed hurts rise to the surface and are healed. It is then no longer necessary for Twos to cover over the blockages to their hearts by being compulsively loving and other-oriented. The Essential qualities of the heart begin to manifest in a balanced and compassionate way that allows Twos to *freely* care for themselves and others.

Personality Type Three: The Motivator

In personality type Three, a primary type, the scenario is a bit different than in types Two and Four, which are secondary types. Each of the primary types is at the Center of its Triad, meaning that it has the most difficulty with the function of that Triad (or that it is most out of touch or most blocked in the expression of the Essential qualities of that function). In the case of Threes, the problem is with the Feeling Center. Threes do have feelings, of course, but their feelings are not properly linked with the other two functions of Thinking and Instinct. (The box around the letter "F" represents this.) It is as if there were a breakdown of communication between the Feeling Center and the other two Centers. As the type in the Center of the Triad, Threes have the most acute problems experiencing the Essential qualities of the heart. Thus, their personalities are highly driven to compensate for the loss of Essential value and identity, among other qualities that come from the heart. Unlike Twos and Fours, Threes remain largely estranged from their Feeling Center, and turn to their Thinking and Moving-Instinctive Centers to come up with ways to give them a sense of value and identity.

As a result, the personality of type Three ends up divided into two modes of operation, feeling or functioning. Most of the time, Threes operate in their "functioning mode" — that is, in some combination of thinking and instinct. When they are in this state, their motto might be "I function, therefore I am." They are competent, capable, and clear-headed, lending average Threes their aura of cool professionalism. However, there are occasions on which they switch to their emotional side and feel things deeply. When they are in "feeling mode," though, average Threes cannot function very effectively: they can only feel.

Many Threes have reported that, even when they are in the average Levels, they cannot function and feel at the same time. They believe that if they feel, then they will not be able to function, and if they function they cannot afford to feel. This state of affairs is often reinforced by the fact that many people, including their parents, have rewarded Threes for their ability to set their feelings aside and perform well.

As demands to perform well increase, average Threes will try to avoid the feeling mode and switch back to the functioning mode as quickly as possible. The further down the Levels they are, the more identified they become with functioning well, and the more threatened and overwhelmed they will be by moments in which their feelings break through. Therefore, they will try to stay out of their feelings as much as possible. The greater the division between their feelings and functioning, the more their feelings become unconscious and the more these unconscious feelings direct their behavior — they will act out compulsively, eventually ruining their ability to function as well.

As Threes become less healthy, the wall between their feeling and functioning modes becomes more and more impenetrable. When this occurs, people and events can affect Threes emotionally, but because their feelings are completely repressed they are not processed. Over time, feelings of jealousy, rage, hostility, and depression begin to accumulate, eventually interfering with their ability to function. This will often cause Threes to become even more frightened of their feelings, leading to further avoidance of them.

If this separation goes on too long, the weight of unprocessed feelings will begin to bring down the functioning of the other two Centers, in one order or the other. When the Thinking Center is imbalanced, unhealthy Threes develop obsessive thinking patterns, particularly about the achievements, possessions, or people that they believe are responsible for their emotional problems. As the Moving Center goes down, unhealthy Threes may exhibit substance abuse, self-neglect, and a paralysis of their ability to engage in effective action.

In developing themselves, healthy Threes do not need to focus on identifying more or less with a particular function (like Twos and Fours), but on integrating their feelings with their other functions — allowing their genuine feelings and bringing them fully into conscious awareness. Healthy Threes need to own their feelings and make sure to acknowledge their real emotional states in any activities that they are engaged in, even if this makes them less effective or less approved of by others in the short run. As they do this, Threes are less and less led by unconscious emotional reactions, and the deeper, Essential qualities of the heart emerge and flower.

Personality Type Four: The Individualist   T E M

Type Four is also identified with the Feeling Center, as indicated by the underlined "F" above. Fours, like Twos, are preoccupied with questions of identity and value, but they resolve the blockage of the Feeling Center in a different way. Twos tend to "cover over" their awareness of feelings of deficiency in the Feeling Center by engaging in activity. Fours, however, attempt to resolve this issue *by thinking about their identity and value.* Even healthy Fours are identified with their feelings and reactions, but their orientation leaves them with a lingering awareness of the blockage in the Feeling Center. They know that something is missing, not flowing.

As we know from the type Four chapter, average Fours use their imaginations to intensify their feeling states, and now we may have more insight into why this is so. Because Fours have built their identities around their emotions, experiencing any deficit of feeling is highly threatening. They must therefore continually use their Thinking Center to artificially stimulate their Feeling Center. In practical terms, this helps explain the Four's penchant for romanticism, eroticism, baroque fantasy, and stormy relationships. Thus, average Fours cultivate a rich fantasy life to maintain and bolster their moods and emotional states, even negative ones. In other words, average Fours get into a certain mood and then think about things to keep them in that mood. Because an underlying awareness of the deficit of the real qualities of the heart is never completely repressed, Fours have great difficulty letting go of any moods, even bad ones, that serve to cover the perceived hole in their feelings.

In Fours who have fallen into the unhealthy range, the blocked Feeling Center mixes not only with their Thinking Center, but also with their Moving-Instinctive Center. Unhealthy Fours may begin to abuse substances or to indulge themselves in whatever ways they think will satisfy their emotional cravings. The Moving-Instinctive Center is co-opted by the distorted emotions into decadent and self-destructive activities that are harmful to their health, well-being, and ability to function. In the worst-case scenarios, unhealthy Fours commit suicide, thus overriding their basic life instinct by the now-compulsive and desperate nature of the emotions.

At the opposite end of the spectrum, healthy Fours are identified with their feelings, but they do not whip them up by means of the wrong use of their Thinking Center. Nonetheless, Fours still sense that something is missing in them, and this often becomes a source of their creativity. However, when healthy Fours stay with the feeling that something is missing in them, the hole in their hearts starts to fill up from within, giving Fours a permanent foundation for a true sense of their value and identity.

Personality Type Five: The Investigator $\overset{\frown}{\underline{\text{T}}}$ F M

Type Five identifies primarily with the Thinking Center, represented by the line under the "T." In the average range, however, Thinking begins to mix with the Feeling Center, and later, in the unhealthy range, it also imbalances the Moving-Instinctive Center.

Even healthy Fives are identified with the mind ("I think, therefore I am"), and begin to identify with their thoughts instead of with the source and background of their thought processes. Their sense of themselves is connected with maintaining a certain mental intensity and with having insights into the nature of things. But Fives can become compulsive about their thinking as a way of compensating for the blockage of the essential qualities of the Thinking Center — especially of inner guidance and quiet mind.

As Fives move into the average Levels, thinking begins to scramble with feelings. Feelings add an emotional charge to Fives' thoughts, making their thoughts feel more alive and real. Identification with ideas, fantasies, and other mental activity becomes more intense and consuming. Thus, average Fives start to live in a reality of their own creation — which is more real to them than their actual lives. As one Five remarked, "I don't need to have a relationship. I can already map the whole thing out in my head. I know what is going to happen." This also leads to the fascination with games, computers, and the alternate realities and mental models that we have described in the type chapter on the Five.

At the same time, the emotional energy becomes so caught up in intensifying a Five's mental activity that it becomes unavailable for its own natural functions. In other words, feeling is not available for feelings. If this trend continues, average Fives become more estranged from their sense of identity and value, and increasingly unable to connect emotionally with others. Deeply identified Fives may not even recognize the need for these things.

In the unhealthy range, the emotionally charged thinking intensifies even further and the Moving-Instinctive Center also becomes imbalanced. The Fives' intense inner world has become so much the dominant reality that they lose awareness of even their basic physical needs: their eating is irregular and unhealthful, their sleep patterns are disturbed, and their hygiene and level of basic comforts are highly limited or virtually nonexistent. They become extremely isolated, eccentric, unkempt, and cut off from human contact, ultimately losing the ability to take care of themselves. Extremely unhealthy Fives are also prone to suicide, which is a complete negation of the life instinct, a total overriding of this Center by the deranged mind.

In the opposite direction, Fives develop by learning to discriminate thoughts from feelings — both by recognizing their feelings as they occur, and by learning to observe their thoughts rather than identifying with them. They are able to do this by learning to include their Moving-Instinctive Center, that is, by becoming more grounded in their bodies and in physical reality. As they become more present and less identified with their thoughts, Fives begin to notice that pure awareness — the quiet mind — can take in their thoughts as well as their feelings, instincts, and all aspects of their inner and outer environment. Gradually, their identification shifts from an attachment to their ideas and thinking processes to the more spacious quality of the quiet mind.

Personality Type Six: The Loyalist $\boxed{T}$ F M

The Six has a pattern parallel to that of the Three, another primary type. In this case, it is thinking rather than feeling that is disconnected from the other two functions (represented by the "T" in a box). As the type in the center of the Triad, Sixes have the most difficulty connecting with the quiet mind or trusting their own inner guidance, their own inner knowing. As a result, just as Threes look outside themselves to establish their identity and sense of worth, Sixes look outside themselves for guidance and support.

Sixes, like Threes, also have two modes of functioning: one is the thinking mode, the other is the "duty mode." When Sixes are in duty mode — when they are driven by some combination of their Feeling and Moving-Instinctive Centers — they resemble Ones and Twos. They are active, service-oriented, committed, and highly responsible to what they feel they *must* do. This mode also causes them to have frequent and powerful emotional reactions that are often acted on. These reactions take place because, while Sixes are in duty mode, their Thinking Center is not engaged in a way that would give them perspective, discernment, and objectivity about what they are experiencing.

By contrast, when they are in thinking mode, Sixes may entertain many different thoughts and ideas, but they seem to be unable to integrate them into the rest of their lives or evaluate them in a balanced way. This is because their thinking is not grounded in the rest of their experience, in their feelings and in their bodies. The anxiety created by this situation causes Sixes to distrust their own thinking processes and to look to other sources outside themselves for guidance.

In evaluating these external sources of guidance, Sixes tend to rely on their emotional reactions and intuitions. We might say that Sixes need to like the messenger in order to fully hear the message. Of course, when Sixes do buy into some system of thought that substitutes for their own internal guidance, it may make their lives easier for a while, but it delays the development of their own ability to know and to feel their own Essential guidance and support.

The feeling quality of Sixes is expressed in their devotion, dedication, and commitment to others whom they trust, much like the Marine who jumps on a hand grenade to save his buddies. Thus, average Sixes are not just "doers" but "doer-feelers." This can result in personal warmth, responsibility, and commitment, but, in the unhealthy range, it can also result in irrational devotion to causes and people — or just the opposite, an irrational prejudice against groups or individuals.

As Sixes move down the Levels, the division between their thinking and their feeling and doing widens; the result is that less healthy Sixes are more desperate for all-encompassing systems of guidance and support. At the same time, because their own thinking is even less connected with their feelings and instincts, it becomes more and more distorted and unrelated to reality. The intense energy of their distorted thinking begins to agitate and poison their feelings and instincts. The results are delusions, paranoia, and burning hatreds born out of irrational fears. When distorted thinking patterns affect their instincts, unhealthy Sixes are likely to act on their delusional ideas. In extreme cases, very unhealthy Sixes may resort to violence, but the violence is not necessarily personal, since it is based on distorted thinking rather than wounded feelings. Such acts can occur for political, ideological, or socioeconomic reasons, or simply to make a point.

In developing themselves, healthy Sixes do not need to focus on identifying more or less with a particular function (like Fives and Sevens), but on integrating their thinking with the other two Centers. Sixes must learn to stay present to their thoughts long enough for them to slow down and allow the "quiet mind" to emerge. This often entails increased anxiety, as it is difficult for Sixes to trust anything other than the thoughts and beliefs they have identified with. But if they fully enter their own inner silence, Sixes discover in themselves the Essential support and guidance they have been seeking.

Personality Type Seven: The Enthusiast   I̲ F M

Personality type Seven is also identified with thinking, as represented by the underlined "T" in the diagram above. Like Fives and Sixes, Sevens are also blocked in the Essential functioning of the Thinking Center: that is, Sevens are notably blocked in "the quiet mind," the ability to stay mentally silent so that real perceptions and inner guidance can arise. To compensate for this blockage, they use their Moving-Instinctive Center to stimulate and intensify their thinking. ("Uh-oh! My mind is starting to quiet down. Let me *do* something right away!")

Although from the outside it may appear that Sevens are identified with doing because they are so active, they are in fact more identified with their thoughts than with what they are doing. Evidence for this can be seen in the fact that although Sevens can be extremely active, they are often thinking about something else while doing whatever they are doing. In average Sevens, their attention is seldom on their current activity; rather, it is focused on what they are anticipating. Left unchecked, this can lead to the scattered quality Sevens often get caught up in.

Of course, if average Sevens are using their doing to stimulate their thinking, they are not able to be satisfied or fully connected with what they are doing *or* to have much space or focus for their thinking. Because of the blockage of real thinking, average Sevens have difficulty taking in impressions adequately. This is one of the main reasons why Sevens seek particular environments and experiences that are stimulating enough to affect them. But rather than wait for the quieter, deeper aspects of mind to arise, they become anxious and engage in activities to intensify any experiences they are having — to stimulate their thoughts through their instincts.

In Sevens, Feeling is the third Center, the open territory: it is the part of themselves that their ego uses the least. This is not to say, of course, that Sevens cannot feel, but that their attention is more occupied by their thinking or doing than by being touched deeply in their hearts — the real meaning of this Center. In the average range, Sevens have feelings, and can be touched, but they tend not to stay with their feelings. They want to be "happy" as soon as possible. Sevens also mistake stimulation and excitement (instinctive qualities) or even hysteria (a fear reaction) for feeling. They begin to associate high levels of stimulation with happiness and well-being. As we have stated in our discussion of the Feeling Triad, the real function of the heart has little to do with our conventional ideas about feeling. In any case, average Sevens are so identified with their thoughts and activities that it often does not occur to them to explore the inner qualities of the heart.

In unhealthy Sevens, however, anxieties have led them to tax their Thinking Center and Moving-Instinctual Center to the limit. To further stimulate thinking, the Feeling Center is also drafted. Unhealthy Sevens can experience major mood swings and rapid alterations of affect. At this stage, hysterical reactions and panic attacks begin to occur. The Feeling Center is driven into the same kind of hyperactivity as is already occurring in the thinking and doing parts of the Seven.

By contrast, to develop themselves, Sevens need to disengage their instincts from their thinking, thus allowing their thoughts to slow down. This inevitably causes anxiety because Sevens are identified with thinking; the quieting of their thoughts feels as if they are disappearing, as if life is draining out of them. If Sevens stay with the process, however, eventually the quiet mind emerges and the need to escape into thoughts and activities disappears. Sevens then become fully open to the magnificence of reality and realize that they have found the fulfillment that they have been seeking.

Personality Type Eight: The Challenger   T F M̲

Type Eight is identified primarily with the Moving-Instinctive Center, represented by the underlined "M." Eights are strongly connected with their physical energy, with their vitality, and with the immediacy of their experiences and reactions: they have an impulse and go with it. Healthy Eights have abundant instinctual energy and powerful drives. They are strongly identified with their body, and want to protect it and do things with it. The instinctual energy is always pushing them into action and makes it difficult for them not to assert themselves.

However, in average Eights, this instinctual energy starts to scramble with their Thinking Center (symbolized by the line between the "M" and the "T"). The combination produces a "shrewd" character that is neither fully spontaneous (Instinctive) nor truly objective (Thinking). Eights constantly strategize their situation, thinking constantly about their instinctual needs: safety, security, money, sex, food, and so forth. Thus, their Thinking Center is no longer free and open to explore reality or to receive inner guidance, nor is their instinctual nature free to respond to the realities of the situation — and for all their calculations, average Eights can make unwise choices for themselves.

In average Eights, the instinctual energy can come across to others as a passionate gusto for life, or as a need to willfully assert themselves. In unhealthy Eights, however, the ego is so identified with the instinctual energy that the Feeling Center is imbalanced along with the Thinking Center. At this stage, their passionate qualities disappear and deteriorate into a hard-hearted quest for control and survival. They stop caring about other people and become calloused even to their own emotional needs. Once imbalanced, their feelings can become dark and vengeful. Their raw instincts, distorted thinking, and wounded feelings may lead them into a raging combat against life. The results can be destructive for all persons involved, as we have seen in the type chapter.

By contrast, this pattern would suggest that Eights would benefit directly from working with their feelings. In the average range, the Eight's feelings are available, although largely untapped. By focusing their awareness on this Center, Eights gain more balance. Thus, many Eights find great healing and satisfaction in doing volunteer work, and by helping the weak and disfranchised. Despite whatever unjust and terrible things may have happened to them, Eights find freedom from their rage and grief by using their instinctual capacities to uplift others who may also have been victims of injustice or abuse.

Eights can also develop themselves by learning to discern their thoughts from their instinctive impulses. As they do so, they begin to discover more inner space: they are still action-oriented, but they find an inner steadiness and peace from which their actions can arise. Further, as their Thinking Center is freed from the dominance of the Instinctive Center, Eights are able to contact their own clarity and inner guidance. These developments at last provide Eights with the sense of Being, strength, and wholeness that they have been seeking.

Personality Type Nine: The Peacemaker   T F M

Nines are the primary type in the Instinctive Triad, and thus have a disconnection between their Moving-Instinctive Center (represented by the letter "M" in the box) and their other two Centers. Like Threes and Sixes, Nines have two modes of functioning that are disconnected from each other in varying degrees. Nines function in either "instinct mode" or in some combination of thinking and feeling that we call "daydream mode."

When they are in their instinct mode, Nines are usually at rest or engaged in activities that do not require the active participation of their thinking and feeling: they follow a routine and their bodies simply perform. Nines report that when they are functioning this way, they are comfortably engaged in their activity or in the sensations of the moment, but they are not thinking or feeling about anything in particular. The body is relaxing, doing what needs to be done, without being inhabited by other parts of the personality. In daydream mode, without a vital connection to their instinctive energy, all experiences are reduced to the same level of stimulation and meaning. Nines can see all possibilities and perspectives while not feeling the weight of their own Being and desires behind any of them. Everything is possible, but nothing is urgent. Nines may have a variety of projects that they have developed to some degree, but they have never generated the inner force necessary to bring them out to the world because they are out of touch with their instinctive energy.

When they are in daydream mode, Nines can be full of thoughts and feelings, philosophical musing, active plans, and fantasies. They can also be quite creative but have trouble advancing or sustaining efforts on their own behalf because they are dissociated from their instinctual energies. While in daydream mode, they do not identify with themselves. Being more grounded in their bodies would make Nines' experiences and accomplishments more real for them, and therefore more fulfilling. Like the two other primary types, they are either in one mode or the other: either comfortable and grounded, but uninterested, or creative and insightful, but disengaged from action.

Just as Threes try to find their value and identity by looking to others, and Sixes seek guidance and support from others, Nines seek grounding and vitality from their interactions and identifications with others. In lieu of carving out a life for themselves, many Nines convince themselves that what they want is to be part of someone else's life. This raises a fundamental contradiction: Nines want to merge with others to incorporate their Being and vitality, but at the same time, their ego structure is set up to maintain their autonomy. Thus, average Nines merge with the other in their imaginations, while possibly neglecting the real relationship and their real connection with the other. On an unconscious level, Nines may not even like the person they wish to merge with, but they are attracted to the other person's strength, vitality, and physical energy — and they may stay in harmful or difficult relationships in order to maintain the connection with that energy.

As with the other primary types, Three and Six, Nines feel threatened when the energies of their Center, in this case instinctual energies, arise. The sense of vague dreaminess and disengagement, which is their usual state of consciousness, suddenly becomes intense and electrified, shattering their peace of mind. As soon as possible, in various ways average Nines will quiet their instinctual upwellings and return to the safety and neutrality of their disengagement. As this state of affairs continues, Nines become increasingly numb, fatigued, and apathetic. Disconnected from the visceral impact of their experiences, less healthy Nines glide through their lives as little more than silent spectators.

In the opposite direction, in order for Nines to discover what they really want from life and to take the steps to actualize those desires, they must break down the barrier between their Moving-Instinctive Center and their Thinking and Feeling Centers. They must realize that they are allowed to claim their own strength. Gradually Nines allow their powerful instinctive energies, especially their anger, to come into consciousness where these energies are transmuted by awareness into the Essential power and stability they have been seeking.

Personality Type One: The Reformer   T F M̂

The ego of type One is primarily identified with a blockage or constriction of their Moving-Instinctive Center, as represented by the underlined "M." Ones consequently are out of touch with their instinctual energy and have trouble feeling their own Being, with its rightful weight and sense of strength. To compensate for this, they draw on emotional energy to stimulate them into action. Anger results from this scrambling of emotional and instinctual energy — nothing gets us motivated like anger. ("Children are starving, and we're not doing anything about it!" "This room is such a mess that I can't stand it anymore! I've got to clean it up.") Of course, all people use their emotions to motivate themselves on occasion, but this is the area in which the average One is most fixated.

But this pattern leaves average Ones far from relaxed, causing them to lose more contact with the flow, presence, solidity, and connectedness that come from the Instinctive Center. Once Ones have become identified with this pattern, they need to stay angry and irritated with themselves and with others to compensate for their felt lack of substantiality. As a result, average Ones cannot act without the interference of subconscious emotional reactions and cannot feel their feelings without acting on them. Despite seeing themselves as rational, they are driven by strong emotional subtexts. Ones need to care passionately about what they do, and they can be exuberant in regard to their positions and projects.

Ones are often characterized as rational thinkers. However,

when we investigate the true function of the Thinking Center — the quiet and open mind — we see that this is not a trait of most Ones. Of course, this has nothing to do with their thinking ability or intelligence; they can be brilliant and capable of pondering profound topics. But the Thinking Center is not part of the primary knot of identifications on which their ego structure is based.

Instead, Ones are *doers* who like practical ideas. They do not spend much time in the pursuit of open-ended inquiry or in the pursuit of knowledge that does not have a practical result. Moreover, Ones, like Nines, may have a comprehensive philosophy of life, but its purpose is to defend and support their actions, not to open them to new possibilities, let alone to the quiet mind. Principles, strong convictions, and rules about life are, in fact, expressions of the Instinctive Center. If we observe ourselves, we will see that strong opinions arise from our "gut." ("Save the whales!" "Business before pleasure!") Of course, ideas may support these views, but their source is not in the Thinking Center.

In unhealthy Ones, the thinking is also taken over by the scrambling of instincts and feelings, leading to irrational and obsessive ideas and inflexible opinions. While average Ones feel guilty when they violate their principles, even in minor ways, unhealthy Ones are able to deceive themselves by rationalizing various compulsive and contradictory behaviors. Their reasoning becomes convoluted in order to justify behavior that they would readily condemn in others.

On the other hand, it is helpful for Ones to focus on the third Center, thinking, by learning to quiet the mind. This allows them to see the relative nature of their own opinions and convictions. There may be much truth in their ideas and proposals, but their approach to that truth is not the only one or necessarily the best one. This helps them find better, more flexible means of communicating the truths that they have perceived. By quieting the mind, Ones dispel their inner judgment and criticism so that they have a more direct relationship with themselves and their environment, enhancing their ability to discern appropriate courses of action.

Ones can also be helped by learning to discern their emotional

The Imbalances of Centers at a Glance

Type	Segregates but is unconsciously motivated by the	Relies on a mix of two other Centers	Divides self into two different modes
Three	Feeling Center	Thinking and Instinctive Centers	Functioning mode and feeling mode
Six	Thinking Center	Feeling and Instinctive Centers	Thinking mode and duty mode
Nine	Instinctive Center	Thinking and Feeling Centers	Sensing mode and daydream mode

The Imbalances of Centers at a Glance

Type	Identifies primarily with the	In the average range, this Center "scrambles" with the	In the unhealthy range, this pattern imbalances the
Two	Feeling Center	Instinctive Center	Thinking Center
Four	Feeling Center	Thinking Center	Instinctive Center
Five	Thinking Center	Feeling Center	Instinctive Center
Seven	Thinking Center	Instinctive Center	Feeling Center
Eight	Instinctive Center	Thinking Center	Feeling Center
One	Instinctive Center	Feeling Center	Thinking Center

responses from their instinctual impulses. They do not try to get a substitute sense of Being from their passions or convictions, and they learn to stay with the sense of deficiency in their Moving-Instinctive Center. As they do so, they come in contact with the Essential solidity, steadiness, and autonomy of the Instinctive Center. Their actions become more conscious and directed without being tense. At the same time, as their Feeling Center is freed from its "knot" with the Instinctive Center, deep experiences of Essential value and connectedness arise. Ones no longer feel that they must strive after perfection to "earn" their existence. They feel profound compassion for others as well as for themselves.

The table above may make the relationships between the Centers more clear.

THE DEEPER MEANING OF THE PATTERNS

If we study the illustration of the Imbalance of Centers in this chapter more closely, we will be able to uncover a number of interesting patterns that have important practical implications.

First, if we take the model of the Hornevian Groups (see *PT*, 433–36), we will see that what distinguishes each Hornevian Group is that each group has the third Center in common. Specifically, the *Withdrawn Types* (Four, Five, and Nine) have the Instinctive Center as the third or undeveloped Center, while their Thinking and Feeling Centers are knotted together in the average range. Because the withdrawn types are not identified with their bodies and their instincts, it comes as a surprise to these types that a real sense of interiority (as opposed to an imaginary one) can only be experienced through the sensations of the body. Each of these three types mistakes for real depth the fantasies, thoughts, and moods that are the result of the mixing and imbalancing of the Thinking and Feeling Centers.

The *Compliant Types* (One, Two, and Six) have the Thinking Center as the third or undeveloped Center. In the average range, their egos are identified with some connection between their Instinctive Center and their Feeling Center. All of these types lack the openness of perception and genuine inner guidance that can only come from a quiet and receptive mind. They substitute beliefs, systems, rules, and algorithms for the fluidity and boundlessness of real thinking and inner guidance. These types also have the most difficulty with ambiguity and uncertainty in various areas of their lives. They would like certitude and have a strong desire to know where they stand with people and with abstract systems and values.

The *Assertive Types* (Three, Seven, and Eight) all have the Feeling Center as the third or undeveloped Center. In the average range, these types are identified with a connection between their Thinking and Instinctive Centers. The real function of the Feeling Center, of the heart, is to give us the ability to be touched and affected by our experiences. It also provides the source of our value and identity by giving us a sense of genuine connection with ourselves and others. The Assertive Types compensate for their lack of identification with this Center by using intense activity to get some sense of stimulation. Intense interaction replaces being really open to and affected by experience. Further, ego inflation through accomplishment, winning, and status replaces the authentic value and identity that the heart alone can give.

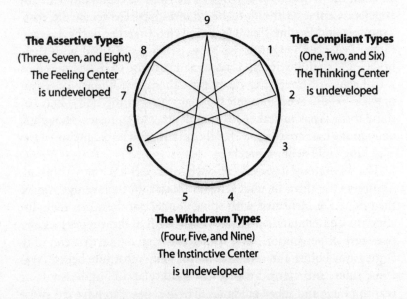

The Hornevians Reveal the Undeveloped Center

Therapeutic Strategies and the Centers

It is extremely important as part of our "general maintenance" and growth to fortify our third Center by using it properly. Working on the third Center gives us greater stability so that when we do engage on a deeper level of Work, there is something else present that is not part of the two-Center "knot" of identifications that we are taking to be ourselves. This also explains why it is so much easier for people functioning in the average range to work on themselves than it is for unhealthy people. When a person becomes unhealthy, all three Centers are imbalanced and brought into the formatory defensive structure. To meddle with any of them threatens the entire ego defensive system. A helpful therapeutic strategy for an unhealthy person must therefore provide support to all three Centers, although even in extreme cases, without proper attention to the third Center, there is little opportunity to make an opening in the person's defenses. The person will lack the perspective that would enable him or her to work on the entanglement of the other two Centers.

For most people who are functioning in the average range, working on the third Center will rapidly bring objectivity and balance into the personality. Real, lasting breakthroughs, however, will not occur until we can also focus on the second Center. If a person continues working only on the third Center without addressing the scrambling of the other two, they may become more stable, but they will generally be unable to sustain further development toward Essential realization.

The daily background practice is based on developing the third Center and is given by their Hornevian Group, as we have just seen. Thus, *Withdrawns* (Fours, Fives, and Nines) need to engage the body, *Compliants* (Ones, Twos, and Sixes) need to work with the quiet mind, and *Assertives* (Threes, Sevens, and Eights) need to open the heart.

Along with this background practice, a secondary focal point is needed to unscramble the personality knot, given by the Harmonic Group. The *Competency Group* (Ones, Threes, and Fives) secondarily need to work on opening up their feelings. The catalyst for their growth will be practices that allow them to experience moments of grief and the release of blocked feelings. For the *Reactive Group* (Fours, Sixes, and Eights), the secondary practice will involve quieting the mind and reframing their thinking and perceptions. The catalyst for their growth will be practices that allow them to see the distortions in their perceptions and interpretations of reality. For the *Positive Outlook Group* (Twos, Sevens, and Nines) the secondary therapeutic strategy will be aimed at grounding the person in their physical body and allowing whatever energy is locked there to flow. The catalyst for their growth will be practices that allow them to release the fears and emotional blockages trapped in their bodies through a direct experience of their bodily sensations. The attentive reader may notice, however, that for the Primary types (Three, Six, and Nine) the background practice and secondary focus will be on the same Center. As we have seen, their inner work involves opening and reintegrating their segregated Center with the other two.

The practices and therapeutic strategies for people functioning in the average range of each type are given in the following chart. Please note that for a person in the unhealthy range, the suggestions will be less helpful, and it will be necessary to turn to a therapist or some other sort of "surrogate" Center for the proper support.

Although a wide variety of therapeutic strategies are suggested by the imbalance of Centers, it is awareness alone that has the power to activate and harmonize them. The degree to which we are not present is the degree to which we are caught in the particular knot of our personality type. When our awareness is sufficiently developed and expanded to include all three functions together, something miraculous happens: we discover that our true identity lies beyond the realm of any of these Centers. Because our lower Centers have become unscrambled and come into balance, our Higher Intellectual and Emotional Centers are able to break through and transform our awareness. We find our true identity;

Practices and Therapeutic Strategies for the Types

Type	Regular practice should focus on	Pursue a therapeutic strategy that
One	Cultivating quiet mind	Allows grieving and processing of feelings, especially frustration and resentment
Two	Cultivating quiet mind	Releases blocked energy in the body, especially repressed need and hostility
Three	Opening the heart	Allows grieving and processing of feelings, especially of inadequacy and shame
Four	Grounding in the body	Reframes distorted thinking patterns and perceptions, especially negative interpretations of self and others
Five	Grounding in the body	Allows grieving and processing of feelings, especially of rejection and futility
Six	Cultivating quiet mind	Reframes distorted thinking patterns and perceptions, especially those caused by anxiety and projection
Seven	Opening the heart	Releases blocked energy in the body, especially repressed sadness and regret
Eight	Opening the heart	Reframes distorted thinking patterns and perceptions, especially denial of fear and vulnerability
Nine	Grounding in the body	Releases blocked energy in the body, especially repressed rage and fear

we have value and guidance, and we feel grounded in ourselves and in the very heart of Being. We find that what we truly are is something precious, beautiful, and mysterious beyond anything we could have imagined.

Perhaps we can understand from this discussion that our mental and emotional health and, ultimately, our degree of self-realization, depend on the unscrambling and alignment of our three Centers. We may also see that when we are in the full sway of our personality, we are identified with only one Center, and a scrambled Center at that. When we are able to function with two Centers, we begin to have some perspective and objectivity about our situation. But only when we have engaged all three Centers are we truly objective, truly in contact with reality. Further, if we have our three Centers aligned, we can be acted on by our Higher Centers

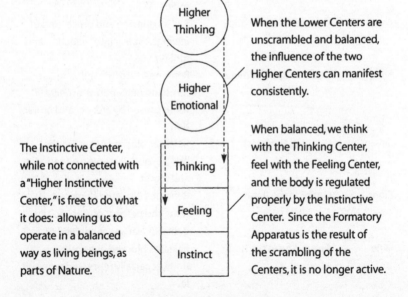

When the Lower Centers are unscrambled and balanced, the influence of the two Higher Centers can manifest consistently.

The Instinctive Center, while not connected with a "Higher Instinctive Center," is free to do what it does: allowing us to operate in a balanced way as living beings, as parts of Nature.

When balanced, we think with the Thinking Center, feel with the Feeling Center, and the body is regulated properly by the Instinctive Center. Since the Formatory Apparatus is the result of the scrambling of the Centers, it is no longer active.

The Unscrambled Centers

— the Centers of higher intelligence and grace (called "baraka" by the Sufis).

Once we are three-Centered, we have all the capacities that are the natural birthright of human beings. We are grounded and autonomous by residing fully in our Being. We are open-hearted, joyful, and compassionate, and we are able to discern and discriminate exactly what we need to do from moment to moment. Further, each of these aspects functions harmoniously, supporting the others with an intelligence that is greater than the sum of its individual parts. A three-Centered person is capable of responding to the needs of the situation and is no longer driven entirely by unconscious feelings of deficiency or fear.

Of course, we cannot "will" our Centers into balance, but we can learn to relax more fully into ourselves by cultivating Presence and by consistently seeking the truth of our situation. Thus, the Centers reveal another reason why being present and aware is crucial to Inner Work: *Presence is the medium in which the three Centers can be unified.* It is not the task of our egos to bring about this unification; indeed, the ego, being partial, cannot create wholeness. Our task is to show up with as much Presence as possible, so that we can be worked on by grace. We make ourselves available to Presence, for Presence alone can harmonize the instincts, the heart, and the mind in such a way as to create a whole and complete human being. This is the goal of real Inner Work.

Another way we can look at the Centers is to see their proper function, to understand what they bring to the complete human being when they are no longer scrambled. The spiritual teacher A. H. Almaas* has written extensively on the many qualities of the Essential Self and on the relationship between the structures of ego, and the deeper aspects of our Essential nature. From his per-

---

* Hameed Ali, writing under the pen name of A. H. Almaas, is the founder of the Ridhwan School, or the Diamond Approach, which is a dynamic blend of traditional spiritual approaches made more powerful by the inclusion of modern depth psychology. See the Bibliography for references to his works.

spective, each of the Centers brings a different quality necessary for the realization of the Essential Self.

The *Thinking Center* in its right functioning brings openness and the quality of "allowing." Basically, the mind becomes quiet and allows whatever impressions are occurring to take place. When the mind becomes quiet, we do not to try to fend off the impressions of the moment by filling up our awareness with inner chatter or imaginary pictures. Whatever is here is here, and we feel secure and supported within that context.

The *Feeling Center* "tastes" experience, enabling us to be fully engaged with the experience. It is in the heart Center that the quality of the moment is experienced. We connect with our experiences through whatever degree of openness and sensitivity we are able to allow in our hearts. If our heart is not included, we are not touched by the quality of the experiences that we are having. The Feeling Center is also the part of us that loves the truth. By including the heart, we love the truth of whatever is happening and will not be satisfied with less.

The function of the *Instinctive Center* is to ground presence. Without Presence, we might allow our impressions with an open mind and experience them deeply through our hearts, but we will become identified with them. We will become lost in them. By remaining grounded in our bodies, we are conscious of the fact that there is a being who is having the experience. Then we are fully here, occupying the moment and feeling our aliveness; we welcome our experience and fully participate in it. At the same time our minds are open, spacious, and receptive to the perceptions that are taking place, inner or outer.

When our awareness is sufficiently developed and expanded to include the three functions together, something miraculous happens: we discover that our true identity lies beyond the realm of any of these Centers. In Gurdjieffian terms, our Higher Intellectual and Emotional Centers are able to transform our awareness because our Lower Centers have become unscrambled and come into balance. We find our true identity; we have value, guidance; we feel grounded in ourselves and in the very heart of Being. We find that we are truly precious, beautiful, and mysterious beyond anything we could have suspected.

The ultimate nature of the Essential Self is beyond the perceived reality of all three Centers. It is not thinking, feeling, or instinct: it encompasses all three. Essence is a quiet spaciousness beyond the distortions of fixation: it is the very source of awareness from which everything arises.

CHAPTER 8

Psychological Categories

The Enneagram reaches out in many directions because it is a symbol of that most elusive and complex thing, human nature. Wherever human beings express themselves, the Enneagram can be used to further our understanding. Because it is a symbol of the psyche, it touches on everything that has been created by the psyche. It connects to many widely different fields because it reflects how we humans connect to ourselves, to others, and to the world around us. Like human nature, the Enneagram encompasses a great deal.

The Enneagram is both exciting and somewhat overwhelming: it takes us beyond psychology into so many other areas of human endeavor. It is ancient yet modern; personal yet universal; esoteric and mystical yet scientific and objective; psychological in scope yet spiritual in overtone; simple to understand yet mysterious and complex. The following illustration indicates some of the Enneagram's connections with other bodies of knowledge.

From the Scientific Tradition	From the Mystical Traditions
Academic psychology	Early Greek philosophy
Freud and followers	Pythagoreans
Jung and followers	Middle Eastern cultures
Horney, Maslow	Islam
Fromm and cultural psychology	Sufism
Quantitative psychology	Gurdjieff and The Work

Questionnaire and	Ichazo and Arica
test validation	Mythology
Therapeutic uses	Astrology
Interpersonal relations	Numerology
Personnel management,	Cabala
advertising, and other	Symbolism
practical applications	Chakras
Philosophy	Meditation techniques
Political science, journalism	Spiritual direction and counseling
Cultural criticism, sociology	Theology and religious studies

The Universality of the Enneagram

Lack of space, as well as our own limited time and abilities, does not allow these connections to be developed any further here. Nevertheless, the cross-fertilization of the many different ideas stimulated by the Enneagram will continue as the Enneagram becomes more widely known. Naturally, there is no telling where these connections will lead, although any discoveries will be enriching not only for those directly involved but for everyone.

In this chapter we examine how the Enneagram corresponds with the personality disorders cataloged in the *Diagnostic and Statistical Manual of Mental Disorders,* fourth edition *(DSM-IV),* the primary reference work for mental health professionals. It is valuable to demonstrate in detail the correlations between the Enneagram and the work of Freud, Jung, Karen Horney, Erich Fromm, Abraham Maslow, Timothy Leary, Theodore Millon, and Myers-Briggs, to name only a few areas for future work.

THE ENNEAGRAM AND THE *DSM-IV*

One of the most amazing aspects of the Enneagram is how well it corresponds with other typologies, particularly those devised by psychiatry and psychology. The fact that it does so is one of the most persuasive indications that the Enneagram is mapping objective truths about human nature. In a sense, the findings of modern psychology corroborate many of the insights provided by the Enneagram — and what is even more extraordinary, the Enneagram validates and clarifies some of modern psychology's findings.

It is also fascinating that psychology has been intuitively moving toward a dynamic typology like the Enneagram. From different theoretical points of view, psychologists have been inching toward a comprehensive, systematic understanding (and a clearer presentation) of character types, although it has taken time for academic psychology to overcome its bias against types and typologies. Insights that those familiar with the Enneagram take for granted have become exciting new discoveries for psychologists.

Two brief quotations from a leading psychiatrist involved with the formulation of the *DSM-III(R)*, an earlier version of the *DSM-IV*, indicate that psychiatry has been moving toward something like the Enneagram.

> There is [the] implicit and reasonable assumption that traits and their disordered counterparts [the personality disorders] exist on continua, which means that the distinction [between normal traits and personality disorders] is inherently arbitrary. Recognition of the universality of character types and the importance of documenting them is, I think, the single most important accomplishment of *DSM-III*. [John G. Gunderson, M.D., in Frosch, ed., *Current Perspectives on Personality Disorders*, 20–21]
>
> I believe the main virtue of *DSM-III* is that its multiaxial format will allow better study of the relationships between personality and symptoms and that — if not in *DSM-IV*, then in some future diagnostic text — we may eventually be ready to place the personality disorders ... arranged as outgrowths or extensions of the various personality types. [34]

We feel that the work done here and in *Personality Types* will provide important contributions to the above-mentioned "future diagnostic text." The Enneagram is already a "multiaxial" typology that can accommodate all the personality disorders and neurotic disorders presented in the *DSM-IV* while also correlating the personality types and personality disorders.

Furthermore, our work on the Continuum of nine Levels of Development provides further evidence for the "reasonable assumption" that "traits and their disordered counterparts [the personality disorders] exist on continua." Many of the discoveries that contemporary psychologists working in the vanguard of their field anticipate have already been made with the Enneagram. What remains is to demonstrate the correspondences between it and the *DSM-IV* (and other typologies) and to communicate the potential of the Enneagram to psychologists in language they can accept and use.

⤙

Before we compare each of the Enneagram's personality types with the personality disorders described by the *DSM-IV(R)*, let us first define "traits" and "personality disorders."

> *Personality traits* are enduring patterns of perceiving, relating to, and thinking about the environment and oneself that are exhibited in a wide range of social and personal contexts. Only when personality traits are inflexible and maladaptive and cause significant functional impairment or subjective distress do they constitute Personality Disorders. [*DSM-IV*, 630]

In lay terms, personality traits (such as anger, shyness, excitability, and empathy, for example) are the building blocks of our personalities. Traits constitute the larger patterns that make up much of our individual and interpersonal life. However, if our normal traits turn "inflexible and maladaptive" — if they become negative and destructive to ourselves or others or both — they become the basis for personality disorders.

Since the personality types of the Enneagram include the healthy and average Levels of Development, they encompass more than the personality disorders described by the *DSM-IV* that focus only on the pathological end of the Continuum.

In correlating the Enneagram with the *DSM-IV*, we have discovered that the personality disorders correspond to only certain Levels of each type, not to an entire type. Two or more disorders often appear within each type, although sometimes at different Levels. Traits start to become "inflexible and maladaptive" beginning at Level 5, and these increasingly disordered traits cause significant conflicts as they deteriorate into the traits that emerge in the unhealthy Levels. Hence, more than one personality disorder can (and often does) correspond to one of the Enneagram personality types because the personality disorders are based on maladaptive traits as they appear at different Levels of Development.

For example, a single personality disorder may appear at Levels 5 and 6, another does not show up until Level 7, and yet another at Level 9 — all within the same personality type of the Enneagram. While the *DSM-IV* would regard these as three different (although related) personality disorders, from our point of view we can see that these three disorders are parts of a larger whole, parts of a single personality type that has become unhealthy.

There are different gradations and patterns within the neurotic process itself: a person with a personality disorder beginning at Level 6 would be less unhealthy than someone with a personality disorder at Level 8. In certain cases the same person may later deteriorate from a Level 6 disorder to a Level 8 disorder; in other cases, closely related disorders could exist at the same time in the same person — for instance, someone might have disorders corresponding to Levels 7 and 8 as well as disorders that are attributable to their wing. Thus, understanding that the personality disorders are part of a larger whole — a personality type at different Levels of Development — will provide a much clearer idea of the status and direction of patients' pathologies and will help simplify the psychiatric "differential diagnoses" that are often intuitively made to fit individual cases.

If therapists understand the personality disorders in the context of the different Levels of Development within a personality type, they can be more insightful about their patients' past difficulties, present condition, and future prognosis. Psychologists may design better therapies for the different disordered personality types and interact more effectively in group therapy with people of many different types. In short, if therapists understand the interrelatedness of the various personality disorders, they may have a much clearer understanding of their patients.

This chapter is necessarily more technical than the average reader may need or want. Nevertheless, it is essential to demonstrate that the Enneagram types and the psychiatric disorders correlate, for two reasons. The first reason is to help establish the Enneagram's intellectual credentials so that it will gain wider acceptance with mental health professionals and the educated general public. It must be shown that the Enneagram does not contradict the established findings of psychiatry; in fact, we will see the reverse: by providing greater context for the psychiatric categories, the Enneagram clarifies them.

Second, correlating the Enneagram and the personality disorders acts as a much-needed corrective for some of the misinformation in circulation about the personality types themselves. A number of incorrect correlations have been made in dissertations and books about the Enneagram: while these correlations may be of interest primarily to Enneagram teachers and writers, they should also be of interest to everyone who believes in the validity and usefulness of the Enneagram.

The issue of which types go with which disorders is important because the disorders are the result of average traits that have deteriorated into inflexible and maladaptive traits. If a teacher or author mistakes which disorders correlate with which type, it is also highly likely that he or she will misattribute the traits from which the disorders emerge. To put this another way, just as apples do not grow on lemon trees, each disorder is not arbitrary: part of the *entire pattern of traits* makes up a type as a whole. If the disorders are mistakenly assigned to the types, this can only obscure the picture of the type as a whole, leading to misdiagnoses and mistaken notions of the types.

In this chapter, the nine Levels of Development are given for each personality type along with the corresponding personality disorders that appear at each Level. Because of space limitations, generally only one excerpt from the dominant personality disorder of the *DSM-IV* has been included for each type to indicate how the systems correspond. For additional information, refer to the *DSM-IV* itself, using the page references provided in parentheses.

Interested readers may also want to turn to *Personality Types* at the corresponding Level to see how the psychiatric categories correlate to the descriptions we have given. For instance, the *DSM-IV* Passive-Aggressive Personality Disorder is listed under personality type Six. In the section describing the Ambivalent Pessimist (*PT*, 235–39) are references to the passive-aggressive traits of the average Six. The description and the psychiatric text illuminate and supplement each other. Rather than comment here on each *DSM-IV* excerpt individually, we have added short interlinear comments in brackets as well as page references to *Personality Types*.

Personality Type Two: *The Helper*

Levels of Development

Level 1: The Disinterested Altruist	
Level 2: The Caring Person	
Level 3: The Nurturing Helper	
Level 4: The Effusive Friend	
Level 5: The Possessive Intimate	
Level 6: The Self-Important "Saint"	Somatization Disorder (446)
	Histrionic Personality Disorder (655)
Level 7: The Self-Deceptive Manipulator	Hypochondriasis (462)
Level 8: The Coercive Dominator	
Level 9: The Psychosomatic Victim	Conversion Disorder, Hysterical Neurosis (452)

Histrionic Personality Disorder
(Type Two Beginning at Levels 4–5)

"The essential feature of Histrionic Personality Disorder is pervasive and excessive emotionality and attention-seeking behavior. This pattern begins by early adulthood and is present in a variety of contexts.

Individuals with Histrionic Personality Disorder are uncomfortable in situations in which they are not the center of attention. Often lively and dramatic, they tend to draw attention to themselves and may initially charm new acquaintances by their enthusiasm, apparent openness, or flirtatiousness. . . . This need is often apparent in their behavior with a clinician (for example, flattery, bringing gifts, providing dramatic descriptions of physical and psychological symptoms that are replaced by new symptoms with each visit [PT, 82].) [Twos and Sevens share different aspects of the Histrionic Personality Disorder and are often confused; see Chapter 5 for their similarities and differences.]

The appearance and behavior of individuals with this disorder are often inappropriately sexually provocative and seductive. The behavior is directed not only toward persons in whom the individual has a sexual or romantic interest, but occurs in a wide variety of social, occupational, and professional relationships beyond what is appropriate for the social context (PT, 72, 77, 84).

. . . Individuals with this disorder are characterized by self-dramatization, theatricality, and an exaggerated expression of emotion. They may embarrass friends and acquaintances by an excessive public display of emotions, for example, embracing casual acquaintances with excessive ardor, sobbing uncontrollably on minor sentimental occasions, or having temper tantrums." (DSM-IV, 655)

Somatization Disorder (Type Two Beginning at Level 6)

"The essential feature of Somatization Disorder is a pattern of recurring, multiple, significant somatic complaints. A somatic complaint is considered to be clinically significant if it results in medical treatment (for example, the taking of medication) or causes significant impairment in social, occupational, or other important areas of functioning. The somatic complaints must begin before age thirty and occur over a period of several years. The multiple somatic complaints cannot be fully explained by any known general medical condition or the direct effects of a substance. . . .

Associated features. Individuals with Somatization Disorder usually describe their complaints in colorful, exaggerated terms, but specific factual information is often lacking. They are often inconsistent historians, so that a checklist approach to diagnostic interviewing may be less effective than a thorough review of medical treatments and hospitalizations to document a pattern of frequent somatic complaints. Individuals often seek treatment from several physicians concurrently, which may lead to complicated and sometimes hazardous combinations of treatments. Prominent anxiety symptoms and depressed mood are very common and may be the reason for being seen in mental health settings." (*DSM-IV,* 446)

Histrionic (types Two and Seven), Borderline, and Antisocial Personality Disorders (type Eight) are the most frequently associated Personality Disorders (*DSM-IV,* 446–47). Note that the Antisocial Personality Disorder corresponds to the Eight, the type in the Two's Direction of Disintegration, and Borderline Personality shows up frequently in type Four, the Two's Security Point.

Personality Type Three: *The Achiever*

Levels of Development
Level 1: The Authentic Person
Level 2: The Self-Assured Person
Level 3: The Outstanding Paragon
Level 4: The Competitive Status-Seeker
Level 5: The Image-Conscious Pragmatist

Level 6: The Self-Promoting Narcissist   Narcissistic Personality
                                                 Disorder (658)
Level 7: The Dishonest Opportunist
Level 8: The Malicious Deceiver
Level 9: The Vindictive Psychopath

Narcissistic Personality Disorder
(Type Three Beginning at Level 6)

"The essential feature of Narcissistic Personality Disorder is a pervasive pattern of grandiosity (*PT,* 116), need for admiration (*PT,* 117–18), and lack of empathy that begins by early adulthood and is present in a variety of contexts (*PT,* 120).

Individuals with this disorder have a grandiose sense of self-importance. They routinely overestimate their abilities and inflate their accomplishments, often appearing boastful and pretentious. They may blithely assume that others attribute the same value to their efforts and may be surprised when the praise they expect and feel they deserve is not forthcoming. Often implicit in the inflated judgments of their own accomplishments is an underestimation (devaluation) of the contributions of others. They are often preoccupied with fantasies of unlimited success, power, brilliance, beauty, or ideal love. They may ruminate about "long overdue" admiration and privilege and compare themselves favorably with famous or privileged people.

. . . Individuals with this disorder generally require excessive admiration. Their self-esteem is almost invariably very fragile. They may be preoccupied with how well they are doing and how favorably they are regarded by others (*PT,* 112–13). This often takes the form of a constant need for attention and admiration. They may expect their arrival to be greeted with great fanfare and are astonished if others do not covet their possessions. They may constantly fish for compliments, often with great charm. A sense of entitlement is evident in these individuals' unreasonable expectation of especially favorable treatment. . . . This sense of entitlement combined with a lack of sensitivity to the wants and needs of others may result in the conscious or unwitting exploitation of others (*PT,* 120). . . . They tend to form friendships or romantic relationships only if the other person seems likely to advance their purposes or otherwise enhance their self-esteem (*PT,* 121).

Individuals with Narcissistic Personality Disorder generally have a lack of empathy and have difficulty recognizing the desires, subjective experiences, and feelings of others. They may assume that others are totally concerned about their welfare. . . . They are often contemptuous and impatient with others who talk about their own problems and concerns. . . . When recognized, the needs, desires, or feelings of others are likely to be viewed disparagingly as signs of weakness or vulnerability. Those who relate to individuals with Narcissistic Personality Disorder typically find emotional coldness and lack of reciprocal interest. . . .

Associated features. Vulnerability in self-esteem makes individuals with Narcissistic Personality Disorder very sensitive to 'injury' from criticism or defeat. Although it may not show outwardly, criticism may haunt these individuals and may leave them feeling humiliated, degraded, hollow, and empty. They may react with disdain, rage, or defiant counterattack. . . . Sustained feelings of shame or humiliation and the attendant self-criticism may be associated with social withdrawal, depressed mood, and Dysthymic or Major Depressive Disorder." (*DSM-IV,* 658) This can also be seen as part of the movement to Nine at Levels 6 through 8. In some cases, Threes "burn out" and slump into an anhedonic depression for long periods of time. In other cases, efforts to get out of the depression may cause their moods to go up and down, superficially like a manic-depressive Seven, although the roots of the depression of these two types are quite different. See Chapter 5 for more about the narcissistic personality (Three) and the traits displayed by the average to unhealthy Seven.

Personality Type Four: *The Individualist*

Levels of Development

Level 1: The Inspired Creator	
Level 2: The Self-Aware Intuitive	
Level 3: The Self-Revealing Individual	
Level 4: The Imaginative Aesthete	
Level 5: The Self-Absorbed Romantic	Avoidant Personality Disorder (662)
Level 6: The Self-Indulgent "Exception"	Narcissistic Personality Disorder (658)
Level 7: The Alienated Depressive	Borderline Personality Disorder (650)
Level 8: The Emotionally Tormented Person	Major Depressive Episode (320)
Level 9: The Self-Destructive Person	

Avoidant Personality Disorder (Type Four Beginning at Level 5)

"The essential feature of Avoidant Personality Disorder is a pervasive pattern of social inhibition, feelings of inadequacy, and hypersensitivity to negative evaluation that begins by early adulthood and is present in a variety of contexts.

Individuals with Avoidant Personality Disorder avoid work or school activities that involve significant interpersonal contact because of fear of criticism, disapproval, or rejection. Offers of job promotions may be declined because the new responsibilities might result in criticism from coworkers. These individuals avoid making new friends unless they are certain they will be liked and accepted without criticism. Unless they pass stringent tests proving the contrary, other people are assumed to be critical and disapproving. Individuals with this disorder will not join in group activities unless there are repeated and generous offers of support and nurturance. Interpersonal intimacy is often difficult for these individuals, although they are able to establish intimate relationships when there is assurance of uncritical acceptance (*PT,* 153). . . .

Because individuals with this disorder are preoccupied with being criticized or rejected in social situations, they have a markedly low threshold for detecting such reactions (*PT,* 154–55). If someone is even slightly disapproving or critical, they may feel extremely hurt. They tend to be shy, quiet, inhibited, and "invisible" because of the fear that any attention would be degrading or rejecting. They expect that no matter what they say, others will see it as 'wrong,' and so they may say nothing at all.

They react strongly to subtle cues that are suggestive of mockery or derision. Despite their longing to be active participants in social life, they fear placing their welfare in the hands of others (*PT,* 152). Individuals with Avoidant Personality Disorder are inhibited in interpersonal situations because they feel inadequate and have low self-esteem. Doubts concerning social competence and personal appeal become especially manifest in settings involving interactions with strangers. These individuals believe themselves to be socially inept, personally unappealing, or inferior to others (*PT,* 161). They are unusually reluctant to take personal risks or to engage in any new activities because these may prove embarrassing. . . . Someone with this disorder may cancel a job interview for fear of being embarrassed by not dressing properly. Marginal somatic symptoms or other problems may become the reason for avoiding new activities.

Associated features. Individuals with Avoidant Personality Disorder often vigilantly appraise the movements and expressions of those with whom they come in contact. Their fearful and tense demeanor may elicit ridicule and derision from others, which in turn confirms their self-doubts. They are very anxious about the possibility that they will react to criticism with blushing or crying. They are described by others as being 'shy,' 'timid,' 'lonely,' and 'isolated.'. . . some They desire acceptance and affection and may fantasize about idealized relationships with others (*PT,* 151–52)." (*DSM-IV,* 662)

Personality Type Five: *The Investigator*

Levels of Development

Level 1: The Pioneering Visionary	
Level 2: The Perceptive Observer	
Level 3: The Focused Innovator	
Level 4: The Studious Expert	
Level 5: The Intense Conceptualizer	
Level 6: The Provocative Cynic	
Level 7: The Isolated Nihilist	Schizotypal Personality Disorder (641)
	Schizoid Personality Disorder (638)
Level 8: The Terrified "Alien"	
Level 9: The Imploded Schizoid	Schizophrenia (274)

Schizotypal Personality Disorder (Type Five Beginning at Level 7)

"The essential feature of Schizotypal Personality Disorder is a pervasive pattern of social and interpersonal deficits marked by acute discomfort with, and reduced capacity for, close relationships as well as by cognitive or perceptual distortions and eccentricities of behavior. This pattern begins by early adulthood and is present in a variety of contexts.

Individuals with Schizotypal Personality Disorder often have ideas of reference (i.e., incorrect interpretations of casual incidents and external events as having a particular and unusual meaning specifically for the person) (*PT,* 199–200). These should be distinguished from delusions of reference, in which the beliefs are held with delusional conviction. These individuals may be superstitious or preoccupied with paranormal phenomena that are outside the norms of their subculture. They may believe that they have special powers to sense events before they happen or to read others' thoughts. . . . Perceptual alterations may be present (for example, sensing that another person is present or hearing a voice murmuring his or her name). Their speech may include unusual or idiosyn-cratic phrasing and construction. It is often loose, digressive, or vague, but without actual derailment or incoherence (*PT,* 193). Response can be either overly concrete or overly abstract, and words and concepts are sometimes applied in unusual ways (for example, the person may state that he or she was not 'talkable' at work).

These individuals are often considered to be odd or eccentric because of unusual mannerisms, an often unkempt manner of dress that does not quite 'fit together,' and inattention to the usual social conventions — for example, the person may avoid making eye contact, wear clothes that are ink-stained and ill-fitting, and be unable to join in the . . . banter of coworkers (*PT,* 200).

Individuals with Schizotypal Personality Disorder experience interpersonal relatedness as problematic and are uncomfortable relating to other people. Although they may express unhappi-ness about their lack of relationships, their behavior suggests a decreased desire for intimate contacts. As a result, they often have no or few close friends or confidants other than a first-degree rela-tive. They are anxious in social situations, particularly those in-volving unfamiliar people. They will interact with other people when they have to, but they prefer to keep to themselves because they feel that they are different and just do not 'fit in.'" (*DSM-IV,* 641–42)

Personality Type Six: *The Loyalist*

Levels of Development

Level 1: The Valiant Hero	
Level 2: The Engaging Friend	
Level 3: The Committed Worker	
Level 4: The Dutiful Loyalist	
Level 5: The Ambivalent Pessimist	Passive-Aggressive Personality Disorder (733)

Level 6: The Authoritarian Rebel

Level 7: The Overreacting Dependent	Dependent Personality Disorder (665)
Level 8: The Paranoid Hysteric	Paranoid Personality Disorder (337)
Level 9: The Self-Defeating Masochist	Borderline Personality Disorder (650)

Passive-Aggressive Personality Disorder
(Type Six Beginning at Level 5)

"The essential feature is a pervasive pattern of negativistic attitudes and passive resistance to demands for adequate performance in social and occupational situations. . . . These individuals habitually resent, oppose, or resist demands to function at a level expected by others. This opposition occurs most frequently in work situations but can also be evident in social functioning. The resistance is expressed by procrastination, forgetfulness, stubbornness, and intentional inefficiency, especially in response to tasks assigned by authority figures (*PT*, 237–39). . . . These individuals feel cheated, unappreciated, and misunderstood and chronically complain to others (*PT*, 241–42). When difficulties appear, they blame their failures on the behaviors of others (*PT*, 240–41). They may be sullen, irritable, impatient, argumentative, skeptical, and contrary. Authority figures — for example, a superior at work, a teacher at school, a parent, or a spouse who acts the role of a parent — often become the focus of discontent.

Because of their negativism and tendency to externalize blame, these individuals often criticize and voice hostility toward authority figures with minimal provocation. They are also envious and resentful of peers who are viewed positively by authority figures. These individuals often complain about their personal misfortunes. They have a negative view of the future and may make comments such as 'It doesn't pay to be good' and 'Good things don't last' (*PT*, 238, 244–45). These individuals may waver between expressing hostile defiance toward those they view as causing their problems and attempting to mollify these persons by asking forgiveness or promising to perform better in the future (*PT*, 243).

Associated features. These individuals are overtly ambivalent, wavering indecisively from one course of action to its opposite. They may follow an erratic path that causes endless wrangles with others and disappointments for themselves. An intense conflict between dependence on others and the desire for self-assertion is characteristic of these individuals." (*DSM-IV*, 733–34)

Personality Type Seven: *The Enthusiast*

Level 1: The Ecstatic Appreciator
Level 2: The Free-Spirited Optimist
Level 3: The Accomplished Generalist
Level 4: The Experienced Sophisticate
Level 5: The Hyperactive Extrovert   Histrionic Personality
                                             Disorder (655)

Level 6: The Excessive Hedonist
Level 7: The Impulsive Escapist   Hypomanic Episode (335)
Level 8: The Manic-Compulsive   Manic Episode (328)
                                             Bipolar Disorders (350)

Level 9: The Panic-Stricken Hysteric

Histrionic Personality Disorder
(Type Seven Beginning at Level 5)

"The essential feature of Histrionic Personality Disorder is pervasive and excessive emotionality and attention-seeking behavior. This pattern begins by early adulthood and is present in a variety of contexts. [Sevens have much of the following in common with Twos; see Chapter 6 for the differences between these two types.]

Individuals with Histrionic Personality Disorder are uncomfortable or feel unappreciated when they are not the center of attention. Often lively and dramatic, they tend to draw attention to themselves and may initially charm new acquaintances with their enthusiasm, apparent openness, or flirtatiousness. These qualities wear thin, however, as these individuals continually demand to be the center of attention. They commandeer the role of 'life of the party.' If they are not the center of attention, they do something dramatic, for example, make up stories or create a scene to draw the focus of attention to themselves (*PT*, 277).

. . . These individuals have a style of speech that is excessively impressionistic and lacking in detail. Strong opinions are expressed with dramatic flair, but underlying reasons are usually vague and diffuse, without supporting facts or details. For example, an individual with Histrionic Personality Disorder may comment that a certain individual is a wonderful human being, yet be unable to provide any specific examples of good qualities to support the opinion (*PT*, 276).

Associated features. Individuals with Histrionic Personality Disorder have difficulty achieving emotional intimacy in romantic or sexual relationships. Without being aware of it, they often act out a role, for example, the 'victim' or the 'princess,' in their relationships to others. . . . These individuals may also alienate friends with demands for constant attention. They often become depressed and upset when they are not the center of attention. They may crave novelty, stimulation, and excitement and have a tendency to become bored with their usual routine (*PT*, 276). These individuals are often intolerant of, or frustrated by, situations that involve delayed gratification, and their actions are often directed at obtaining immediate satisfaction (*PT*, 283–84). Although they often initiate a job or project with great enthusiasm, their interest may lag quickly. Longer-term relationships may be neglected to make way for the excitement of new relationships (*PT*, 281)." (*DSM-IV*, 655)

Manic Episode (Type Seven Beginning at Level 7)

"A Manic Episode is defined by a distinct period during which there is an abnormally and persistently elevated, expansive, or irritable mood (*PT*, 282–83). . . . The mood disturbance must be accompanied by at least three additional symptoms from a list that includes inflated self-esteem or grandiosity, decreased need for sleep, pressure of speech, flight of ideas, distractibility, increased involvement in goal-directed activities or psychomotor agitation, and excessive involvement in pleasurable activities with a high potential for painful consequences (*PT*, 283, 285–86). . . .

The elevated mood of a Manic Episode may be described as euphoric, unusually good, cheerful, or high. . . . The expansive quality of the mood disturbance is characterized by unceasing and indiscriminate enthusiasm for interpersonal, sexual, or occupational interactions. . . .

Manic speech is typically pressured, loud, rapid, and difficult to interrupt. Individuals may talk nonstop, sometimes for hours on end, and without regard for others' wishes to communicate. Speech is sometimes characterized by joking, punning, and amusing irrelevancies. The individual may become theatrical, with dramatic mannerisms and singing. . . . If the person's mood is more irritable than expansive, his or her speech may be marked by complaints, hostile comments, and angry tirades (*PT*, 283–84).

The increase in goal-directed activity often involves excessive planning of, and excessive participation in, multiple activities (for example, sexual, occupational, political, religious). . . . The person may simultaneously take on multiple new business ventures without regard for the apparent risks or need to complete each venture satisfactorily. Almost invariably, there is increased sociability (for example, renewing old acquaintances or calling friends or even strangers at all hours of the day or night) without regard to the intrusive, domineering, and demanding nature of these interactions. . . .

Expansiveness, unwarranted optimism, grandiosity, and poor judgment often lead to imprudent involvement in pleasurable activities such as buying sprees, reckless driving, foolish business investments, and sexual behavior unusual for the person . . . (*PT*, 285–86)." (*DSM-IV*, 328–29)

Personality Type Eight: *The Challenger*

Levels of Development

Level 1: The Magnanimous Heart	
Level 2: The Self-Confident Person	
Level 3: The Constructive Leader	
Level 4: The Enterprising Adventurer	
Level 5: The Dominating Power-Broker	
Level 6: The Confrontational Adversary	
Level 7: The Ruthless Outlaw	Antisocial Personality Disorder (645)
Level 8: The Omnipotent Megalomaniac	
Level 9: The Violent Destroyer	

Antisocial Personality Disorder
(Type Eight Beginning at Level 7)

"The essential feature of Antisocial Personality Disorder is a pervasive pattern of disregard for, and violation of, the rights of others that begins in childhood or early adolescence and continues into adulthood. . . .

. . . Individuals with Antisocial Personality Disorder fail to conform to social norms with respect to lawful behavior. They may repeatedly perform acts that are grounds for arrest (whether they are arrested or not), such as destroying property, harassing others, stealing, or pursuing illegal occupations (*PT*, 323–24). [We have learned anecdotally from therapists working with prison populations that there are a disproportionate number of Eights incarcerated]. Persons with this disorder disregard the wishes, rights, and feelings of others. They are frequently deceitful and manipulative in order to gain personal profit or pleasure (for example, to obtain money, sex, or power). They may repeatedly lie, use an alias, con others, or malinger. A pattern of impulsivity may be manifested by a failure to plan ahead. . . . Individuals with Antisocial Personality Disorder tend to be irritable and aggressive and may repeatedly get into physical fights or commit acts of physical assault (including spouse beating or child beating) (*PT,* 325). . . . These individuals may also display a reckless disregard for the safety of themselves or others. This may be evidenced by their driving behavior (for example, incidents of recurrent speeding, driving while intoxicated, and multiple accidents). They may engage in sexual behavior or substance use that has a high risk for harmful consequences. They may neglect or fail to care for a child in a way that puts the child in danger.

Individuals with Antisocial Personality Disorder also tend to be consistently and extremely irresponsible. . . . Financial irresponsibility is indicated by acts such as defaulting on debts, failing to provide child support, or failing to support other dependents on a regular basis. Individuals with Antisocial Personality Disorder show little remorse for the consequences of their actions (*PT,* 325). They may be indifferent to, or provide a superficial rationalization for, having hurt, mistreated, or stolen from someone (for example, 'life's unfair,' 'losers deserve to lose,' or 'he had it coming anyway'). . . . They generally fail to compensate or make amends for their behavior. They believe that everyone is out to 'help number one' and that one should stop at nothing to avoid being pushed around. . . ." (*DSM-IV,* 645–46)

Personality Type Nine: *The Peacemaker*

Levels of Development

Level 1: The Self-Possessed Guide
Level 2: The Receptive Person
Level 3: The Supportive Peacemaker
Level 4: The Accommodating Role-Player
Level 5: The Disengaged Participant   Passive-Aggressive Personality Disorder (733)

Level 6: The Resigned Fatalist	Dependent Personality Disorder (665)
Level 7: The Denying Doormat	Schizoid Personality Disorder (638)
Level 8: The Dissociating Automaton	Dissociative Disorders (477)
Level 9: The Self-Abandoning Ghost	

Dependent Personality Disorder (Type Nine Beginning at Level 6)

"The essential feature of Dependent Personality Disorder is a pervasive and excessive need to be taken care of that leads to submissive and clinging behavior and fears of separation. This pattern begins by early adulthood and is present in a variety of contexts. The dependent and submissive behaviors are designed to elicit caregiving and arise from a self-perception of being unable to function adequately without the help of others. [Much of this is in common with the Six: both types can become dependent and submissive, although in different ways and for different reasons.]

Individuals with Dependent Personality Disorder have great difficulty making everyday decisions (for example, what color shirt to wear or whether to carry an umbrella) without an excessive amount of advice and reassurance from others. These individuals tend to be passive and to allow other people (often a single other person) to take the initiative and assume responsibility for most major areas of their lives (*PT*, 358). Adults with this disorder typically depend on a parent or spouse to decide where they should live, what kind of job he or she should have, and which neighbors to befriend. . . . [Sixes, by contrast, react for and against those they are dependent on and are rarely 'passive' or completely dependent, as Nines tend to be. The dependency of Sixes is based on their need for reassurance against anxiety, whereas the passive dependency and lack of interest in decision making is based on the desire of Nines that things not change and that they never be upset.]

Because they fear losing support or approval, individuals with Dependent Personality Disorder often have difficulty expressing disagreement with other people, especially those on whom they are dependent (*PT*, 353–54). These individuals feel so unable to function alone that they will agree to things that they feel are wrong rather than risk losing the help of those to whom they look for guidance. They do not get appropriately angry at others whose support and nurturance they need for fear of alienating them. . . .

Individuals with this disorder have difficulty initiating projects or doing things independently (*PT*, 363). They lack self-confidence and believe they need help to begin and carry through tasks. They will wait for others to start things because they believe that as a rule others can do them better. . . . There may be a fear of becoming or appearing too competent, because they believe this will lead to abandonment. . . .

. . . They are willing to submit to what others want, even if the demands are unreasonable (*PT*, 362–63). Their need to maintain an important bond will often result in imbalanced or distorted relationships. They will make extraordinary self-sacrifices or tolerate verbal, physical, or sexual abuse. . . . They will 'tag along' with important others just to avoid being alone, even if they are not interested or involved with what is happening. . . ." (*DSM-IV*, 665–66)

Schizoid Personality Disorder (Type Nine Beginning at Level 7)

"The essential feature of Schizoid Personality Disorder is a pervasive pattern of detachment from social relationships and a restricted range of expression of emotions in interpersonal settings (*PT*, 362). . . .

Individuals with Schizoid Personality Disorder appear to lack a desire for intimacy, seem indifferent to opportunities to develop close relationships, and do not seem to derive much satisfaction from being part of a family or other social group. They prefer spending time by themselves, rather than being with other people.

They often appear to be socially isolated or 'loners' and almost always choose solitary activities or hobbies that do not include interactions with others. . . . [Nines share this disorder with Fives, who also display strong schizoid tendencies. Unhealthy Nines are not always recognized as schizoid because they seek a relationship they can depend on, but having found some source of security with another, they maintain the relationship primarily in their imaginations. They detach from the real person so that they will remain untroubled by their feelings — especially of anger — and the actual requirements of the relationship.] They prefer mechanical or abstract tasks, such as computers or mathematical games. They may also have very little interest in having sexual experiences with another person. . . .

Individuals with Schizoid Personality Disorder often seem indifferent to the approval or criticism of others and do not appear to be bothered by what others may think of them (PT, 356). . . . They usually display a 'bland' exterior without visible emotional reactivity and rarely reciprocate gestures or facial expressions, such as smiles or nods. They claim that they rarely experience strong emotions such as anger or joy. They often display a constricted affect and appear cold and aloof. [Average to unhealthy Nines are increasingly disengaged emotionally and dissociated from reality.] However, in those very unusual circumstances in which these individuals become at least temporarily comfortable in revealing themselves, they may acknowledge painful feelings, particularly related to social interactions.

Associated features. Individuals with Schizoid Personality Disorder may have particular difficulty expressing anger, even in response to direct provocation, which contributes to the impression that they lack emotion (PT, 358–59). Their lives sometimes seem directionless, and they may appear to 'drift' in their goals (PT, 356–57). Such individuals often react passively to adverse circumstances and have difficulty responding appropriately to important life events. . . ." (DSM-IV, 638–39)

Personality Type One: *The Reformer*

Levels of Development

Level 1: The Wise Realist	
Level 2: The Reasonable Person	
Level 3: The Principled Teacher	
Level 4: The Idealistic Reformer	
Level 5: The Orderly Person	
Level 6: The Judgmental Perfectionist	Obsessive-Compulsive Personality Disorder (669)
Level 7: The Intolerant Misanthrope	
Level 8: The Obsessive Hypocrite	Obsessive-Compulsive Disorder (417)
Level 9: The Punitive Avenger	

Obsessive-Compulsive Personality Disorder (Type One Beginning at Level 6)

"The essential feature of Obsessive-Compulsive Personality Disorder is a preoccupation with orderliness, perfectionism, and mental and interpersonal control at the expense of flexibility, openness, and efficiency (*PT,* 394–97). . . .

Individuals with Obsessive-Compulsive Personality Disorder attempt to maintain a sense of control through painstaking attention to rules, trivial details, procedures, lists, schedules, or form to the extent that the major point of the activity is lost (*PT,* 396). They are excessively careful and prone to repetition, paying extraordinary attention to detail and repeatedly checking for possible mistakes. . . . The perfectionism and self-imposed high standards of performance cause significant dysfunction and distress in these individuals (*PT,* 395–96). . . .

Individuals with Obsessive-Compulsive Personality Disorder display excessive devotion to work and productivity to the exclusion of leisure activities and friendships. This behavior is not accounted for by economic necessity. They often feel that they do not have time to take an evening or a weekend day off or to go on an outing or to just relax. They may keep postponing a pleasurable activity, such as a vacation, so that it may never occur. When they do take time off for leisure activities or vacations, they are very uncomfortable unless they have taken along something to work on so they do not 'waste time.' There may be a great concentration on household chores (for example, repeated excessive cleaning so that 'one could eat off the floor'). (*PT,* 392). . . .

Individuals with Obsessive-Compulsive Personality Disorder may be excessively conscientious, scrupulous, and inflexible about matters of morality, ethics, or values (*PT,* 397–98). They may force themselves and others to follow rigid moral principles and very strict standards of performance. They may also be mercilessly self-critical about their own mistakes. Individuals with this disorder are rigidly deferential to authority and rules and insist on quite literal compliance, with no rule bending for extenuating circumstances (*PT,* 397–98). . . .

Individuals with Obsessive-Compulsive Personality Disorder are reluctant to delegate tasks or to work with others. They stubbornly and unreasonably insist that everything be done their way and that people conform to their way of doing things. They often give very detailed instructions about how things should be done (for example, there is one and only one way to mow the lawn, wash the dishes, build a doghouse) and are surprised and irritated if others suggest creative alternatives. At other times they may reject offers of help even when behind schedule because they believe that no one else can do it right (*PT,* 392–93).

Associated features. They are prone to become upset or angry in situations in which they are not able to maintain control of their physical or interpersonal environment, although anger is typically not expressed directly (*PT,* 378–79, 392). . . . On other occasions, anger may be expressed with righteous indignation over a seemingly minor matter. . . .

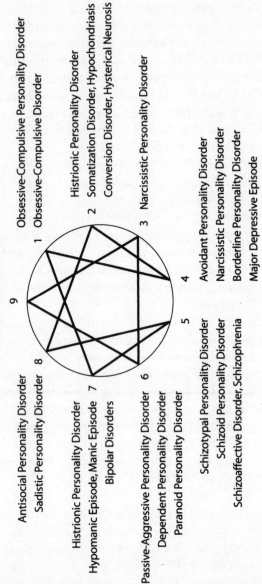

Dependent Personality Disorder
Schizoid Personality Disorder
Dissociative Disorders

9

Obsessive-Compulsive Personality Disorder
1   Obsessive-Compulsive Disorder

Histrionic Personality Disorder
2   Somatization Disorder, Hypochondriasis
Conversion Disorder, Hysterical Neurosis

3   Narcissistic Personality Disorder

4

Avoidant Personality Disorder
Narcissistic Personality Disorder
Borderline Personality Disorder
Major Depressive Episode

5

Schizotypal Personality Disorder
Schizoid Personality Disorder
Schizoaffective Disorder, Schizophrenia

8

Antisocial Personality Disorder
Sadistic Personality Disorder

7

Histrionic Personality Disorder
Hypomanic Episode, Manic Episode
Bipolar Disorders

6

Passive-Aggressive Personality Disorder
Dependent Personality Disorder
Paranoid Personality Disorder

The Enneagram and the DSM-IV Disorders

Individuals with this disorder usually express affection in a highly controlled or stilted fashion and may be very uncomfortable in the presence of others who are emotionally expressive. Their everyday relationships have a formal and serious quality, and they may be stiff in situations in which others would smile and be happy, for example, greeting a lover at the airport (*PT*, 394)." (*DSM-IV*, 669–71)

CHAPTER 9

Advanced Topics

THE ORIGINS OF TYPE

Nobody knows for sure what creates an individual's personality type. It seems that both heredity *and* our early childhood relationships with our parents (or other significant people) are the two most important sets of influences, both of which are highly complicated and not completely understood by science. Heredity seems to provide us with a basic *temperament,* while our early relationship with our parents further crystallizes our temperamental predisposition and heavily influences how healthy or unhealthy we are as we begin life. Of course, there are many more potential influences on type, but for practical purposes, they are not relevant here. Every person has a basic personality type, and that type holds the key to understanding the self and others.

Most Enneagram teachers would probably agree that the origins of type are unknown. It seems clear that our type is the result of partly genetic, partly prenatal, and partly learned conditioned factors. It seems clear that much (but not all) of our personality has been formed virtually from birth, if not before.

Parenting counts for a great deal, but, in our opinion, parenting in itself is not the decisive factor that determines which type a child will become. The personality types of the parents clearly do not "create" the personality type of the child. If genetics alone were responsible for determining type, we would expect that all of the children born of a particular set of parents would be the same personality type, or at least that there would be more of one or two types produced by this set of parents than of others. But this is not what we see in real life. There seems to be a genetic wild card that makes it impossible to predict type based on the types of the parents. In other words, if we know the types of the parents, we cannot predict the children's types. Fortunately, there can be no "type engineering" of subsequent generations based on Enneagram information, or with any other typology or method of which we are aware.

The innate and genetic structures that lead to the development of type are usually referred to as one's *temperament*. In a sense, we arrive in a particular family having been dealt certain cards, and we must find a way to make the most of the basic building blocks. Of course, the temperament one has is not the result of a conscious choice, nor is it the result of a conscious or unconscious choice on the part of our parents. The conscious choices we have made regarding our personality come later in our development and have to do with the formation of our identity, particularly the creation of a "sense of self" that both allows and disallows certain feelings and characteristics within us.

The temperament expresses itself early in life in three general ways; scientists define the temperament types as "high responders," "low responders," and "in-between responders." In terms of the Enneagram, these three groups correspond to the three Hornevian Groups (see *Personality Types,* 433–36), the aggressives with the high responders, the withdrawns with the low responders, and the compliants with the in-between responders. For example, Eights, Sevens, and Threes are clearly high responders who have an abundance of energy, making them eager — and sometimes hyperactive — participants in their world.

The idea of temperament throws light on another problem in childhood development, the question of "fit" between the temperament of the child and that of the parents. A high responder child can be extremely challenging to the parents if they are low responders themselves, or if they are dysfunctional such that their neuroses allow little energy for coping with a high-energy child. The reverse might also be true: the parents could be high responders while the child is a low responder. Again, the temperamental fit between generations would be difficult, especially if it is not taken into account. Thus, the fundamental questions are "How good is the temperamental match between the parent and the child? How are the needs of the child matched with the needs of the parents? How realistic are the expectations of the parents for their child, given the innate temperament of the child they are actually presented with? How can the child be validated and mirrored when given a 'poor' match?"

While our parents do not determine our type or basic temperament, parents usually play an extremely significant role in the crystallization of their child's overall personality pattern, especially in determining the Level of Development (see Chapter 4) at which the consciousness and identity have emerged. While our parents may not determine our type, *they determine how healthy or unhealthy we are as individual representatives of our type.*

For instance, a child born into a dysfunctional family will most likely have to learn to defend oneself and build an identity in whatever degree of dysfunction exists. Destructive, abusive, or neglectful parents will, of course, make a major difference in the kinds of adaptations the child will have to make. His or her Essential being will have to contract far more, and will be much more highly defended than would optimally be the case.

Children have to "shut down" to the degree of dysfunction of their family in order to defend themselves; the extent to which a person has shut down can be measured by the Level of Development at which the child functions. Thus, two children of the same basic temperament will crystallize at different Levels of Development depending on the differences of health or unhealth in their family of origin. For example, one child will function at a lower Level than another child of the same type who has been born into a better functioning family.

Our work on the Enneagram therefore confirms the common-sense observation that the quality of parenting (and other environmental factors such as health, education, and availability of resources) has a tremendous impact on the level of functioning or dysfunctioning of a child. A person's type doesn't tell us anything about the quality of parenting that the child received. However, with the help of the Levels of Development, we can have an idea of the family's degree of dysfunction by seeing how deeply defended and dysfunctional the child needed to become in order to adapt to it and find a degree of safety within it.

THE DOMINANT AFFECT GROUPS

The Dominant Affect Groups are important for transformational work because they reveal the unconscious emotional background we bring to all areas of our lives. In technical language, these have to do with "object-relations" theory.

Modern psychological theory has identified three fundamental "affects" — universal emotional states that are major building blocks of the personality. They are *attachment, frustration,* and *rejection.**

All human beings are constantly operating in all three of the affective states, regardless of their specific personality type. Further, they are mutually dependent: to have one is to have them all. Nevertheless, each Enneagram type operates primarily out of one of these particular affects; some types are more typically "attach-

---

* This concept comes from a field of psychology called *object-relations theory.* The basic idea behind object-relations theory is that the ego self only exists in relation to something else. In the first three years of life, we begin to distinguish and separate aspects of our experience, in the process of learning to distinguish our identity from that of others; this phenomenon was discovered in the course of studying the interactions of infants with their mothers. Noted ego developmental psychologists, such as Margaret Mahler, learned that initially the baby cannot distinguish herself from her mother or from anything else for that matter. The baby's consciousness exists in what is called an "undifferentiated state." There is only immediate experience without a distinct sense of a separate self. Gradually, the baby recognizes that her universe consists of a self and someone else (of course, the mother, or "the nurturing figure"). The baby then begins to separate some of her many experiences and qualities, assigning some to herself and some to the other. Further, psychologists learned that this unconscious pattern remained active as the ground for all the subsequent developments of the personality.

ment-based," some are more "frustration-based," and some are more "rejection-based."

Attachment represents the desire of the ego to maintain a comfortable and stable relationship with people or things that are identified with. Simply put, we want to hold on to whatever works well for us, be it a person, a job, a self-image, a feeling state, or a comfortable chair.

The *Attachment-Based Group* includes types Three, Six, and Nine. These types have problems with deeply held attachments to people, situations, or states that are "working" for them. *Threes* have learned to adjust their self-image and feelings to become more acceptable to and be valued by others. In this way, they hope to hold on to whatever attention and affection is available to them. They become attached both to the positive regard of whomever in their life they turn to for validation, and to whatever means they believe are necessary to keep the other's approval. *Sixes* have learned to associate certain relationships, social situations, groups, and beliefs with their security and safety. They invest themselves in these attachments and defend them, even when they may actually be harmed by them. (For example, a Six may stay in a bad marriage or a job out of a belief that it is necessary for security.) *Nines* became attached to an inner sense of well-being, a comfort zone, that they associate with autonomy and freedom. Nines may see their relationship with an idealized other or a comforting routine or a favorite food or a television show as a source of their stability and inner peace. Whatever the source, Nines do not want their comfort zone to be tampered with or changed

Frustration relates to our feeling that our comfort and needs are not being sufficiently attended to. The self is experienced as "hungry" — uncomfortable, restless, dissatisfied, impatient, or needy. These feelings arise from deeply conditioned patterns from our childhood. A person may actually be getting his needs met in ways he may not recognize, but still feel frustrated due to this background patterning. In fact, even if the person's needs are consciously met, he will often find something else to become frustrated about. This is because *the person's identity is partially based on being frustrated.* Sometimes we also reverse the pattern and become the one who frustrates others as a way of defending against our own feelings of frustration.

The *Frustration-Based Group* includes types One, Four, and Seven. None of these types ever seems to be able to find what it is looking for; they all can quickly become disenchanted with whatever previously has seemed to be the solution to their desires.

Ones are frustrated that the world is not more sensible and orderly than it actually is, and that others do not have the integrity that Ones believe they themselves have. They feel that others are constantly thwarting their efforts to improve things. Ones feel "Nothing is done quite well enough — everything fails to measure up to my standards." *Fours* are frustrated that they have not been adequately parented, and unconsciously expect valued others to protect and nurture them. When others fail to live up to their unrealistic expectations, Fours become frustrated and disappointed. Fours think "I never get what I need — everyone disappoints me." *Sevens* are frustrated because they pin their hopes for happiness on specific experiences that ultimately fail to satisfy them, moving on to something new with equal ardor and high hopes for fulfillment, usually only to be disappointed again. They feel "I can't find what will satisfy me — I've got to keep looking and going after it."

The *Rejection-Based Group* includes types Two, Five, and Eight. In this pattern, the self is unconsciously seen as small, weak, and potentially victimized, and others are seen as powerful, abusive, and rejecting. All three of these types go through life expecting to be rejected and so they defend themselves against this feeling in various ways. They repress their own genuine needs and vulnerabilities, attempting to offer some service, ability, or resource as a hedge against further rejection. *Twos* feel that they must be so good that others will not reject them. They cover over a feeling of underlying worthlessness and the fear that they are not really wanted by trying to please others so much that others will not dare reject or abandon them. Unlike Twos who feel that they are good, *Eights* feel that they are innately bad, and will likely be rejected unless they are so powerful and in control of life's necessities that others will dare not reject them. Further, Eights adopt a "tough" stance toward life — in effect, bracing themselves for rejection and trying not to care in the event that they actually are rejected. *Fives* feel negligible, on the sidelines of life, and they therefore must compensate by knowing something or have some special skill so useful to others that they will not be rejected. Like Eights, Fives also reduce the pain of rejection by cutting off from their feelings about it.

All three of these types offer some service or skill as a way of staving off rejection. Twos offer their caring and affection; Eights offer their strength; and Fives offer their knowledge and expertise.

We can also use this information for our personal growth by seeing what the antidote to our most troublesome object-relation affect is. Thus, the antidote for the feeling of Ones that their own efforts or the efforts of others are never sufficient is *acceptance of reality.* The antidote for Fours' feeling that they cannot get their needs met adequately is *self-renewing equanimity,* and the antidote for Sevens' feeling that they cannot find or get enough of what they want is *gratitude for what is available.* Likewise, the an-

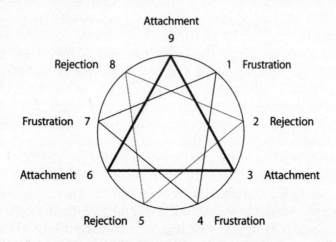

The Enneagram of Dominant Affect Groups

tidote for Twos' feeling that they are loved for only their service to others is *to love themselves and others regardless of others' reactions to them.* The antidote to Eights' feeling that they must control to protect themselves from any further hurt is a *self-surrendering open-heartedness,* and the antidote to Fives' hoarding quest for mastery is *nonattached compassion and clarity.* The antidote for Threes' attachment to "performance" is *an authentic humility and self-regard,* the antidote for Sixes' ambivalent attachment to others is their *courageous self-reliance,* and the antidote to Nines' comfortable complacency is their *love of life and growth itself.*

These antidotes might be a focal point for your meditation and self-observation during the day. The longer you contemplate them, the more their power to dissolve your old personality patterns will reveal itself. Remember, however, that the dominant affects (stemming from our object-relations patterns) are among the deepest, most fundamental building blocks of our ego identity, so we cannot do away with them by force of will. We can, however, lessen their negative impact by bringing awareness to them and *by being aware of their opposites,* these nine powerful antidotes.

We can further anchor and maintain our growth by being aware of (and meditating on) three principal spiritual attitudes for each Dominant Affect Group. No matter what type we are, we can benefit greatly by contemplating these attitudes — we do not have to be a Three to be aware of being authentic, or a Five to contemplate being compassionate. But focusing on the attitudes associated with our basic type can give us a profound new grounding from which to consolidate and expedite our growth and transformation.

Types 1, 4, 7	Need to reflect on the qualities of **acceptance, forgiveness, and gratitude** as a way of transforming their difficulties with their underlying feelings of *frustration*
Types 2, 5, 8	Need to reflect on the qualities of **unconditional positive regard for themselves and others, compassion,** and **self-surrender** as a way of transforming their difficulties with their underlying feelings of *rejection*

Types 3, 6, 9   Need to reflect on the qualities of **authenticity, courage,** and **self-possession** as a way of transforming their difficulties with their underlying feelings of *attachment*

EACH TYPE'S "MISSING PIECE"

There is a paradoxical and exciting element to the structure of the Enneagram that is best considered after the types are well understood — but which is a key to rapid growth with this system.

We have discovered that the healthy Levels, especially Level 1, of the type in the Direction of Disintegration indicate what our type most needs for our personal development. Under normal circumstances, we tend to act out in the Direction of Disintegration because we unconsciously know that what we need for our healing and wholeness is symbolized by that type — even though we cannot yet fully integrate that quality into our personality structure. When we become more healthy, however, we also begin to be in the position to access and claim our most needed qualities — to seize the capstone of our psyche, as it were.

However, for a person in his or her average Levels, the qualities of the Missing Piece are too "ego alien" and thus cannot be owned without disrupting the person's self-image in fundamental ways. None of the types can therefore claim its Missing Piece immediately or in a balanced way because none has not sufficiently laid the psychological groundwork for such a development. For example, Sevens most need to learn the lessons of acceptance and self-discipline, but they "cannot get there from here" if they move directly to One. A direct move to One results not in learning these higher lessons but in acting out average to unhealthy behavior, which is why we consider this a move in the Seven's "Direction of Disintegration." Only after doing a considerable amount of transformational work will the Seven be in a position to assimilate the healthy lessons of type One consistently.

For all the types it is highly instructive to take note of the Level 1 qualities of the type in the Direction of Disintegration for our type since it will reveal *what we most need for our completion*. We can then see our personality trying to imitate and compensate for this quality — as well as observe ourselves in those authentic moments when we actually attain it. The following chart will make some of these qualities clearer.

The Characteristics of Each Type's "Missing Piece"

Type One	Needs most to learn from Four to listen to and trust one's unconscious impulses and inspirations
Type Two	Needs most to learn from Eight to recognize one's own strength and to fully claim one's presence in the world
Type Three	Needs most to learn from Nine how to be instead of constantly doing, achieving, or performing
Type Four	Needs most to learn from Two to love oneself and others unconditionally
Type Five	Needs most to learn from Seven that life is a joy and that the universe is benevolent
Type Six	Needs most to learn from Three to be inner-directed and to respect oneself
Type Seven	Needs most to learn from One to accept life as it is and to live for a higher purpose
Type Eight	Needs most to learn from Five humility and one's true place in the larger scheme of things
Type Nine	Needs most to learn from Six to rely on oneself and to grow in adversity

THE INTERCONNECTED ENNEAGRAM

Thinking about the positive image of human nature that the Enneagram holds out to us can inspire us to embark on the journey, or to renew our commitment to it. Being aware of the characteristics of health helps us recognize these traits in ourselves so that our journey toward integration will be swifter and more sure. Yet we cannot simply list the healthy traits we find in each type with the recommendation that people acquire them. The healthy potentials symbolized by the Enneagram (or by any other typology, for that matter) are not a checklist of assets that can be acquired piece-meal, like a Chinese menu of virtues from which we select one from this column and another from that. The development of the person is more complex, demanding dynamic integration and bal-ance. As we move in the Direction of Integration, one strength bal-ances another, new potentials come into play, and another capac-ity emerges to ensure the harmony of those that have already been acquired.

It is not enough to be adaptable to the environment (a trait of the healthy Three), for example, since it is possible to adapt in ways that conceal one's identity. Adaptability alone is not a sole criterion for psychological health since, under certain circum-stances, the ability to adapt may well not indicate psychological growth but its reverse, a stultifying conformity. As desirable as adaptability may be, it must be *counterbalanced* by other quali-ties. In the case of an integrating Three, it is balanced by steadfast-ness to commitments, a trait of the healthy Six, the type in the Three's Direction of Integration.

The challenge is to balance all the strengths from all the types as we come in greater contact with our essential self. Remarkably, the Enneagram indicates the proper progression for this balancing evolution for each type. For example, we find that the healthy Eight's self-assertion must be balanced by the healthy Two's empa-thy. But empathy for others alone is not enough lest it deteriorate into sentimentality. The Two's empathy must be counterbalanced by the Four's honest self-appraisal. Yet honest self-appraisal is not enough lest it deteriorate into self-absorption. The Four's self-awareness must be counterbalanced by the One's objectivity — and yet that is not enough lest objectivity deteriorate into rigid logic. We could continue this way around the Enneagram, point-ing out how each type's strengths are called forth to balance the strengths of the other types.

The progression of the Direction of Integration is what we need to balance our strengths and growing virtues. Thus, while acquiring the healthy traits of our type is necessary, possessing them alone is not enough for a full and balanced life. The process of living out of one's Essence allows many different capacities of the psyche to emerge. There is no one state of "health" that can be prescribed for everyone, nor is there a final state of "health" common to all — but an ongoing process of growth and unfolding of each individual.

The problem is that the ego tends to identify itself with certain states, and to resist the ongoing flow of the unfolding self. Thus, it is extremely common to have an extraordinary experience of Essence, and then have our egos use it to make us feel more important, or to reinforce our pride, or even to feel more sexually desirable. With spiritual maturity, however, we understand that we do not own or create Essential qualities, but that they are always available to us, as we need them. When we are more open and centered, these qualities manifest themselves and flow freely through us. If we could allow ourselves to experience this truth on a regular basis, our lives would be transformed. All religions teach that there is nothing to cling to: when we are free of attachments, there is no more personal agenda, and we constantly manifest Divine attributes. Life is a joy and a continual participation in and exploration of a mystery — the mystery of existence.

As we continue with our Inner Work, we need to be aware that it is the nature of the personality to cling to the past, to the familiar, and to whatever is known. But whenever we do so, the qualities that are present in the moment pass us by. Instead of being refreshed by our experiences, we are most often drained by them; instead of seeing the rich texture and color of a brick wall in the sunlight, or smelling the aroma of cooking food, or hearing the symphony of sounds around us, we are gradually worn down by the effort to resist reality. Perhaps even more insidious is the fact that every gift that we receive can turn into a trap if we try to hold on to it, especially if we try to claim it as part of our personality. The lightness of joy, the exquisite moment of beauty, the simple instant of peace and freedom — if held on to — only add to the weight and opacity of our egos. Our experience becomes less alive, and our holding on to memories prevents us from claiming whatever treasures may await us in *this* moment.

While letting go of painful states is something we can all see the value of, it is often more difficult to let go of identifying with positive states. The reason we would consider doing so is because identifying with positive states causes them to degenerate into their opposite. Being present brings many gifts, but they change from moment to moment — and even gifts can become traps if they are clung to.

To retain any one of the gifts of the Enneagram, therefore, we need to be open to all of them, while identifying with none of them. When we identify with a gift, incorporating it into our self-image and forgetting to stay connected to *now*, the gift inevitably becomes a pale imitation of what it was.

It is useful to remember that the Enneagram is a symbol that *moves*. Gurdjieff insisted that it is a living symbol — a diagram of perpetual motion. The inner lines represent the dynamic movement of awareness itself, reflecting the fact that it is the nature of reality to change from instant to instant. Nothing in nature remains static. Only our minds wish to stand still (although, ironically, they are anything but static themselves).

Thus, the interconnected nature of the Enneagram teaches us that we cannot rest on our laurels. The principle of the interconnected Enneagram is that each type will eventually degenerate into its opposite unless it is counterbalanced by the strengths of the type in its Direction of Integration.

The chart below can therefore be read as follows. For example, type One can be read as, "Having a higher purpose in life . . . degenerates into being led by rigid ideas and principles . . . unless we are open to a joyous acceptance of reality at Seven." But at Seven, "A joyous acceptance of reality . . . degenerates into a hunger for more experiences . . . unless we are open to the sacredness of each experience at Five," and so forth.

The Interconnected Enneagram

Type		Degenerates into	Unless
One	Having a higher purpose in life ...	being led by rigid ideas and principles ...	we are open to a joyous acceptance of reality at Seven.
Seven	A joyous acceptance of reality ...	a hunger for more experiences ...	we are open to the sacredness of each experience at Five.
Five	Openness to the sacredness of each experience ...	being led by elaborate and useless interpretations of reality ...	we are fully grounded in reality and committed to practical, constructive action at Eight.
Eight	Being fully grounded and committed to practical, constructive action ...	an aggressive pursuit of control and self-importance ...	we are open to a devoted service to others, symbolized by Two.
Two	A devoted service to others ...	manipulating others to fulfill one's own needs ...	we are open to being completely truthful about who we are and what we are doing, at Four.
Four	Being completely truthful about who we are and what we are doing ...	being led by subjective states and emotional neediness ...	we are open to having a higher purpose in life at One.
Three	A humble self-love and esteem of one's true value ...	self-aggrandizement and ego glorification ...	we are open to commitment to others and the assumption of responsibility for our life, at Six.

Six	Being committed to others and taking responsibility for life ...	defending one's self from others and being fearful about one's own capacities ...	we are open to a complete trust in Being and a surrender to reality, symbolized by Nine.
Nine	A complete trust in Being and surrender to reality ...	passivity and self-neglect ...	we are open to a humble self-love and esteem for our true value, at Three.

CHAPTER 10

Recommendations

THE PROCESS OF TRANSFORMATION

Spiritual tradition and modern psychology offer many techniques and practices for cultivating Presence or awareness — qualities we discussed in Chapters 1 and 2 as essential for real growth and development. Ultimately, all of these techniques aim at getting people in contact with the real qualities of the Centers: grounded presence, vitality, and connectedness from the Instinctive Center; authenticity, value, true identity, and real love from the Feeling Center; and Quiet Mind, receptivity, and openness from the Thinking Center.

Gurdjieff taught that there have been three traditional paths, associated with the Three Centers, that are available to the person who sought genuine transformation. Historically, anyone attempting to reach self-realization had to retire from worldly life and submit to rigorous disciplines for many years. These three ways were undertaken in monasteries or in solitude, and if followed wholeheartedly, could produce transformation.

The first of these is the *Way of the Fakir*, followed by the person who struggles to overcome the body and mortify the flesh, such as the ascetic who sits out in the sun all day, or who lives alone in a cave or in a secluded hermitage of some kind. This way often involves strenuous physical work and discipline to overcome the body and its sensual demands and distractions. One distinctive aspect of it is that the ascetic must give up normal social life and retire from the world to take up this path of mortification. This way focuses on the Instinctive Center.

The second is the *Way of the Monk,* or the Way of Devotion, what in Hinduism is called Bahkti Yoga. In traditional Christianity, we see this way practiced in devotion to the Virgin Mary or to the Sacred Heart of Jesus, or in a personal devotion to the saints; elements of this way are present in the charismatic movement and, in various Eastern sects, in devotion to one's guru. This way involves transforming the feelings into something higher: by giving up the grosser forms of emotionality and transforming them into a pure form of transcendental love, the person is united with God in ecstatic rapture. Many Sufi schools also employ "second way" teachings by directing the feelings to greater and greater devotion to the Beloved: by setting one's heart on the Beloved, the seeker is transformed. This way corresponds to the Feeling Center.

The third way is the *Way of the Yogi,* or the Way of Knowledge and of quieting the mind. Buddhism travels this path as a way of having insight into how the mind functions. One learns to observe the mind in order to quiet it so that one can become completely still and unattached to all earthly things. This path is involved with a search for inner emptiness and quiet spaciousness beyond all transient manifestations. This way corresponds to the Thinking Center.

We have related these three paths to the three Centers of the Enneagram, as you can see in the illustration on the opposite page.

These three major spiritual ways are capable of producing profound results, if they are followed wholeheartedly. But Gurdjieff and others have said that there is also a hidden Fourth Way, a way that works on *all three Centers at once.* He called it the Way of the Sly Man because seekers on the Fourth Way do not retreat from life into a monastery as seekers on the first three ways must do. Rather, they live ordinary lives in the world while practicing their spirituality in a private and personal way hidden from the view of others. No one working beside such a person would know that he or she was doing anything special or out of the ordinary. The "sly person" uses the occurrences of ordinary life as the raw mate-

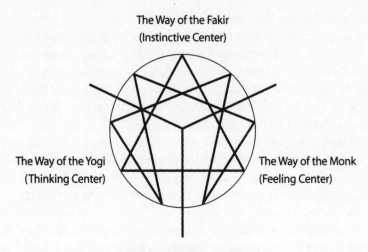

The Way of the Fakir
(Instinctive Center)

The Way of the Yogi
(Thinking Center)

The Way of the Monk
(Feeling Center)

The Three Traditional Ways

rial for Work without standing out or drawing attention to him-
or herself.

Nonetheless, the Fourth Way seeker throws himself into his
spiritual practices with the same integrity and intensity of purpose
that he would if he lived in a monastery; indeed, the person on a
Fourth Way path approaches the whole world as if it were a monastery. The everyday conditions of his life become his lessons.

The Fourth Way is a means of service that Gurdjieff said becomes available and operative when the world is in a crisis, or
when Earth reaches a shock point in its evolution. When we come
to a critical juncture in the evolution of life on the planet, the
Fourth Way is given as a special help to humankind. Gurdjieff also
taught that the Enneagram is the symbol of the Fourth Way, and
when it appears, it means that the Fourth Way has been opened. It
is the sign that humans need to respond to an extraordinary challenge — to make a major leap in consciousness. For that reason,
more help is made available from on High, so to speak.

From this perspective we can understand that the Enneagram is
much more than an interesting way to classify people. Combined
with practices to cultivate our awareness, it can be a powerful tool

for transforming the ego. This map of the soul — and the profound spirituality that it represents — may be preparing us to assume tremendous responsibilities in the near future, in ways that we can scarcely imagine. In a world that is more Spirit-centered, our ego projects must take their proper place. We believe that the Enneagram is a tool that can help humanity prepare for such a fundamental shift in human consciousness.

Whether we are considering the Enneagram on this greater scale or are simply looking to improve our lives in basic ways, one fact is certain: we change. Either we move forward or we move backward, but it is not possible to stay the same. If our change is to be toward growth, we must learn to desire what is truly right for us and have the courage not to succumb to our fears. Knowing ourselves so that we will know what will be truly good for us is our surest guide.

Although our work emphasizes the importance of cultivating awareness and presence as the key to transformation, many people have requested more specific suggestions for using the Enneagram in their growth and development. Naturally, no general recommendations can apply to all individual cases, so you must personalize these suggestions just as you must personalize the descriptions themselves. These recommendations are not a substitute for self-knowledge and are, at best, a means of "priming the pump" for personal growth. They are merely another source of insight. For real change to occur, you will always need awareness, self-discipline, and perseverance. A set of recommendations will not in itself cause improvements in anyone's life.

These suggestions are not exhaustive, nor are they meant to be. But the recommendations may help focus your attention on typical problems so that you will be less controlled by unconscious tendencies in your personality. They may also be helpful in Enneagram study groups, in therapy, or as the basis for discussion with family and friends about yourself and your type.

In a sense, sets of recommendations should be unnecessary: the descriptions suggest dozens of areas that can be used as starting points for change and growth. If, for instance, you are a Six and read that average Sixes "begin to get suspicious, and react against their supporters or authorities through indirect passive-aggressive behavior, giving contradictory, mixed signals" (Chapter 3, p. 99), you might attempt to learn how passive-aggressive you have been, if you are suspicious, whether you react against others, give mixed signals, and so on. Used in this way, virtually every paragraph of *Understanding the Enneagram* or *Personality Types* can be not only a source of insight into ourselves but, by implication, a source of recommendations about what we can do to grow.

But, of course, knowing the automatic tendencies of our personality type is only a first step — although an absolutely necessary one. Indeed, it may well be that many people do not consider their habitual patterns to be a problem at all. Without insight and more objective feedback, most people are highly unaware of the potentially negative results of their unconscious behavior. And even if we have already come to know ourselves, probably much more remains to be seen.

> Books can provide valuable information and advice, they can give us new insights, they can encourage. But knowledge alone is not enough to change us. If it were, the most knowledgeable people would be the best people, and we know from our own experience that this is not so. Knowledge would be virtue, and it is not. Knowing more about ourselves is but a means toward the goal of being happy and leading a good life, but the possession of knowledge alone cannot bestow virtue, happiness, or fulfillment on us. Books cannot provide answers to all the problems which confront us or impart the courage necessary if we are to persevere in our search. For these things, we must look both within and beyond ourselves. [*PT,* 10]

Whether or not we grow as persons depends on our having insight into our genuine attitudes and behaviors, as well as having the motivation to persevere in the process of self-observation and Inner Work. Seeing ourselves as we really are takes courage because it necessarily involves stirring up — and consciously dealing with — our ego defenses, our anxiety, and our underlying hurt, shame, and grief. Encountering these parts of ourselves is never easy, and we can use all the help we can get. If this chapter is simply a first step in the right direction, then, as limited as it is, it will be valuable.

RECOMMENDATIONS FOR PERSONALITY TYPE TWO

1. First and foremost, remember that if you are not addressing your own needs, it is highly unlikely that you will be able to meet anyone else's needs without problems, underlying resentments, and potential rejections. Further, you will be less able to respond to people in a balanced way if you have not gotten adequate rest, and taken care of yourself properly. It is not selfish to make sure that you are okay before attending to others' needs — it is simply common sense.

2. Try to become more conscious of your own motives when you decide to help someone. While doing good things for people is certainly an admirable trait, when you do so because you expect the other person to appreciate you or do something nice for you in return, you are setting yourself up for disappointments. Your type has a real danger of falling into unconscious codependent patterns with loved ones, and they almost never bring you what you really want.

3. While there are many things you might want to do for people, it is often better to ask them what they really need first. You are gifted at accurately intuiting others' feelings and needs, but that does not necessarily mean that they want those needs remedied by you in the way you have in mind. Communicate your intentions; be willing to accept a "no thank you." Someone deciding that she does not want your particular offer

of help does not mean that she dislikes you or is rejecting you.

4. Resist the temptation to call attention to yourself and your good works. After you have done something for others, do not remind them about it. Let it be: either they will remember your kindness themselves and thank you in their own way or they will not. Your calling attention to what you have done for them only puts people on the spot and makes them feel uneasy. It will not satisfy anyone or improve your relationships.

5. Do not always be "doing" for people and above all do not try to get people to love you by giving them either gifts or undeserved praise. On the other hand, do not pointedly withdraw your service when others do not respond to you as you would like. Do not make what you do for others depend on how they respond to you. Help others when they ask for it, especially helping them to become more capable of functioning on their own.

6. It is tempting to make new friends and to want to enjoy their company. While it is exciting to feel the flush of a new love, your service to those who already depend on you may suffer. Moreover, your primary commitments (to spouse and children, for example) must be honored first before you spend time cultivating new relationships.

7. Beware of looking for specific signs of affection from others. While you may be able to show your love freely, others may feel less comfortable with overt displays of affection. *This does not mean that they do not care about you* — only that they have a different way of expressing their care. Learn to recognize other ways that people show their appreciation.

8. Do not be possessive of your friends; share them with others just as they have shared themselves with you. Remember: if the love among you is genuine, there will be enough to go

around for everyone. Genuine love is the only commodity that can be given away endlessly without ever running out.

9. Beware of "rescue missions." You have a tender heart and are drawn to help people who are suffering or in trouble. Also beware of rescuing people so that they will be grateful to you for your help, or worse, "fixing" them so that they can become your boyfriend or girlfriend. Do not allow your passion of pride to cause you to believe that your love will instantly change a troubled person into a perfect spouse.

10. To love others selflessly is an extraordinary achievement — one of human nature's very highest powers. If you have achieved the ability to love others unselfishly, you are already an extraordinary individual. If you develop your great capacity to care about others, you will never go far wrong — in fact, you will do a great deal of good in life. Others are probably already seeking you out because you possess what everyone wants: the ability to love and appreciate others for who they are.

RECOMMENDATIONS FOR PERSONALITY TYPE THREE

1. For our real development, it is essential to be truthful. Be honest with yourself and others about your genuine feelings and needs. Likewise, resist the temptation to impress others or inflate your importance. You will impress people more deeply by being authentic than by bragging about your successes or exaggerating your accomplishments.

2. Develop charity and cooperation in your relationships. You can do this by taking time to pause in a busy day to really connect with someone you care about. Nothing spectacular is required — simply a few moments of quiet appreciation. When

you do so, you will become a more loving person, a more faithful friend — and a much more desirable individual. You will feel better about yourself.

3. Take breaks. You can drive yourself and others to exhaustion with your relentless pursuit of your goals. Ambition and self-development are good qualities, but temper them with rest periods in which you reconnect more deeply with yourself. Sometimes taking three to five deep breaths is enough to recharge your battery and improve your outlook.

4. Develop your social awareness. Many Threes have grown tremendously by getting involved in projects that had nothing to do with their own personal advancement. Working cooperatively with others toward goals that transcend personal interest is a powerful way of finding your true value and identity.

5. In their desire to be accepted by others, some average Threes adapt so much to the expectations of others that they lose touch with what they are really feeling about the situation. Develop yourself by resisting the tendency to adjust to others' expectations. It is imperative that you invest time in discovering your own core values.

6. Support and encourage others. Instead of looking for attention and admiration yourself, give your attention and admiration to others, especially when they deserve it. Paradoxically, you will feel better about yourself when you learn to appreciate (and support) others. Your relationships will be happier and more satisfying if they are not based on competition but on cooperation. You will become even more desirable as a friend when you give as much attention and affirmation as you receive.

7. You have great energy and a good sense of humor, are good at organizing events, and create excitement, usually simply by your presence and high spirits. Use these qualities for the wel-

fare of the groups you belong to and for individual members of these groups, making sure that members are developing themselves and their best capacities.

8. Threes tend to become depressed when they fail to meet their notion of success, or enraged when they feel that others are slighting them in some way. Unrealistic expectations of themselves are at the root of their problems — both in their careers and in many of their relationships. If this applies to you, be aware of how inflated your expectation of acclaim might be. If people find merit in whatever you have accomplished, they will let you know about it. And even if they do not, it is not necessarily indicative of your true worth.

9. It is usually difficult for Threes to admit that they have problems or are "in over their heads." Much of the deceit associated with your type results from your denial that you are suffering or that you are not qualified to do something. If unchecked, this tendency can get you into big trouble. You can avoid many of the traps of your type by simply letting others know when you have reached your limit of understanding, ability, or endurance.

10. As is true of all the types, Threes have spiritual capacities and can develop themselves into the best persons they can be. Many of your strengths already lie in this direction, so follow them. Do not become distracted by comparing yourself with anyone else or by fretting about anyone else's success. When you focus your attention and abilities on doing worthwhile work (especially when it benefits others), you are well on your way to being your best, and comparisons with anyone else become completely beside the point. In short: learn to accept yourself — and do not worry about anyone else.

RECOMMENDATIONS FOR PERSONALITY TYPE FOUR

1. Do not pay so much attention to your feelings; they are not a true source of support for you, as you probably already know. Remember this advice: "From our present perspective, we can also see that one of the most important mistakes Fours make is to equate themselves with their feelings. The fallacy is that to understand themselves they must understand their feelings, particularly their negative ones, before acting. Fours do not see that the self is not the same as its feelings or that the presence of negative feelings does not preclude the presence of good in themselves" (*PT,* 172). Always remember that your feelings are telling you something about yourself as you are at this particular moment, not necessarily any more than that.

2. Avoid putting off things until you are "in the right mood." Commit yourself to productive, meaningful work that will contribute to your good and that of others, no matter how small the contribution may be. Working consistently in the real world will create a context in which you can discover yourself and your talents. Actually, you are happiest when you are working — that is, activating your potentials and realizing yourself. You will not find yourself in a vacuum, so connect — and stay connected — with the real world.

3. Self-esteem and self-confidence will develop only from having positive experiences, whether or not you believe that you are ready to have them. Therefore, put yourself in the way of good. You may feel that you are never ready to take on a challenge of some sort, that you always need more time. (Fours typically never feel that they are sufficiently "together," but they must nevertheless have the courage to stop putting off their lives.) Even if you start small, commit yourself to doing something that will bring out the best in you.

4. A wholesome self-discipline takes many forms, from sleeping regular hours to working regularly to exercising regularly, and has a cumulative, strengthening effect. Since it comes from you, a healthy self-discipline is not contrary to your freedom or individuality. On the other hand, sensuality, excessive sexual experiences, alcohol, drugs, excess sleep, and fantasizing have a debilitating effect on you, as you already know. Therefore, practice healthy self-discipline and stay with it.

5. Avoid lengthy conversations in your imagination, particularly if they are negative, resentful, or even excessively romantic. These conversations are essentially unreal and at best only rehearsals for action — although, as you know, you almost never say or do what you imagine you will. Instead of spending time imagining your life and relationships, begin to live them.

6. Talk openly with someone you trust. This need not be a therapist, although it might be. You need both to express your feelings spontaneously and to have someone react honestly. You may well discover that you are not as different or as much of an outsider as you sometimes feel you are. Paradoxically, one of the surest ways of "finding yourself" is by being in a relationship with someone else.

7. Community service of some kind will make you less self-conscious and give you a better perspective on yourself. There are good things in you that you have kept hidden, possibly even from yourself. Find out what they are by getting involved in practical service.

8. Do not succumb to self-pity or to complaining about your parents, thoughts of your unhappy childhood, your unfulfilled past, your failed relationships, and how no one understands you. Someone would likely understand you if you made a real effort to communicate. (One of your unhealthy claims is that you have been damaged by your upbringing and are therefore exempt from having realistic expectations of any sort placed

on you.) Use your self-knowledge to be aware of the true effects of your negative attitudes.

9. Do not take everything so personally, thinking that every remark is aimed at you. And even if one occasionally is, do not go over it in your mind. After all, a critical or hostile remark does *not* reflect the whole truth about you. Usually, people are too busy worrying about themselves to scrutinize your thoughts or behavior in such detail. If in doubt, get reality checks from others — ask them what they meant.

10. Beware of the harshness of your own self-talk. You tend to say and do things to yourself that you would never dream of saying or doing to anyone else. Learn to notice the inner voices of contempt and self-rejection that you entertain. Cliché though it is, become a friend to yourself. Stand up for yourself and give yourself a chance.

RECOMMENDATIONS FOR PERSONALITY TYPE FIVE

1. Learn to notice when your thinking and speculating take you out of the immediacy of your experience. Your mental capacities can be an extraordinary gift, but they can also be a trap when you use them to retreat from contact with yourself and others. Stay connected with your physicality.

2. You tend to be extremely intense and so high-strung that it's difficult to relax and unwind. Make an effort to learn to calm down in a healthy way, without drugs or alcohol. Exercising or using biofeedback techniques will help channel some of your tremendous nervous energy. Meditation, jogging, yoga, and dancing are especially helpful for your type.

3. You see many possibilities but often do not know how to choose among them or judge which is more or less important. When you are caught in your fixation, a sense of perspective

can be missing, and with it the ability to make accurate assessments. At such a time, it can be helpful to get the advice of someone whose judgment you trust while you are gaining perspective on your situation. Doing this can also help you trust someone else, a difficulty for your type.

4. Notice when you are getting intensely involved in projects that do not necessarily support your self-esteem, confidence, or life situation. It is possible to follow many different fascinating subjects, games, and pastimes, but they can become huge distractions from what you know you really need to do. Decisive action will bring more confidence than learning more facts or acquiring more unrelated skills.

5. Fives tend to find it difficult to trust people, to open up to them emotionally, or to make themselves accessible in various ways. Their awareness of potential problems in relationships may tend to create a self-fulfilling prophecy. It is important to remember that having conflicts with others is not unusual and that the healthy thing is to work them out rather than reject attachments with people by withdrawing into isolation. Having one or two intimate friends whom you trust enough to have conflicts with will enrich your life greatly.

6. Try to be more cooperative with others and less a loner. Although it goes against the grain, it will be instructive for you to learn to be supportive and nurturing to people. And, where possible, yield to others graciously without feeling that you have been beaten intellectually or have been put into a vulnerable position.

7. Some Fives tend to make others feel ill at ease. Because they are so intensely involved in what interests them and find their own ideas so fascinating, they tend to forget the social niceties that help others be comfortable with them. If this applies to you, remember that your very brilliance may be intimidating to many (indeed, it is probably something you are proud of and use to distance yourself from people). Rather than being

encouraged to share your interests, others can be put off unnecessarily.

8. You tend to look down on those who you think are less intelligent than you. However, even if other people are not as intelligent, this does not automatically mean that they are stupid or their ideas are worthless. Try to be more accepting of their intellectual limitations without being cynical or harsh in your judgments. Also remember that there are different kinds of intelligence and that even if your intellectual gifts are superior to those of others, it does not give you the right to be condescending or abrasive to anyone else. Use your gifts for others, not against them.

9. If others begin to avoid you or react to you antagonistically, consider the possibility that you — rather than they — have begun the antagonisms. Examine yourself to discover what you may have contributed to your interpersonal conflicts.

10. You have an enormous capacity for understanding. Think of ways to develop your compassion for others, to understand what they are going through from their point of view. By using your insight into people with compassion and caring, your own more gentle feelings will emerge to soften your hard edges. You will become more trusting, relaxed, and happier if you identify with other people rather than standing back and observing them. Do not use only your head — use more of your heart: it will give purpose and meaning to your knowledge and make you a more fulfilled person.

RECOMMENDATIONS FOR PERSONALITY TYPE SIX

1. Remember that there is nothing unusual about being anxious since everyone is anxious — and much more often than you might think. Learn to be more present to your anxiety, to ex-

plore it, and to come to terms with it. Work creatively with your tensions without turning to excessive amounts of alcohol (or other drugs) to allay them. In fact, if you are present and breathing fully, anxiety can be energizing, a kind of tonic that can help make you more productive and aware of what you are doing.

2. You tend to get edgy and testy when you are upset or angry, and you can even turn on others and blame them for things you have done or brought on yourself. Be aware of your pessimism: it results in dark moods and negative thought patterns that you tend to project on reality. When you succumb to this self-doubt, you can become your own worst enemy and may harm yourself more than anyone else does.

3. Sixes tend to overreact when they are under stress and feeling anxious. Learn to identify what makes you overreact. Also realize that almost none of the things you have feared so much has actually come true. Even if things *are* as bad as you think, your fearful thoughts weaken you and your ability to change things for the better. You can't always manage external events, but you *can* manage your own thoughts.

4. Work on becoming more trusting. There are doubtless several people in your life you can turn to who care about you and who are trustworthy. If not, go out of your way to find someone trustworthy, and allow yourself to get close to that person. This will mean risking rejection and arousing some of your deepest fears, but the risk is worth taking. You have a gift for getting people to like you, but you are unsure of yourself and may be afraid of making a commitment to them. Therefore, come down clearly on one side of the fence in your relationships. Let people know how you feel about them.

5. Others probably think better of you than you realize, and few people are really out to get you. In fact, your fears tell you more about your attitudes toward others than they indicate about others' attitudes toward you.

6. You are highly responsible in many areas, but you can be afraid of accepting responsibility for mistakes. You may fear others will jump down your throat, but most people respect those who take responsibility for their actions, *especially* if they have made a mistake. If you try to pass the buck, you may succeed only in alienating others and in undermining the respect they have for you.

7. You want to feel secure, but this will never be possible unless you are secure with yourself. You need to focus on becoming more self-affirming — developing a realistic belief in yourself and your own abilities. If you do not believe in yourself, other people probably will not either. A good way to do this is by getting more grounded in your body and allowing your fretting mind to become more quiet. When this happens, you will naturally feel more confident and supported by life.

8. Examine your attitudes toward authority. Do you reflexively rebel and resist authority? Do you seek it out, hiding behind an "I was only following orders" attitude? For most Sixes, issues with authority are highly charged. The greater your awareness is of your unconscious attitudes in this department, the more you will be able to recognize the authority of your own inner wisdom.

9. Be fair with others and tell them what is on your mind, lest you appear indecisive or defensive. Any of the alternatives cause conflicts and tensions in your relationships.

10. Most of your issues have to do with finding reliable sources of guidance and support outside yourself. It is good to remember that many of these sources can be useful up to a point, but none of them can provide the kind of unwavering stability and unerring wisdom you want. Only your own true nature can give you a deep sense of solidity and capacity in the world, because only the spontaneous intelligence of your own soul can respond to each unique situation freshly. So be grateful for the many sources of support in your life, but lean on them less.

You have within you everything you need to move through life with dignity and grace.

RECOMMENDATIONS FOR PERSONALITY TYPE SEVEN

1. Recognize your impulsiveness, and get in the habit of observing your impulses rather than giving in to them. This means letting most of your impulses pass and becoming a better judge of which ones are worth acting on. The more you can resist acting out your impulses, the more you will be able to focus on what is really good for you.

2. Learn to listen to other people. They are often interesting, and you may learn things that will open new doors for you. Also learn to appreciate silence and solitude: you do not have to distract yourself (and protect yourself from anxiety) with constant noise from the television or the stereo. By learning to live with less external stimulation, you will learn to trust yourself. You will be happier than you expect because you will be satisfied with whatever you do, even if it is less than you have been doing.

3. You do not have to have everything this very moment. That tempting new acquisition will most likely still be available tomorrow (this is certainly true of food, alcohol, and other common gratifications — that ice-cream cone, for instance). Most good opportunities will come back again — and you will be in a better position to discern which opportunities really are best for you.

4. Always choose quality over quantity, especially in your experiences. The ability to have experiences of quality can be learned only by giving your full attention to the experience you are having *now*. If you keep anticipating future experi-

ences, you will keep missing the present one and undermine the possibility of ever being satisfied.

5. Make sure that what you want will really be good for you in the long run. As the saying goes, watch what you pray for since your prayers may be answered. In the same vein, think about the long-term consequences of what you want since you may get it only to find that it becomes another disappointment — or even a source of unhappiness.

6. Happiness usually comes indirectly, as a by-product of giving yourself to something worthwhile. When people are actively engaged with their present experience and have their priorities right, they easily become happy without seeking happiness as their primary goal. Therefore, making being happy your main goal in life will almost guarantee that real, abiding happiness will continue to elude you.

7. Beware of your tendency to get out of control. It is easy for you to do so because you are naturally enthusiastic about everything. You have a great deal of energy and strong appetites. Your type's deepest fear is of being deprived, but by pursuing every exciting possibility that comes along without adequate discrimination, you will inevitably be deprived not only of the happiness you seek but of many other things besides.

8. You can be very funny and entertaining. Your sense of humor, wit, and quick mind are a source of pleasure for you and others. However, watch what you say. Avoid any tendency to say more than you mean for effect or to get a reaction from others. You may well hurt people and damage your relationships just for the sake of getting off a quip or for having the last word. It is not worth ruining friendships and hurting people just to get a laugh.

9. In a similar vein, remember that it is not your job to keep yourself or other people "up" all the time. Seek out friends

with whom you can feel free to express other sides of your feelings. While your capacity for high sprits is always welcome, you are most compelling to others when you are more real and more grounded. Cultivate depth, and do not be afraid of your sorrow. What you are running from has already happened, and you are still here and living your life.

10. One of your highest psychological and spiritual capacities is for joy and for feeling intense gratitude for all that you have. Remember to take time to be grateful and to allow yourself to be enthralled by existence: your sense of wonder at the beauty and preciousness of life will lead you into unexpected realms. Prepare to be surprised.

RECOMMENDATIONS FOR PERSONALITY TYPE EIGHT

1. It goes against the grain, but act with self-restraint. You show true power when you forbear from asserting your will with others, even when you could. Your real power lies in your ability to inspire and uplift people. You are at your best when you take charge and help everyone through a crisis. Few will take advantage of you when you are caring, and you will do more to secure the loyalty and devotion of others by showing the greatness of your heart than you ever could by displays of raw power.

2. It is difficult for Eights, but learn to yield to others, at least occasionally. Often little is really at stake, and you can allow others to have their way without fear of sacrificing your power, or your real needs. The desire to dominate everyone all the time is a sign that your ego is beginning to inflate — a danger signal that more serious conflicts with others are inevitable.

3. Remember that the world is not against you. Many people in your life care about you and look up to you, but when you are in your fixation, you do not make this easy for them. Let in the affection that is available. Doing this will not make you weak, but it will confirm the strength and support in you and your life. Also remember that by believing that others are against you and reacting against them, you tend to alienate them and confirm your own fears. Take stock of the people who truly are on your side, and let them know how important they are to you.

4. Eights typically want to be self-reliant and depend on no one. But, ironically, they depend on many people. For example, you may think that you are not dependent on your employees because they depend on you for their jobs. You could dismiss them at any time and hire other workers. Everyone is expendable in your little kingdom — except you. But the fact is that you are dependent on others to do their jobs too, especially if your business concerns grow beyond what you can manage alone. But if you alienate everyone associated with you, you will eventually be forced to employ the most obsequious and untrustworthy operatives. When you do, you will have reason to question their loyalty and to fear losing your position. The fact is that whether in your business world or your domestic life, your self-sufficiency is largely an illusion.

5. Eights typically overvalue power. Having power, whether through wealth, position, or simple brute force, allows them to do whatever they want, to feel important, to be feared and obeyed. But those who are attracted to you because of your power do not love you for yourself, nor do you love or respect them. While this may be the Faustian bargain you have made, you will nevertheless have to pay the price that whatever power you accumulated will inevitably be at a cost to you, physically and emotionally.

6. Learn to serve a higher purpose than your self-interest. Family and relationships provide a means for doing this in the lives of most people. Giving and receiving the love of a spouse and of children is the higher purpose that helps most people transcend themselves to find meaning in their lives. But if everything is reduced to serving your self-interest, the possibility of self-transcendence is eliminated — and with it the possibility of deep happiness, spiritual growth, and many other values. Maintaining a grossly inflated ego is the only way many Eights have of staving off meaninglessness — a meaninglessness, however, that their lifestyles frequently create.

7. If a Higher Power exists, there is something greater than you, and something to surrender to. But self-surrender is one of the most difficult concepts for Eights to accept. If you do not believe in God, is your nonbelief based on genuine intellectual convictions or merely on the fact that you do not want to give up your ego and the things you enjoy? A great deal may depend on your answer to this question.

8. If you have fallen into the lower Levels of your type, and, because of your own pain, you have been harsh, ruthless, or caused pain and injury to others, then you have reason to turn your life around while you still can. A life lived on the lowest level of human functioning — at the level of the beast — results in an end similar to that suffered by other animals, an ultimately meaningless existence and a lonely death. Things do not have to go that way. Trust in your essential goodness and be open to the possibility of real transformation.

9. One of your greatest potentials is your ability to create opportunities for others. When Eights use their power to create hope and prosperity for everyone, they are respected and remembered for being the benefactors they truly are. Therefore, if you are in a position of power and have great resources at your disposal, and if you use them magnanimously, you will

have no one to fear. Rather than make enemies, you will make fervent allies. Rather than question the loyalty of others, you can count on it with assurance. And even if you are taken advantage of by someone, the greatness of what you may have accomplished can never be taken away or forgotten. Indeed, others will see to it that it is not. If you look out for other people's needs, they will look out for yours.

10. Think of the harm you can do to others; then think of the good. By which do you wish to be remembered?

RECOMMENDATIONS FOR PERSONALITY TYPE NINE

1. It is worth examining your type's tendency to go along with others, doing what they want to keep the peace and be nice. Will constantly acquiescing to the wishes of others provide the kind of relationships that will really satisfy you? Remember, it is impossible to love others if you are not truly present to them. This means that you have to be yourself, that you (paradoxically) have to be independent so that you can really be there for others when they need you.

2. Exert yourself. Force yourself to pay attention to what is going on. Do not drift off or tune out people, or daydream. Work on focusing your attention to become an active participant in the world around you. Try to become more mentally and emotionally engaged.

3. Recognize that you also have aggressions, anxieties, and other feelings that you must deal with. Negative feelings and impulses are a part of you and they affect you emotionally and physically whether or not you acknowledge them. Furthermore, your negative emotions are often expressed inadvertently and get in the way of the peace and harmony you want

in your relationships. It is best to get things out in the open first, at least by allowing yourself to become aware of your feelings.

4. Although this will be very painful for you, if your marriage has ended in divorce or if you are having problems with your children, you must honestly examine how you have contributed to these problems. Examining troubled relationships will be extremely difficult because the people involved have been close to your heart. The feelings you have for others endow you with much of your identity and self-esteem. But if you really love others, you can do no less than examine the role you have played in whatever conflicts that have arisen. In the last analysis, the choice is simple: you must sacrifice your peace of mind (in the short run) for the satisfaction of genuine relationships (in the long run).

5. Exercise frequently to become more aware of your body and emotions. (Some Nines run around doing errands and think that they are getting enough exercise.) Regular exercise is a healthy form of self-discipline and will increase your awareness of your feelings and other sensations. A body awareness will allow you to concentrate and focus your attention in other areas of your life as well. Exercise is also a good way to get in touch with and release aggression.

6. Repressing your feelings will lead to somatization reactions — unexplained headaches, backaches, nausea, and other bodily ailments. Sudden migraines, crying spells, panic attacks, and fear of going out into public (agoraphobia) are examples of physiological and psychological problems caused by repressed emotions. It will be difficult to seek help for these if you need to, but it may be necessary. Do not be afraid. Your life will be richer and you will be more truly at peace if you do.

7. Do not use drugs or alcohol to tranquilize you, except at times of great crisis. They may spare you from anxiety, but at the

cost of dulling the very awareness and ability to cope that you are trying to develop. Using tranquilizers is, for Nines, like "bringing coals to Newcastle" — not something you really need, only something you think you need to spare yourself discomfort. Coping with crises not only will increase your self-esteem but will be a real sign to others that you are truly a strong person and that they will be able to look to you for support at times of crisis in their lives.

8. To the degree that they are repressed as individuals, one of the greatest tragedy for Nines is that they may come to the end of their lives and realize that they have never really lived. It's as if their lives have happened to someone else: they haven't really lived them themselves. They may realize (if only faintly) that they were "asleep" most of the time. Do not live like this. Accept your life and learn to feel the magnitude of what it is to be alive. If you give up your presence, you give up much of your life.

9. Trust yourself to ventilate your anger and fears with your spouse and friends. (Standing up to others and expressing feelings is threatening to many of the personality types, so you are not alone.) Have confidence that you will not damage your relationships by expressing yourself. Think of the comfort of knowing that your relationships are solid, that your family and friends will respond to you, and that you can be yourself and grow as an individual. This is a basis for genuine reassurance and comfort.

10. One of your greatest assets is your receptivity to people: others feel calm, safe, and accepted around you. But they will love you and seek you out even more if they also feel that you understand them and are attentive to their needs. Listen to people carefully and get to know them as they really are. The love you have for them — and they for you — will be that much more real and that much more valuable.

RECOMMENDATIONS FOR PERSONALITY TYPE ONE

1. Learn to relax. Take some time for yourself, without feeling that everything is up to you or that what you do not accomplish will result in chaos and disaster. Mercifully, the salvation of the world does not depend on you alone, even though you may sometimes feel it does.

2. You have a lot to teach others and are probably a good teacher, but do not expect others to change immediately. What is obvious to you may not be as obvious to them, especially if they are not used to being as self-disciplined and objective about themselves as you are about yourself. Many people may also want to do what is right and may agree with you in principle, but for various reasons, they simply cannot change right away. The fact that others do not change immediately according to your prescriptions does not mean that they will not change sometime in the future. Your words and above all your example may do more good than you realize, although they may take longer than you expect. So have patience.

3. It is easy for you to work yourself up into a lather about the wrongdoings of others. And it may sometimes be true that they are wrong. But what is it to you? Your irritation with them will do nothing to help them see another way of being. Similarly, beware of your constant irritation with your own "shortcomings." Does your own harsh self-criticism really help you to improve? Or does it simply make you tense, nervous, and self-doubting? Learn to recognize the attacks of your superego and how they undermine you rather than help you.

4. It is important for you to get in touch with your feelings, particularly your unconscious impulses. You may find that you are uneasy with your emotions and your sexual and aggressive impulses — in short, with the messy human things that make

us human. It might be beneficial to keep a journal or to get into some kind of group therapy or other group work both to develop your emotions and to see that others will not condemn you for having human needs and limitations.

5. Your Achilles' heel is your self-righteous anger. You get angry easily and are offended by what seems to you to be the perverse refusal of others to do the right thing — as you have defined it. Try to step back and see that your anger alienates people so that they cannot hear many of the good things you have to say. Further, your own repressed anger may well be giving you an ulcer or high blood pressure and is a harbinger of worse things to come.

6. One of the most difficult things for Ones to learn is to allow people to be as they are and to come to decisions on their own. It is tempting to tell people what you think they should do — and while you may well be right, your good intentions can go astray when you try to impose rules or principles to every situation. Acting wisely involves knowing how much to say and when to say it; it involves knowing what your listener can accept and learn from, and this can never come from a set of rules. The wisest thoughts do no good unless others are ready to hear them. Therefore, let a living wisdom be your guide, not your rules or your "rightness."

7. Listen to others: they are often right, too. And even if they are not, there is almost always some kernel of truth to the point of view they are expressing. By listening to others, you not only will learn more but will become a more informed and sensitive teacher. When you speak, others will know that they are listening to a human being, not a logic machine.

8. Perfectionists drive others crazy. There is probably no single, absolutely correct way of doing everything — from washing dishes to ironing a shirt to laying out a garden, to every other activity in life. Many things can be done differently without any disadvantages. Moreover, perfectionism that is nothing

more than a useless pickiness undermines the confidence others have in you when you advise them about something truly important. In short, it is necessary to discriminate between those times when perfection is a useful standard and when it is not.

9. Unhealthy Ones tend to be obsessive in their thoughts and compulsive in their actions, and even average Ones begin to manifest elements of these kinds of behavior. Try to resist both tendencies as soon as you become aware of them; if yielded to, they will lead you into increasingly destructive behavior. In particular, be aware of the desire for total orderliness and control of your environment since it is a harbinger of other, darker disorders. (An exaggerated orderliness is often a displacement for the fear of losing control in some other area of your life.) Try to find out what is really bothering you and tackle those problems; do not waste your energy on the thousand little annoyances you tend to spend yourself on.

10. A person does not have to be perfect to be good. Give yourself the true satisfaction of becoming human, not inhumanly perfect.

CHAPTER 11

Personality, Essence, and Spirituality

Naturally, it takes years of work on oneself to get to know anything real about ourselves; we may think we are finding out a great deal, through self-observation and by applying the other teachings and techniques of The Work [Gurdjieff's teaching]. . . . What we think we have discovered about ourselves is very superficial at first, so that real self-knowledge only comes after years of patient effort. But such effort is immensely worthwhile in every particular, because it not only transforms us, it transforms our whole life for us; because as our level of being changes, so does our life change, too. We become different people *inside,* and this is reflected by the way life treats us *outside.*

This is an esoteric law . . . and explains why it is only ourselves who can make anything really worthwhile of our lives. It is no good looking to external factors or agencies to do this for us. Such things cannot change our level of being, and so life remains just as it was before, despite whatever we may be doing or thinking. It is only when we begin to really work on ourselves, and change our habitual ways of thinking and feeling, that anything real or permanent can happen to us. For self-change is the basic pre-requisite for external change. And self-change can only come about as a result of self-knowledge and work on oneself. (H. Benjamin, *Basic Self-Knowledge,* 163–64)

Providing accurate knowledge of ourselves was the purpose of *Personality Types,* just as it is the purpose of the Enneagram itself. The lesson that had to be learned was the wastefulness of ego inflation. As valuable as this lesson was, there was much more to be said: the Enneagram can also guide us to spiritual dimensions by helping us move beyond personality. We have already alluded to the fact that genuine fulfillment (which is to be found primarily within a spiritual context) lies in the ability to discover our Essential nature.

> We must be willing and able to go beyond ego to reach out to something more, to experience the parts of ourselves that have nothing to do with the agendas of our personalities. At the same time, we must also be willing to experience the limitation and pain that our ego's habits are causing us.
>
> Self-transcendence is difficult and frightening because it entails going into unknown territory, feeling, thinking, and acting in ways foreign to our personality, contrary to our past habits, at odds with our old attitudes and identity, and free of the old wounds and defenses of our childhood. In a sense, self-transcendence is a rebirth, a true transformation, the coming into being of a new person who is learning to leave the old ways behind and strike out into a new world. . . .
>
> In the last analysis, learning how to transcend the ego involves nothing less than learning how to be open to love. Only love has the power to save us from ourselves. Until we learn to truly love ourselves and others — and to accept the love of others — there can be no hope of lasting happiness or peace or redemption. It is because we do not know how to love ourselves properly that we lose ourselves so easily in the many illusions ego sets before us. (*PT,* 460–61)

Cataloging the illusions that "ego sets before us" was the very stuff of the descriptions in *Personality Types* and in this book. It is now time to turn our attention to that other path — toward higher states that open out to us once we have seen through the veils and illusions of the ego, to that upward spiral by which we awaken to Essence.

Describing "living in Essence" is much more difficult than describing personality types, for one fundamental reason. Most of the ego states described in *Personality Types* are unfree; they involve degrees of compulsion, of losing ourselves in illusions and mechanical responses. Since they are relatively fixed states ("fixations"), they are also relatively easy to describe, once you know what to look for. However, Essence results in states that are marked by *freedom,* and as such they are dynamic and ever-evolving — not only as an expression of life but, in a true sense, as life-giving states themselves. If we can analyze the qualities of a truly free person, of someone living in a state of liberation, we will learn more about "living in Essence."

> The unfolding of essence becomes the process of living. Life is no longer a string of disconnected experiences of pleasure and pain, but a flow, a stream of aliveness. One aspect manifests after another, one dimension after another, one capacity after another. There is a constant flow of understanding, insight, knowledge, and states of being. (Almaas, *Essence,* 178)

As we become healthier by overcoming our characteristic fears and by acting on our right desires, our ego becomes more flexible and transparent as we gradually move up the Levels of Development. To attain Level 1, the Level of Liberation, is to come into contact with our Essence, our Essential self, our true nature in all of its magnificence.

The astonishing thing is that *we actually get our Basic Desire when we move to the Level of Liberation* (Level 1). We learn to do this by recognizing where what we seek can truly be found. We understand that our ego, try as it might, cannot fulfill our Basic Desire. For this, we must turn to our Essence — the ground of our being. Although most of us have had some profound experiences of the deep satisfactions of our Essential nature, it usually takes many such experiences to convince the ego of the ultimate bankruptcy of its project. Part of the problem is that, once we have identified with our ego consciousness, it is difficult for us to imagine any alternative, even though it brings no relief and causes us to behave in ways that hurt ourselves and others.

Seeing the truth of this and letting go of our ego agendas is not done once and for all, however, as if we could be liberated from the human condition. We move up and down on the Levels while gradually opening to the type in our Direction of Integration, to our Missing Piece, and to the potentials found there. Thus our liberation is gradual, although with the new state comes the awakening of new capacities. As Almaas says, "One aspect manifests after another, one dimension after another, one capacity after another." We do not move beyond human nature but beyond our delusions about ourselves and about reality. Living in Essence becomes a matter of seeing through our ego and, in so doing, of discovering and maturing our truest self. The search for Essence is not an escape from life but the reverse: a commitment on our most profound level of consciousness to participate in our own creation.

Still, if the idea of "living in Essence" sounds overly esoteric, the Enneagram can help take some of the obscurity out of it. For modern sensibilities, the goal of living in Essence may be strange and off-putting. But if we keep the Enneagram as our frame of reference, we will be less mystified if we think of living in Essence as the same as becoming a fully functioning, integrated person. The goal is *not* to strengthen our ego but to transcend its limitations: in so doing, we become increasingly healthy and we increasingly "live in Essence."

What capacities will we discover in ourselves if we work on ourselves and begin the process of "living in Essence" — whether we call it that or not?

The fact is that the healthiest characteristics of our personalities become accessible to us as we work on ourselves. The more aware we are and the more we avail ourselves of presence, the more Essence supports the healthy manifestations of our personalities. As we become more integrated as human beings, more and more of these qualities become available, not just those of our own type.

Some of the most important healthy traits of each type are displayed on the Enneagram on page 360. These are only some of the strengths we can learn from each other; they are particular to each type although universally accessible. Always keep in mind that many additional healthy traits exist that you will discover as you move in your own unique way beyond your ego identity.

NINE OBSERVATIONS ABOUT SPIRITUAL WORK

In our own explorations of this system, we have made nine observations about the process of uncovering our true nature. These nine observations do not correspond to the nine personality types; they are equally applicable to each, and each type will discover the truth of these points if each pursues his or her journey far enough. These nine observations encapsulate many of the major points we have discussed throughout this book.

Observation 1. Our true nature is Essence. Essence and personality are not separate: personality exists in and is made out of Essence. While we have a personality, it is only a part of the totality of our true Self. Most of the time we are entranced by our personality and do not remember our Essential nature, or who we really are.

Observation 2. Work on ourselves proceeds layer by layer, from the most external forms of personality to the inner core of our Being. The automatic pattern of our personality draws us into contracted, identified states, but by bringing *awareness* to these patterns, we reverse the course. We can start peeling away the layers and uncover our true identity. Awareness (mindfulness) plus the willingness and ability to work through our psychological issues are the keys to our Work.

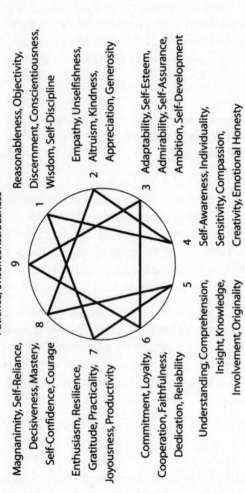

Reasonableness, Objectivity,
Discernment, Conscientiousness,
Wisdom, Self-Discipline

1

Empathy, Unselfishness,
Altruism, Kindness,
Appreciation, Generosity

2

Adaptability, Self-Esteem,
Admirability, Self-Assurance,
Ambition, Self-Development

3

Self-Awareness, Individuality,
Sensitivity, Compassion,
Creativity, Emotional Honesty

4

Understanding, Comprehension,
Insight, Knowledge,
Involvement, Originality

5

Commitment, Loyalty,
Cooperation, Faithfulness,
Dedication, Reliability

6

Enthusiasm, Resilience,
Gratitude, Practicality,
Joyousness, Productivity

7

Magnanimity, Self-Reliance,
Decisiveness, Mastery,
Self-Confidence, Courage

8

Acceptance, Self-Possession,
Receptivity, Groundedness,
Patience, Unselfconsciousness

9

The Enneagram of Healthy Personality

Observation 3. We will succeed in our Work if we are willing to know the truth about what is really occurring in us. Truth allows us to live in reality. We must tell the truth to ourselves, and where appropriate, to others. Being with the truth of our condition brings an ingredient that dissolves the structures we have been trapped in. But we must be willing to name our demons, to count the bars of our prison cell.

Observation 4. We need to be willing to observe our resistance to reality, our attachment to our self-image, and our fear. It is not in our power to transform ourselves, but we can bring awareness to these three major barriers: we can observe them and be *willing* to have them removed from us. It is helpful in our transformational work to pray for healing, and to seek healing with one's heart.

Observation 5. Whenever we work through a particular layer, the issues of the next layer automatically present themselves. The soul has its innate wisdom and yearns to be free. Therefore listen to your heart, your higher mind, and your body. The Self will unfold organically as we bring nonjudgmental awareness to it and stay with the process. There is no finish line; the process will continue as long as we live.

Observation 6. The deeper we go with our process, the more difficult it becomes — at least for a while, and from the perspective of the personality. Initially it becomes more difficult because we uncover deeper and more intense sources of pain. This is because the closer we come to the truth, the more our ego is threatened. Later, difficulties arise because the barriers become more subtle and elusive. However, the deeper we go, the greater the rewards. We become more alive, joyful, and peaceful, and also more determined to be focused.

Observation 7. We must be willing to be uncomfortable for a while if we wish to be released from whatever has bound us. We must remain present to whatever we find — whether it brings us sorrow or ecstasy. Remember that all negative behavior is the result of unprocessed pain. In the course of our Work, we uncover difficult feelings, powerful Essential states, and many qualities of emptiness. The more we can learn to tolerate these different aspects of ourselves, the more quickly and smoothly our Work will progress. The personality cannot tolerate many things, whereas the spirit can embrace everything.

Observation 8. We gradually learn to disidentify with the personality and to identify with our Essence, our true self. This, of course, requires that we be able to recognize our Essence and to distinguish our personality trances from it. We cannot accomplish this by judging, disliking, or trying to get rid of the personality. In fact, those very desires and attitudes are part of personality and are not characteristic of Essence. When the personality is seen in its proper context, its true function reveals itself.

Observation 9. Remember that it is our birthright and our natural state to be wise and noble, to be loving and generous, to esteem ourselves and others, to be creative and constantly renewing ourselves, to be engaged in the world in awe and wonder and in depth, to have courage, to be joyous and effortlessly accomplished, to be strong and effective, to be self-possessed and enjoy an unshakable peace of mind — and above all, to be present to the unfolding mystery of our lives.

THE TRANSFORMATIONAL PROCESS

At the beginning of our transformational work, it is easy to feel frustrated and overwhelmed. It is also easy to begin to see the personality as an enemy that must be defeated, since it is, after all, the repository of the baggage of our past, with its hurts, damage, and disappointments. When we are tempted to think this way, it is beneficial to realize that the personality is not separate from us — in fact, it is an important and legitimate part of ourselves. The problem is simply that *we mistake the part for the whole.* Personality depends on our *identifying* with certain states, feelings, thoughts, and reactions even though whenever we do so, *we expe-*

rience ourselves as less than the totality of who and what we really are.

The spirituality of the Enneagram does not divide us into good (Essence) and bad (personality) but simply recognizes that when we are *identified* with our personalities, we forget that there is much more to us. The personality has the function of closing us down so that we can feel more defended against a threatening and uncertain world. At one time in our lives, in childhood, this response was adaptive and necessary. We had to identify with whatever qualities we found in ourselves in order to defend ourselves more efficiently and to find our place in the world.

But if we were able to stop identifying with our personality right now, who would we be? What would guide our actions? Who or what would be speaking in us? If, all of a sudden, the autopilot that directs many of our actions is no longer in charge, how would we be able to live?

There are no predetermined answers to these questions: we are not discussing the finding of a better formula or more rules to live by. We are talking about *transformation* — changing our state of Being — which requires being aware in the present moment. This inevitably leads to learning how to interfere with our habitual patterns, which in turn entails some degree of discomfort. But if we are willing to allow this discomfort, we can suddenly emerge from the tangle of reactions, plans, self-images, and tensions that constitute our regular life and realize that *we are here. We exist. We are real.* When we experience this recognition, it is like emerging from a fog bank.

Of course, learning to be more present is an art and takes practice — in fact, that's what spiritual practices are about. They help us cultivate awareness so that we can become more present to our lives and the miracles that are unfolding around us at every moment. Because much of the personality operates unconsciously and depends on tension and identification, when we become present it cannot operate in its automatic way, and the deeper qualities of our heart, mind, and body — our Essential nature — manifest themselves. In this state, we see reality more clearly, and when we are in touch with reality, truth governs. In the land of truth, there are no contradictions, no conflicts, no hindrances, and no fears. But first, we must learn to be present.

The personality is always composed of a small fraction of the total range of our potentials. It contains imitations of the real, more expansive qualities of our Essential nature that include joy, love, peace, compassion, strength, understanding, and many other priceless qualities. Moreover, our Essence awakens us to the beauty all around us — to the gifts of nature and the miracle of other people. In every moment there exists treasures and sources of delight, if we could only open to them. In the world of personality we are too consumed with our own projects and preoccupations, worries and hopes, to notice the exquisite pleasure of being alive and the astounding variety of life.

But as we expand more fully into our Essential nature, our senses are awakened — seeing, hearing, smelling, tasting, touching, intuition. The world is more immediate and has a deeper impact on us; everything becomes more vivid and alive. We have all had moments in which a veil seems to have been removed so that the enchantment of even the smallest things touches us deeply. We experience the world once again with the innocence of a child, with all of the awe and mystery of life restored.

When we are functioning in personality, however, our attention is focused on the imagination, looking to the future or toward the past. *Personality is constantly in some kind of reaction to the present moment.* When we are functioning in Essence, we are grounded, present, and receptive to the moment. We see precisely what is necessary, and with exquisite economy, we are able to do it without unnecessary effort or resistance. We are capable, substantial, and real.

Further, because it is not what is real in us, but merely a construct in our minds, personality does not have any authority or power in itself. When we are lost in personality, it is not surprising that we often feel powerless, confused, and unsafe because we are basing our identity on an artificial construct. (If we are identified with something that is not real, then many things are going to be extremely threatening.) Our entire identity structure has been built up in our memory and imagination, whereas our true power and authority come from our Essence, from our contact with the Divine. And yet, ironically, we fear and resist opening to that which is most real in us. When we trust in the process and give ourselves over to it, however, our authentic self comes forth. The result is real integrity, love, authenticity, creativity, understanding, guidance, joy, power, and serenity — all of the qualities we are forever demanding that personality supply.

The part of this process that is so difficult to understand is that we do not have to *do* anything to experience our true nature. The almost magical part is that our old personality patterns change without effort on our part in proportion to the depth of awareness that we bring to them. All we need to do is to *stop identifying* with the agendas of our personality. The effort is in waking up and letting go; the rest will take care of itself.

Thus, no matter how entranced in our personality we are, the amazing thing about Inner Work is that *things begin to change rapidly as we bring awareness to the compulsive aspects of our personalities*. The more we allow ourselves to feel the pain of our self-abandonment, the Essential qualities that we have been longing for begin to arise in us. The unfinished business of childhood begins to resolve itself in our psyches and our hearts begin to heal. When this happens, the ego matures and becomes a suitable vessel for further transformation. But until some degree of personality completion has taken place regarding the losses and vicissitudes of childhood, any spiritual attainment we have will be either fleeting or illusory.

Of course, the very fact of being receptive to spirituality can vastly accelerate the process of healing the deficits in our early development, provided we do not use spirituality as an evasion for going through the whole healing process. And, by the same token, using the tools of psychology to heal the gaps in our development gives us the capacity to sustain spiritual states of consciousness.

These two processes — the psychological and the spiritual — are therefore connected and need not be considered separate; they are stages in the full development of the complete human being.

From this perspective, to say that one is interested in spirituality but not psychology (or vice versa) is like saying that you want to learn to be a writer but are not interested in spelling or grammar, or that you want to be a doctor but don't care about biology. Psychology that does not address people's spiritual hungers is not going to lead to any complete and satisfying result — it's like climbing halfway up a mountain or taking a dish out of the oven when it's only half-baked. We derive some benefits but don't reach the final goal. Psychology without spirituality is arid and ultimately meaningless, while spirituality without grounding in psychological work leads to vanity and illusions. Either way, disappointment and deception result. To be most effective, spirituality and psychology need to go hand in hand to reinforce the best in each other.

Another challenge is the common belief that to live in Essence is to have left personality entirely behind. This is not the case since both personality and Essence are integral parts of each other, two sides of the same coin — the whole self.

In the best of all possible worlds the acquired habits of personality would be available to one's Essential nature and would help one to function adequately in the social context in which he or she lived, and for a realized being this undoubtedly is the case. The ordinary person, unfortunately, lacks the ability to make use of personality to carry out Essential wishes. What is Essential can manifest only in the simplest instinctive behavior and in primitive emotions.

All this is not to say that essence is always noble and beautiful while personality is an alien crust of useless cultural barnacles. According to Gurdjieff, "as a rule a man's essence is either primitive, savage and childish, or else simply stupid." The essences of many are actually dead, though they continue to live seemingly normal lives. The development of essence to maturity, when it will embody everything that is true and real in a person's being, depends on work on oneself, and work on oneself depends on a balance between a relatively healthy essence and a personality that is not crushingly heavy. . . . Both are necessary for self-development, for without the acquisition of personality there will be no wish to attain higher states of consciousness, no dissatisfaction with everyday existence; and without essence there will be no basis of development. (Speeth, *The Gurdjieff Work*, 48–49)

As one becomes liberated from the negative aspects of personality, Essence becomes developed. Or, more aptly, the balance between Essence and personality shifts from personality to Essence until more of the self is living out of Essence (that is, authentically, from the depths of its being). The personality remains ready to be employed as a useful and necessary tool, but only as an extension and expression of the deeper, Essential self — a self that, because it is an expression of Essence, remains unfathomable to the ego mind.

The full development and expression of the true self is what we seek, and this cannot be done in a vacuum. Because we cannot live without form, our human Essence must express itself through the forms of our personality type, just as talents must be expressed in action if talent is to be developed. A dancing master does not become so perfect a dancer that the master no longer dances. Dancing is not forsworn as evidence of having achieved perfection: on the contrary, mastery is expressed by losing the self in the dance.

If we are fortunate, we are nurtured and guided in our development toward a stable, well-integrated ego, one that is therefore ripe for transformation. The idea is not to return to the infantile state but to mature as adults so that we can move ahead with the process of transformation. In the famous phrase of Jack Engler, "You have to be somebody before you can be nobody." It is necessary that we develop a whole, well-integrated personality before we can "give it up" in the transformational process. The healthy, well-functioning human ego plays a crucial role in the process of self-realization, and so our developmental deficiencies must be healed if our transformative experiences are to have any lasting effect.

Thus, personality is as necessary to the development of the soul as Essence, and it is to be used for living in the world and for contributing to it. The aspects of personality that are more congruent with our Essence are the *healthy* personality states we find at Levels 1 to 3 for each type. Moreover, those personality states themselves develop to become finer expressions of our Essential self as we continue to evolve. Once we have begun to integrate and to live in Essence more habitually, we become the master of our ego and are increasingly able to express ourselves freely and appropriately. Ego no longer controls us: Essence speaks through personality.

The danger is that many students begin to identify with Essential states — in effect, creating a new ego identity. For example, we can have an extraordinary spiritual experience and feel liberated from our usual sense of ourselves only to have identification cause our usual sense of self to claim the experience and make it part of our self-image. One moment we feel an abiding serenity and oneness with the universe, and the next, identification with the ego subtly slips in and we are telling ourselves how spiritually "advanced" we are. We may even start anticipating how impressed our teacher (or therapist or spouse) is going to be with our new state or new insights. Of course, by this time the experience of immediate awareness and real oneness has been lost.

What needs to happen is to free this aspect of essence for it to become a station, to become permanently available, so that it is there when its mode of operation is needed. Therefore, all of the issues around identity and selfhood must be seen and understood, including the need for or attachment to identity. The true self exposes all misunderstanding and conflicts around identity and selfhood. Resolving the issues around the essential self eliminates all identification; or rather, identification becomes a free, conscious movement. (Almaas, *Essence,* 170)

Every experience of presence, of true nature, helps us see reality more objectively. It prepares us for the next movement toward liberation, so that we can move yet again in self-transcendence toward more freedom and abide more deeply in our Essential self. Looked at one way, this movement is from state of consciousness to state of consciousness, yet looked at another way, the movement becomes increasingly free of all attachments to those very forms.

Life continues to be a process of creative discovery. The process of learning, unfolding, and expansion never stops. Essence continues to unfold, new dimensions arise, new modes of experience and insight emerge, new capacities manifest. . . . The shift of identity from personality to essence is nothing but the realization of the true self, the high self of essence. . . . Practical action becomes the action of the true being. There is efficiency, economy, simplicity, directness. One fully lives in the world but is constantly connected to the Beyond, the Supreme Reality. (Almaas, *Essence,* 179)

The move to Essence is not an escape from ourselves but the growth of freedom from those aspects of ourselves that have made us unfree and subject to suffering. The move to Essence is a supremely positive thing — not a negation of our individuality, but the occasion in which we become deeply alive and connected with the depths of ourselves. We hinted at this in *Personality Types:*

Attaining the goal of a full, happy life, ripe with experiences well used, means that each of us will become a paradox — free, yet constrained by necessity; shrewd, yet innocent; open to others, yet self-reliant; strong, yet able to yield; centered on the highest values, yet able to accept imperfection; realistic about the suffering existence imposes on us, yet full of gratitude for life as it is.

The testimony of the greatest humans who have ever lived is that the way to make the most of ourselves is by transcending ourselves. We must learn to move beyond self-centeredness to make room within ourselves for others. When you transcend yourself, the fact will be confirmed by the quality of your life. You will attain — even if only momentarily — a transparency and a radiance of being which result from living both within and beyond yourself. This is the promise and the excitement of self-understanding. (*PT*, 54–55)

The quality of your life is confirmation that, in the moment of presence, you have attained Essence — your deepest, truest self. The transparency and radiance that result from living in Essence is the sign that Essence is not only desirable but attainable. The state of "transparency" — of openness and unselfconsciousness — makes the Essential self accessible to others. And the "radiance" that results from self-transcendence — self-possession and profound happiness — emanates the many particular qualities of love.

Enlightenment cannot be according to any system. It has to resolve and clarify your own situation. The realization must satisfy and fulfill your heart, not the standards of some system. The liberation must be of you, you personally. . . . The quest does not bring about improvement or perfection. It brings about a maturity, a humanity, and a wisdom. (Almaas, *Essence,* 181–82)

We have seen much the same about the limitations of any system, including the limitations of the Enneagram. While Almaas says that "the quest does not bring about improvement or perfection," he means that the process is one of self-discovery — not of self-improvement. We are correcting a case of mistaken identity, not trying to "fix" our false identity. In fact, when we discover our true nature, and recognize that *we are Essence,* we see that all of the noble qualities we have been seeking are already here — part of us. Just as we saw in Chapter 2, our personalities are a response to the obscuration of the Virtues and Holy Ideas. When we correct our misperceptions, these qualities are rediscovered, and manifest freely again.

Our Essence is always available because at our deepest level, it is what we are. The Enneagram reminds us again and again that if we are on a spiritual path, we must begin to question our basic assumptions about ourselves and our identity. As awareness grows, we will open up to an expanded sense of self that includes more than the preoccupations of our personality, indeed, more than the personality can even imagine.

THE TRIADS AND THE PATHS OF TRANSFORMATION

Each Triad has a defining set of personality issues as well as dominant Essential qualities. We can also delineate nine distinct Paths of Transformation that unlock the issues of the Triads and restore access to our Essential nature. These Paths represent internal attitudes that help to liberate us from some of the limited views of our type, but they are also markers of our progress. As we are able to experience and sustain these inner orientations, we can be reassured that we are making progress.

The key issues of the Instinctive Triad involve resisting reality by maintaining imaginary boundaries to define the self. We create these imaginary boundaries because, once we have become estranged from our Essential nature, we lose our feeling of substantiality — of being a real, palpable presence in the world. Because we do not occupy a real space, we must construct an imaginary one and then protect it. Much of the work with this Center involves the recognition of these imaginary boundaries and their artificial nature. When we are able to do this, we begin to reexperience ourselves as Presence, as something real and as spaciousness. Thus, there is no need to maintain false boundaries.

The three paths connected with the Instinctive Triad are *Self-Remembering* (at point Nine), *Self-Surrender* (at point Eight), and *Acceptance* (at point One). We see that when we are actually occupying our instinctive functions, we know that we are here directly — we remember that we exist right now (self-remembering). We fully experience our "is-ness," and it is not based on stories or pictures of ourselves held in the mind. We are engaged with reality, with a complete immediacy.

Supporting this are the Paths of Transformation for types Eight and One. From Eight we experience *Self-Surrender,* which entails a dissolving of the imaginary ego boundaries such that we no longer experience ourselves as one object in a universe of objects. Instead we know that our presence, the very ground of our being, is also the ground of everything else that we can perceive. Because we are at one with the universe, we no longer need to defend ourselves from it or to continue our personal struggle against it. We know that our Essential nature cannot be overcome or destroyed, and we find deep purpose and confidence in being the instrument of a Higher Will.

From type One, we experience *Acceptance.* We accept our own inner condition exactly as it is, without reacting to it or defending against it. We end the inner war between the parts of ourselves that are driven by frustrated desires and those that would banish or condemn those desires. We know that neither side reflects the truth of our Essential being, although they both reflect a partial truth. As we become more accepting of ourselves, we find that we are in a more direct relationship with reality. Like type Eight, we see that the presence from which our being springs is the same presence that underlies everything around us, and that there is no need to judge or separate ourselves from any of it. This does not reduce our capacity to discern or to choose wise actions; rather, it increases that capacity infinitely.

The Feeling Triad is concerned with issues around the maintenance of a false or assumed self as a defense against the loss of our Essential identity and sense of value. At the Center of this Triad, *Authenticity,* connected with type Three, is the Path of Transformation that dissolves the false self-image and reveals the narcissistic nature of most of our projects and agendas. At the same time, authenticity opens the door to our true identity such that we fully experience the preciousness of who and what we are and that our identity is a given — we do not need to create it.

From Two, we experience proper *Self-Nurturing,* which certainly does not mean self-indulgence or acting out infantile cravings. Rather, self-nurturance is the ability to realistically assess our genuine needs and then to take action to address them without waiting for others to do so. Self-nurturing also entails self-regulation in the sense that we are able to soothe our own needs and states by staying in contact with our hearts. This keeps us sensitive to our authentic needs and keeps us sensitive to the needs and boundaries of others. Proper self-nurturing also prevents us from becoming dependent on the goodwill, positive opinions, or affection of others.

From Four we experience *Forgiveness,* which is most simply the ability to let go of the events of the past and to move on with one's life. We stop clinging to old hurts and resentments, thereby opening up space in our hearts to be affected by people and events freshly, without the dense filters of residual emotional reactions from our childhood. Rather than holding the world responsible for our frustrations, we begin to understand the forces in ourselves that perpetuate them. When we do this, we experience our lives and our identities as they truly are — as a process, a flow.

The Thinking Triad is concerned with the strategies we develop to move forward in life, to protect ourselves from dangers, and to acquire the things that we need for our well-being. We engage in these strategies because our egos have separated from our Essential capacity to know. At the Center of this Triad is the Path of Transformation for point Six, *Courage.* This is a quality that does not come from ignoring fears, rather, it arises naturally from the Essential quality of knowing — what we have been referring to as "the quiet mind." When we are receptive to the Essential quality of the quiet mind, our ego's strategies for survival and gratification are revealed as superfluous or even counterproductive. We perceive things simply and directly, without the fearful interpretations of the imagination, and we are able to act from the sense of spaciousness and possibility that the support of the quiet mind affords. We do not have to devote all of our energies to figuring out how to support and protect ourselves and our loved ones; rather, we become attuned to a more subtle form of direction that arises from the quiet of our own awareness.

At point Five, we experience true *Understanding*, which should not be confused with intellectual understanding, although that can be an aspect of it. Rather, understanding entails a *gestalt*, an immediate and complete apprehension of truth that is felt in all of the parts of oneself. Understanding in this sense is direct knowing, in which we know something through intimate contact with our experience, not through distancing ourselves as "outside observers." This kind of understanding allows us to make wise choices and supports our courage to move forward in life.

At point Seven, we experience the *Gratitude* that occurs when the mind is open and fully receptive to the impressions of the moment. When this takes place, we are deeply satisfied and nourished by all the contents of our immediate experience. We understand that there is no need for the mind to wander elsewhere seeking "greener pastures" because what is here and now completely supports us and fills us. We become exquisitely sensitive to every subtle sense impression so that the many hidden treasures and delights of each moment reveal themselves to us. To fully allow a color or a quality of light or a sensation to register in our consciousness is to allow ourselves to feel the ecstasy of existence. We can entertain any experience, thought, or impression without desiring more of it or feeling the need to seek something else to take its place. Further, we are aware that the supply of rich impressions is inexhaustible. Gratitude is the antithesis of "scarcity thinking" — we are secure in the knowledge that we will have whatever we need, and more. Our capacity for true spontaneity and a deep sense of joy arise to heal the ego's impulsiveness and feelings of frustration. Instead of scrambling after whatever we believe will make us feel better, gratitude enables us to savor each moment of our lives.

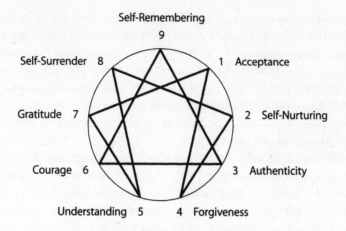

The Paths of Transformation

THE NINE TYPES AND THEIR ESSENTIAL QUALITIES

As we have seen, contacting our Essence is always a matter of recognizing our identifications, fears, and resistances, and bringing our attention to our experience in the here and now. As we do so, we become increasingly aware of a vast number of Essential qualities that arise perfectly to support whatever issues we are facing. Indeed, the more we move up the Levels of Development and are less encumbered by our ego identities, the more we have access to all of the Essential qualities.

Our Essential nature, however, is vast and subtle; it manifests in a multitude of ways and at a variety of levels. Here we are most concerned with the qualities of Essence that are "closer" to the surface — that is, more generally accessible to our daily awareness. These aspects arise to support our Inner Work any time we remember ourselves and come back to some contact with Presence. The Enneagram delineates some of the most important of these qualities, and by describing them, we may be able to see how they constantly support our transformation. Each of the nine points can be thought of as contributing an important ingredient for our development. We may also begin to see how the personality attempts to fill in the gaps in our development by imitating them. Over time, we can develop an increased sensitivity to these states, which gradually enables us to identify with our True Nature instead of our personality.

Of course, as with everything else in this book, reading about the Essential qualities or having an intellectual understanding of them is not the same as having a direct experience of them. For that, consistent practice is needed, preferably with the support of others as we have previously mentioned. Also note that the Essential aspects described here are only a departure point and are by no means complete or definitive.

From point Eight, we experience Essential *Strength*. Strength is an expansive energy, and when it is manifesting we feel large, solid, capable, and alive. Not surprisingly, Essential strength arises in defense of our souls — it protects our process and its integrity. It provides a foundation and ground that gives us the ability to discriminate present, real experience from projections and reactions from the past, as well as to tolerate more painful, subtle, or empty states. Without this quality, we may have profound experiences, but we will not be able to embody or sustain them in any meaningful way.

From point Nine, we experience a sense of *Unity* or *Wholeness*. We know that we are not only connected with everything else, but that we are not a "separate object." We directly experience the oneness of reality, and our Essential union with all creation. Further, we understand that this unity is dynamic, alive, and ever-changing. We know love as the force that breaks through all false boundaries and identities to restore this experience of wholeness. The realization of this state brings a deep satisfaction and contentment — a profound sense of well-being. We feel at peace with reality and with our place in it. We are able to function effectively in the world while knowing that what we are is "beyond" the world.

From point One, we experience *Wisdom*. This quality is related to the Buddhist concept of *right action*. Wisdom manifests as brilliant intelligence, an ability to see exactly what is needed in the moment and to act accordingly. This intelligence is not based on any set of principles, guidelines, or rules but rather arises spontaneously whenever it is needed. It gives us the ability to respond to situations effectively, with an economy of energy — neither too much nor too little. Further, when we are manifesting this quality, we are able to communicate our insights clearly and authoritatively. We are patient, steady, capable, and radiant.

From point Two, we experience *Unconditional Love*. This quality gives us a tremendous freedom from the inherent neediness of the ego. Knowing that we are connected to the very source of love, and that we cannot lose it, allows us to interact with other human beings in whatever way the moment dictates, without any concern that we will be disliked or rejected. Further, when we are truly and authentically experiencing love as part of our Essential nature, we see that love does not belong to anyone, including ourselves, and we recognize that everyone around us is also a manifestation of love. We know that it is not our duty to go around "loving" everyone, but to live in the presence of love such that others may also remember that they too are in the presence of love. Further, love is a tremendously powerful force for dissolving all that is false in us. Few of our illusions about ourselves or others can stand long in the presence of real love. In this respect, we see how love represents the active or dynamic part of truth, and that love and truth are intimately related.

From point Three, we experience Essential *Value*. When we are manifesting this quality of Essence, we do not need to do anything to feel valuable or worthwhile. We do not need to work at developing our self-esteem because we fully experience our intrinsic value as Being. We feel the profound pleasure and satisfaction of existing — a sense of enjoyment pervades our entire presence. This aspect predisposes us to behave benevolently toward others: experiencing our own Essential value, we do not need to manipulate others or our environment in order to see ourselves in any particular light. We experience ourselves as a shining presence — starlike, a source of radiance in the world.

From point Four, we experience *Equanimity*. Once we open to the riches of the heart and to the inexhaustible wonder of living in truth, we are filled from moment to moment with a kaleidoscope of powerful impressions, sensations, and feelings. Equanimity gives us the capacity to contain all of these ever-changing qualities without being swept into emotional reactions about them. Because the nature of spirit is ever-changing, our experience of ourselves and of life is also constantly changing. Equanimity allows the identity of the Essential self to participate in the cornucopia of experiences and inner qualities without clinging to or fearing any of them, and without regretting their passing. In this way, the sense of oneself continually deepens so that powerful experiences are fully realized yet do not overwhelm the Essential identity. We are able to feel both the heights of ecstasy and the full intensity of suffering without becoming lost in either.

From point Five, we experience the Essential quality of *Direct Knowing*. This quality is quite distinct from the ego's form of thinking, which is generally characterized by inner talk or inner visualization, often accompanied by a process of sorting information and "data retrieval." In direct knowing, however, the mind is silent and open, and we are supported by the awareness that we will know whatever we need to know as we need to know it. Even the acquisition of new information, skills, or experiences will be guided by an inner knowing that does not arise from the ego's feelings of insufficiency. Direct knowing arises out of a direct experience of the pristine empty space of mind: it allows us to be free of attachment to any particular perspective. We know that in different moments and situations different perspectives may be more useful, and that our Essence will guide us to the perspective that is most suitable. This inner clarity allows us to be unattached to the phenomenal world: when we are functioning in this capacity, we see all objects and events as arising and disappearing within a vast and unfathomable mystery. We see the world as a dance of exquisite gestures and movements within the shining void.

From point Six, we experience Essential *Will*. This quality manifests as a sense of being embedded in reality — solidly supported by the ground of Being. It gives us a capacity for endurance and persistence in our Work, and an ability to confront situations without anxiety. We feel as if we are supported by a solid ocean of Presence that guides us. Further, we do not need to fill our minds with plans and strategies, because we are directed by a well of inner guidance that functions harmoniously with our circumstances and with our environment. It brings a sense of unshakable confidence and a clear sense of direction. The more we open to this quality, the more actively it manifests in our world, leading us exactly to the experiences we most need for our development.

From point Seven, we experience Essential *Joy*. When this quality manifests, we are filled with an expansive, sunny presence that lets us know that we are moving in the right direction. We feel grateful for the wonderful and mysterious gift of our lives, and we experience a profound wonder and curiosity about our journey. We deeply feel the presence of our true spiritual home and feel it calling us back. As Essential joy arises in us, we know where true value lies, and we are fortified to do whatever is necessary to re-

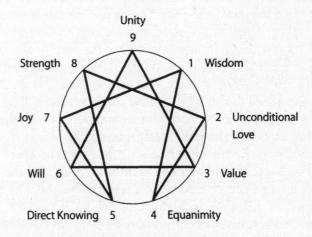

The Enneagram of Essential Qualities

turn to what our heart truly desires. We know what we love and joyfully open to deeper aspects of our True nature.

CONCLUSION

The Enneagram guides us toward nothing less than learning how consciously to surrender the ego self of personality to the greater Self so that we can become conscious participants in the sacred mystery of life. In reality, it entails the surrender of nothing — our personality — in order to receive the gift of everything — the life of the Spirit. But the first step on that path involves being willing to observe ourselves so that we can stop playing out the unconscious dictates of our personality.

The process of growth by any name it is called — living in Essence, the growth of virtue, or the movement toward integration — is evolutionary, an upward spiral that has no final state of completion since to become completely possessed of all virtues would be to become God — an impossibility. (Our call, in a religious frame of reference, is to become "like God" — to attain some degree of the virtues that God alone possesses to an absolute degree.) If some see this never-ending quest for increasing virtue (or personal strengths) as a frustrating chase after an unreachable goal, it is because they have not experienced the deep fulfillment that results from self-realization. If integration is thought of as merely collecting a set of impractical virtues as if they were merit badges being added to a collection, then the enterprise will be unsatisfying. But the true situation is far from this. Acquiring the strengths of virtue brings about the enlargement of the person. By acting virtuously and by "living in Essence," the person becomes capable of living more deeply and consciously as master of the self. New depths are being opened in the integrating person. The creation of inner resources, the experience of oneself as enlarged, more potent, and creative is tremendously fulfilling. In this sense, the saying that "virtue is its own reward" has new meaning: the reward of virtue is the happiness that comes from the realization that we are living out of our Essential self and that in doing so we are bringing more of ourselves into being.

Yet it will always remain true that realizing the value of self-transcendence can be found only in the individual's innermost heart. In the moment of self-transcendence, we discover that over and above liberation from the ego, self-transcendence gives us another, deeper reward by creating both the capacity and the desire for more of itself.

By integrating, we are constantly moving in the direction of increasing life. And nothing in life is more fulfilling than cooperating in the process of creation. Integrating persons become co-creators of that most vast yet intimate mystery, the human spirit. From only a psychological point of view, the capacity to be a co-creator bestows on human nature enormous dignity. But from a spiritual point of view, this capacity has a more profound meaning because to move in the direction of increasing life is to move toward Being itself. With each step we take toward Being, we also find that Being supports our quest. In the end, the quest for the self and its deepest Essence culminates in meeting the Divine.

Bibliography

Almaas, A. H. *Essence: The Diamond Approach to Inner Realization.* York Beach, Me.: Samuel Weiser, 1986.

———. *Facets of Unity: The Enneagram of Holy Ideas.* Berkeley, Calif.: Diamond Books, 1998.

———. *The Pearl beyond Price: Integration of Personality into Being: An Object Relations Approach.* Berkeley, Calif.: Diamond Books, 1988.

———. *The Point of Existence: Transformations of Narcissism in Self-Realization.* Berkeley, Calif.: Diamond Books, 1996.

Anthony, Dick, Bruce Ecker, and Ken Wilber, eds. *Spiritual Choices: The Problem of Recognizing Authentic Paths to Inner Transformation.* New York: Paragon House, 1987.

Bayrak al-Jerrahi al-Halveti, Skeikh Tosun. *The Most Beautiful Names.* Putney, Vt.: Threshold Books, 1985.

Benjamin, Harry. *Basic Self-Knowledge.* York Beach, Me.: Samuel Weiser, 1971.

Bennett, J. G., and G. I. Gurdjieff. *Making a New World.* New York: Harper & Row, 1973.

———. *Enneagram Studies.* York Beach, Me.: Samuel Weiser, 1983.

Capps, Donald. *Deadly Sins and Saving Virtues.* Philadelphia: Fortress Press, 1987.

Danner, Victor. *The Islamic Tradition.* New York: Amity House, 1988.

Diagnostic and Statistical Manual of Mental Disorders. 4th ed. (DSM-IV). Washington, D.C.: American Psychiatric Association, 1994.

Faucett, Robert, and Carol Ann. *Personality and Spiritual Freedom.* New York: Doubleday, 1987.

Fine, Reuben. *A History of Psychoanalysis.* New York: Columbia University Press, 1979.

Frosch, James P., ed. *Current Perspectives on Personality Disorders.* Washington, D.C.: American Psychiatric Press, 1983.

Glasse, Cyril. *The Concise Encyclopaedia of Islam.* San Francisco: Harper & Row, 1989.

Greenberg, Jay R., and Stephen A. Mitchell. *Object Relations in Psychoanalytic Theory.* Cambridge: Harvard University Press, 1983.

Guntrip, Harry. *Schizoid Phenomena, Object Relations and the Self.* Madison, Ct.: International Universities Press, 1995.

Gurdjieff, G. I. *Views from the Real World.* New York: Dutton, 1975.

Halevi, Z'ev ben Shimon. *Adam and the Kabbalistic Tree.* York Beach, Me.: Samuel Weiser, 1974.

Horney, Karen. *Neurosis and Human Growth: The Struggle toward Self-Realization.* New York: W. W. Norton, 1950.

———. *Our Inner Conflicts.* New York: W. W. Norton, 1945.

Ichazo, Oscar. *Between Metaphysics and Protoanalysis: A Theory for Analyzing the Human Psyche.* New York: Arica Institute Press, 1982.

———. *Interviews with Oscar Ichazo.* New York: Arica Institute Press, 1982.

Leary, Timothy. *Interpersonal Diagnosis of Personality.* New York: Ronald Press, 1957.

Lilly, John, and Joseph Hart. "The Arica Training." In *Transpersonal Psychologies,* edited by Charles T. Tart. New York: Harper & Row, 1975.

Macquarrie, John. *In Search of Humanity.* New York: Crossroad, 1985.

Maslow, Abraham. *The Further Reaches of Human Nature.* New York: Viking Press, 1971.

Metzner, Ralph. *Know Your Type: Maps of Identity.* New York: Doubleday, 1979.

Millon, Theodore. *Disorders of Personality.* New York: John Wiley, 1981.

Millon, Theodore, and Gerald L. Klerman, eds. *Contemporary Directions in Psychopathology: Toward the DSM-IV.* New York: Guilford Press, 1986.

Naranjo, Claudio. *Character and Neurosis: An Integrative View.* Nevada City, Calif.: Gateways/IDHHB, 1994.

Nicholi, Armand M., ed. *The Harvard Guide to Modern Psychiatry.* Cambridge: Harvard University Press, 1999.

Nicoll, Maurice. *Psychological Commentaries on the Teaching of Gurdjieff and Ouspensky.* Boulder: Shambhala, 1984.

Ouspensky, P. D. *In Search of the Miraculous.* New York: Harcourt, Brace & World, 1949.

Plotinus, trans. by Stephen McKenna. *The Enneads.* New York: Penguin Books, 1991.

Riordan, Kathleen. "Gurdjieff." In *Transpersonal Psychologies,* edited by Charles T. Tart. New York: Harper & Row, 1975.

Riso, Don Richard, with Russ Hudson. *Personality Types: Using the Enneagram for Self-Discovery.* Rev. ed. Boston: Houghton Mifflin, 1996.

Shapiro, David. *Neurotic Styles.* New York: Basic Books, 1965.

Shushud, Hasan. *Masters of Wisdom of Central Asia.* Moorcote, England: Coombe Springs Press, 1983.

Speeth, Kathleen Riordan. *The Gurdjieff Work.* Berkeley, Calif.: And/Or Press, 1976.

Speeth, Kathleen Riordan, and Ira Friedlander. *Gurdjieff: Seeker of the Truth.* New York: Harper & Row, 1980.

Tart, Charles T., ed. *Transpersonal Psychologies.* New York: Harper & Row, 1975.

———. *Waking Up: Overcoming the Obstacles to Human Potential.* Boston: Shambhala, 1986.

Waldberg, Michel. *Gurdjieff: An Approach to His Ideas.* London: Routledge & Kegan Paul, 1981.

Webb, James. *The Harmonious Circle.* New York: G. P. Putnam's Sons, 1980.

ENNEAGRAM DISSERTATIONS

Several doctoral theses have been written about the Enneagram and related matters in the last several years, and the academic work continues.

Some of the following dissertations are concerned with developing and validating a questionnaire based on the Enneagram personality types, while others explore various aspects of the relation between depth psychology and the traditional Arica interpretation of the Enneagram.

This has become a fertile field in which to work at the master's and doctoral levels. There is no doubt the Enneagram's correspondence with the DSM-IV personality disorders and other typologies will continue to sustain research and scholarship.

In the following list, the author's name, title of the thesis, degree awarded, year, institution, and page length (when available) have been given; the volume and page in *Dissertation Abstracts International* and the order number have also been included with each entry. At the end of the list is information about how to order copies of these works.

Beauvais, Phyllis. "Claudio Naranjo and SAT: Modern Manifestation of Sufism." Ph.D., Hartford Seminary, 1973. 264 pages. 35/12-A, p. 8005. GAX75-13868.

Campbell, Richard. "The Relationship of Arica Training to Self-Actualization and Interpersonal Behavior." Ph.D., United States International University, 1975. 115 pages. 36/03-B, p. 1401. GAX75-20244.

Gamard, William Sumner. "Interrater Reliability and Validity of Judgments of Enneagram Personality Types." Ph.D., California Institute of Integral Studies, 1986. GAX86-25584.

Lincoln, Robert L. "The Relation between Depth Psychology and Protoanalysis." Ph.D., California Institute of Transpersonal Psychology, 1983. 429 pages. Research Abstracts International LD00676.

Randall, Stephen. "Development of an Inventory to Assess Enneagram Personality Type." Ph.D., California Institute of Integral Studies, 1979. 112 pages. 40/09-B, p. 4466. GAX80-05160.

Wagner, Jerome. "A Descriptive, Reliability, and Validity Study of the Enneagram Personality Typology." Ph.D., Loyola University, 1981. 283 pages. 41/11-A, p. 4664. GAX81-09973.

Wolf, Steven Raymond. "Effects of the Arica Training on Adult Development: A Longitudinal Study (Stage Theory)." Ph.D., Saybrook Institute, 1985. 46/11-B, p. 4040. GAX85-28854.

Zinkle, Thomas Edward. "A Pilot Study toward the Validation of the Sufi Personality Typology." Ph.D., United States International University, 1975. 91 pages. 35/05-B, p. 2418. GAX74-24529.

For current information and to order copies, consult *Dissertation Abstracts International*, Dissertation Publishing, University Microfilm International, 300 N. Zeeb Road, P. O. Box 1764, Ann Arbor, Michigan 48106, or telephone 800-521-3042. For online searches at libraries, use DATRIX DIRECT: 800-233-6901, ext. 708.

Index

Lilly, John, 31
Living in Essence, 323, 357, 358–59, 367, 368, 370, 380
Love
 and Essential qualities, 376, 377, 380
 importance of, 17
 and purpose of Enneagram, 5, 16, 17
 self-, 17, 319, 356
 and transformation process, 327, 356, 370
Loyalist. See Type Six
Lucas, George, 223
Lust, 57–58
Lynch, David, 224

MacDowell, Andie, 207
McLachlan, Sarah, 217
Mahler, Gustav, 230
Major Depressive Disorder/Episode, 294, 295
Manic Episode, 294, 300, 302–3
Manilow, Barry, 209
Maslow, Abraham, 285
Melancholy, 48
Midler, Bette, 221, 242
Miller, Arthur, 198
Million, Theodore, 285
Misidentification
 and Direction of Disintegration, 191
 individual experience as source of, 191
 and Instinctual Variant, 190
 and Levels of Development, 204
 reasons for, 189–93
 and stress, 190–91, 206
 and traits out of context, 173
 and wing theory, 190, 192, 206
 See also specific type
Missing Piece, for each type, 320–21, 358
Mitchell, Joni, 229
Motivations, 7, 8, 21, 70–71, 72, 192–93. See also specific personality type
Myers, Mike, 240
Mysticism, 5, 33, 34–35, 284–85

Nader, Ralph, 206
Naranjo, Claudio, 5, 10, 31, 72, 137
Narcissisim, 292, 293–94, 295, 372
Neo-Platonism, 33, 34
Neurosis, 154, 288
Nine. See Type Nine

Nonattachment, 50, 319
Nureyev, Rudolf, 226

Object-relations theory, 315, 319
Objectivity, 8, 21
Obsessive Compulsive Personality Disorder, 308–10
O'Connor, Sandra Day, 194
"Octave of Essential Being," 156
"Octave of personality," 156
One. See Type One
Orbison, Roy, 229
Overcompensation, 154, 163. See also Level 6

Paranoid Personality Disorder, 299
Parents/parenting, 12–13, 67, 312–15
Passion, 3, 33, 36, 37, 38, 153. See also specific personality type
Passive Aggressive Personality Disorder, 290, 298, 299–300, 304
Pathology
 and Levels of Development, 155, 156, 166
 See also Level 8; Level 9
Paths of Transformation, 371–75
Pauley, Jane, 197
Peacemaker. See Type Nine
Penn, Sean, 229
Personality
 as artifical construct, 253
 as automatic, 15
 and awareness, 14–15
 components of, 12
 and Dominant Affect Groups, 315–20
 and Essence, 15, 16, 33, 359, 362, 366–68
 and Essential qualities, 250, 376
 functions of, 362, 363
 and identity, 13
 imbalance of Centers as basis of, 252–53
 and Interconnected Enneagram, 323–24
 limitations of, 12
 as mechanism from past, 12
 observations about, 359, 361, 362
 parents' influence on, 12–13
 and Presence, 15
 and purpose of Enneagram, 3, 6, 7, 9, 11, 12, 13–15, 16

Your local bookstore can provide you with copies of all of Don Richard Riso's other books, *Personality Types* (1987, 1996, revised edition with Russ Hudson), *Discovering Your Personality Type: The New Enneagram Questionnaire* (1992, 1995, containing the *Riso-Hudson Enneagram Type Indicator,* RHETI questionnaire), *Enneagram Transformations* (1993), and *The Wisdom of the Enneagram: The Complete Guide to Psychological and Spiritual Growth for the Nine Personality Types* (1999).

To order the self-scoring Offprint of the RHETI, Version 2.5, or to have the RHETI interpreted by an Enneagram teacher trained and certified by Don Riso and Russ Hudson, please contact the Enneagram Institute for a free referral to a teacher in your area.

Don Richard Riso and Russ Hudson offer a comprehensive, three-part Enneagram Professional Training Program. The Training Program is designed to equip serious students of the Enneagram to teach the system and to make applications of it in areas as diverse as business, education, personal growth, relationships, therapy, counseling, and spirituality. Please contact the Enneagram Institute at the address below for more information about their Training Program.

To contact Don Richard Riso and Russ Hudson for information about their business seminars, Enneagram workshops, new publications, and audiotapes, or to have your name added to their mailing list for workshops in your area, please contact:

The Enneagram Institutesm
222 Riverside Drive, Suite 10
New York, New York 10025
Telephone: (212) 932-3306
Fax: (212) 865-0962
E-mail: ennpertype@aol.com
www.EnneagramInstitute.com

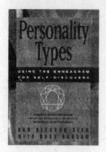